AQA(A)
PSYCHOLOGY
FOR AS

AQA(A)
PSYCHOLOGY
FOR AS

RICHARD GROSS
GEOFF ROLLS

HODDER
EDUCATION
PART OF HACHETTE LIVRE UK

Orders: please contact Bookpoint Ltd, 130 Milton Park, Abingdon, Oxon OX14 4SB. Telephone: (44) 01235 827720. Fax: (44) 01235 400454. Lines are open from 9.00–5.00, Monday to Saturday, with a 24-hour message answering service. You can also order through our website www.hoddereducation.co.uk.

British Library Cataloguing in Publication Data
A catalogue record for this title is available from the British Library.

ISBN: 978 0 340 94661 9

First Published 2008
Impression number   10 9 8 7 6 5 4 3 2
Year   2012 2011 2010 2009 2008

Hachette Livre UK's policy is to use papers that are natural, renewable and recyclable products and made from wood grown in sustainable forests. The logging and manufacturing processes are expected to conform to the environmental regulations of the country of origin.

Typeset by Fakenham Photosetting Ltd, Fakenham, Norfolk NR21 8NN.

Cover © Clément Contet/iStockphoto.com

Printed in Italy for Hodder Education, part of Hachette Livre UK, 338 Euston Road, London NW1 3BH.

Contents

As the title indicates, *AQA(A) Psychology for AS* is written for that particular Specification, but it could also prove useful for students following other Specifications.

Each of the six chapters follows the same basic structure, reflecting precisely aspects of the Specification. As the book's cover makes clear, and as should be apparent now from having looked through the book, the text comes with a CD-ROM, which includes further resources and activities, as described below.

- *Practical Learning Activities* (**PLAs**): these occur several times within each chapter and are designed to help you consider methodological aspects of the research studies and theories that make up the content. This can be done either through questions requiring (usually short) written answers or through suggested practical activities/practicals (which can be fairly specific or more open-ended, leaving room for you and/or your fellow-students to design your own). Either way, you're being asked to consider *How Science Works*, a set of concepts which underpin the whole Specification, designed to help students understand how scientists 'do science' in their attempt to explain the world around them. While psychology displays many characteristics of science in general, it is also unique in being about human behaviour and experience (which includes doing science).

  This is assessed as **AO3** (see below). One of the special problems faced by psychologists as scientists relates to the *ethics* of their research; others include the *culture* and *gender-bias* of their theories and conclusions. These are sometimes included as part of the PLAs and represent a broader view of '*How Psychology Works*'.

- *Assessment checks:* these usually appear at the end of each major sub-section of a chapter and comprise several short-answer questions which test your knowledge of the material covered in that sub-section (they can also be useful as revision exercises). The questions are generally not worded/structured in the way that actual exam questions are – they are often more specific – but they sometimes do resemble possible exam questions (those that would be worth only a few marks).

- *End-of-chapter summaries:* these are detailed summaries, using the same sub-section headings as used in the chapter (following the Specification). They are designed to aid revision as well as initial learning. In the CD-ROM, chapter summaries appear in the form of **schematic summaries** (or **schemas**); these are diagrammatic in nature, combining boxes, links between boxes etc. as well as words. These more visual elements aid memory and reduce a large amount of information to a much smaller, more manageable format. Another way of checking your knowledge and understanding of the topic is to fill the gaps that appear in written summaries: you'll be presented with a sentence that has one or more words missing, and you have to choose from several options the correct word(s) by dragging it into the gap (it only stays there if you have chosen correctly).

- *Other features of the text* include **Key Study** boxes. Although you're not required to know about specific studies, these studies retain a central place within a particular topic. In other words, it is important that you are familiar with them, even though you couldn't be asked about a specific study in the exam. We use a different set of headings (Aim/Hypothesis, Method/Design, Results, Conclusions and Evaluation) for each Key Study, with the Evaluation concentrating on methodological aspects of the investigation. Outside of these Key Study boxes, a theory or piece of research may be evaluated using a different format, namely, positive criticisms (denoted by a ✔) and negative criticisms (denoted by a ✗). Positive and negative criticisms are of equal importance.

- *Other features of the CD-ROM* include (i) a Further Resources section that points you towards weblinks, books and journal articles; (ii) an Exam and Study Skills section, that (a) defines exactly what is meant by AO1, AO2 and AO3, (b) explains mark allocations for AO1 and AO2, (c) provides hints for writing evaluation (AO2), (d) provides some examples of how to write your commentaries for AO2, and (e) offers some tips on how to make the most effective use of your time both before and during the exam; and (iii) Revision Planners.

Just as examiners use 'positive marking', so we are very much on your side. We hope you find this book easy and enjoyable to read, and that it helps you both to learn and to revise what you need to know to achieve a good grade in your AS exam.

Acknowledgements

Both authors would like to thank Lynn Brown for her thorough and efficient copy-editing of the text, Kate Short, for her management of the whole project, and Emma Woolf, for her unstinting support and restrained use of the editorial whip.

RG would also like to thank GR for sharing his pedagogical expertise, as well as his general moral support during a time of great change and uncertainty. It continues to be a pleasure working with you.

GR would like to thank RG for making this monumental task manageable and for being a source of expertise and encouragement throughout.

Dedication

To all psychology teachers, who must provide their students with a safe base while experiencing their own separation anxiety.

RG/GR

Credits

The authors and publishers would like to thank the following for the use of photographs in this volume:

p.5 © Paul Thompson; Eye Ubiquitous/CORBIS; p.16 Carmen Taylor/AP/PA Photos; p.21 © SINER JEFF/CORBIS SYGMA; p.40 © Charles & Josette Lenars/CORBIS; p.42 Martin Rogers/Stone/Getty Images; p.43 SCIENCE PHOTO LIBRARY; p.48 Joyce Robertson; p.57 Bubbles Photolibrary; p.72 © Tim De Waele/Corbis; p.76 Tony Kyriacou/Rex Features; p.77 All Action /EMPICS Entertainment/PA Photos; p117 Life File Photo Library/Andrew Ward; p.129 (top) © David Parry/epa/Corbis; p.129 (bottom) US Army photo; p.137 Anthea Sieveking/Wellcome Photo Library; p.147 Courtesy of Scientific American/© William Vandivert; p.150 (both) Philip G. Zimbardo, Inc; p.157 © 1965 Stanley Milgram; p.158 from the film Obedience, copyright © 1965 by Stanley Milgram and distributed by Penn State Media Sales; p.172 Stephen Ferry/Liaison/Getty Images; p.178 © Bettmann/CORBIS; p.180 © CORBIS SYGMA; p.189 Painting © Salvador Dali, Gala-Salvador Dali Foundation, DACS, London 2007/Photo © Bettmann/CORBIS; p.190 © Woodystock/Alamy; p.192 Archives of the History of American Psychology, The University of Akron; p.199 Courtesy of The Ronald Grant Archive.

Every effort has been made to trace and acknowledge ownership of copyright. The publishers will be glad to make suitable arrangements with any copyright holders whom it has not been possible to contact.

Cognitive psychology: memory

What's covered in this chapter?

You need to know about:

Models of memory

- The multi-store model (MSM) of memory, including the concepts of encoding, capacity and duration
- Strengths and weaknesses of the MSM model
- Working memory
- Strengths and weaknesses of working memory

Memory in everyday life

- Eyewitness testimony (EWT) and factors affecting the accuracy of EWT, including anxiety and age of witness
- Misleading information and the use of the cognitive interview
- Strategies for memory improvement

Models of memory

Memory: what is it?

The term '**memory**' can mean the system of retaining information, the actual storage system or the material that has been retained. Rather than being one process it involves three basic processes (see Figure 1.1), as described below.

1 **Encoding**: the process of transforming a sensory input (e.g. sound or visual image) for it to be registered in memory. There are different ways of encoding different material, depending on the sensory input – for example, by sound, vision or meaning (see also the section on 'Memory improvement', pages 26–29).

2 **Storage**: the process of retaining or holding information in memory until it's required.

3 **Retrieval**: the process of locating information that has been stored and extracting it from memory so we are consciously aware of it.

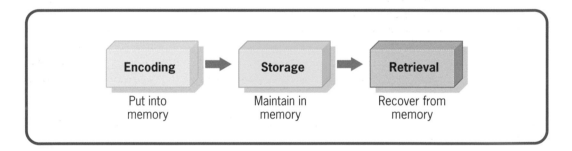

Figure 1.1: Three basic processes in memory

The multi-store model (MSM) of memory (Atkinson and Shiffrin, 1968)
Description

The multi-store model (MSM) was the first attempt to develop a general model of memory (Atkinson and Shiffrin, 1968). The MSM explains how information flows from one storage system to another. The model proposes that there are three permanent structures in memory: sensory memory, short-term memory (STM) and long-term memory (LTM). Each memory storage system is thought to differ in terms of:

● capacity – how much information can be stored

● duration – how long the information can be stored

● encoding – the form in which the information is stored.

The main components of the MSM are described below.

Sensory memory

Sensory memory is the store that retains the impressions of information received through the senses. It's believed that there is a separate sensory store for each sense. For example, when viewing an object, we retain a brief visual image of it even after it has disappeared. The store contains this information for anything from a few milliseconds (visual sensory memory) to about two to three seconds with auditory sensory memory (Crowder, 2003). Information that is paid attention to passes on to STM and LTM (see below) for more permanent storage. Sensory memory is often called the 'gatekeeper' of information since most information perceived by the senses is immediately forgotten.

Short-term memory (STM)

Short-term memory (STM) is an active memory system and contains all the information that you are currently thinking about. It is a place for temporary storage of information received from sensory memory.

Encoding in STM

Information arrives in sensory memory in its original form (e.g. sound, vision and so on). This information needs to be encoded in a form that STM can deal with. For example, if the input into sensory memory is the word 'banana', you could encode this *visually* by thinking of an image of a banana. Alternatively, you could encode it *acoustically* by repeating 'banana' over and over again (probably best done quietly!), or you could encode it *semantically* (through meaning) by applying your pre-existing knowledge of bananas. This might involve thinking about what desserts you can make with bananas or the time you slipped on a banana skin!

One study that investigated coding in STM was that of Baddeley (1966), as covered in Practical Learning Activity 1.1.

How Science Works

Practical Learning Activity 1.1: Replication of Baddeley's (1966) 'cat/mat' study

Baddeley's study examined whether encoding in STM is primarily acoustic (sound) or semantic (meaning). In the study, participants were presented with four word lists:

1 List A – acoustically similar words (such as 'cat', 'mat', 'sat', 'sad')
2 List B – acoustically dissimilar words (such as 'pit', 'day', 'cow')
3 List C – semantically similar words (such as 'big', 'huge', 'tall')
4 List D – semantically dissimilar words (such as 'hot', 'safe', 'foul').

A total of 75 participants heard one list repeated four times. Immediately after this (to test STM), they were given a list that contained all the original words but in the wrong order. Their task was to rearrange the words in the correct order. They found that those participants given List A (acoustically similar) performed the worst (recall of 10 per cent). Recall for the other lists was comparatively good

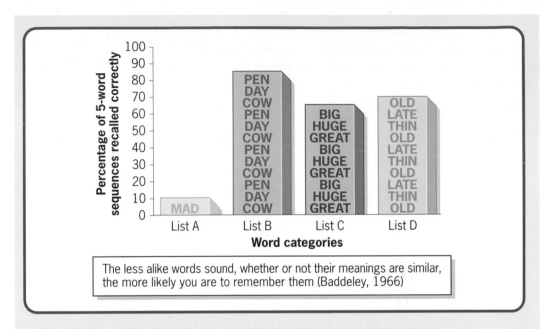

The less alike words sound, whether or not their meanings are similar, the more likely you are to remember them (Baddeley, 1966)

Figure 1.2: Baddeley's 1966 acoustic/semantic (AS) study findings

(60–80 per cent). The conclusion was that since List A was recalled the least efficiently, it would appear that there's acoustic confusion in STM. Therefore, STM tends to be encoded on an acoustic basis.

- What kind of research method was used?
- What are some of the advantages and disadvantages of this method?

(See pages 65–105 of Chapter 3, 'Research methods'.)

Evaluation of research into encoding in STM

✔ The results of Baddeley's study do make 'cognitive sense'. For example, if you were asked to remember a shopping list for a short time you'd probably repeat it aloud (acoustic rehearsal) as you walked to the supermarket.

✗ However, STM is not restricted to acoustic coding. Some semantic coding has been demonstrated in STM. The small difference in recall between semantically similar (64 per cent) and semantically dissimilar (71 per cent) lists suggests that, at best, there's *minimal* semantic coding in STM. We can also remember visual images (e.g. faces) in STM that would be very difficult to encode on the basis of sound. For example, how would your face be encoded acoustically?

Capacity of STM

STM has a limited capacity – that is, we can hold only a small amount of information in it before it's forgotten. **Serial digit span studies** demonstrate this. These are where participants are presented with increasingly long sequences of digits that they have to report back in the correct order (e.g. 26478, 968423, 2975841, and so on). When they fail on 50 per cent of the trials, they've reached their digit span capacity.

Jacobs in his (1887) study of immediate digit span investigated the capacity of STM. He read aloud lists of either letters or numbers. (They had to have only one syllable, so 'w' or '7' weren't used). He increased the length of these lists until participants could successfully recall them only 50 per cent of the time. Jacobs used a wide age range in his sample. He found that:

● STM capacity for digits was 9, whereas for letters it was 7

● STM increased with age – 8-year-olds recalled 7 digits, whereas 19-year-olds recalled 9 digits.

The longest place name in Wales – digit span this!

Jacobs concluded that STM has a limited capacity of between 5 and 9 digits and that age does affect STM capacity, since people may improve their recall strategies with age and/or through practice. He also found that numbers are easier to recall than letters, because there are fewer of them (9) compared to letters (25).

Evaluation of research into capacity of STM

✔ **Replicated research:** Jacob's findings have been replicated by Miller (1956), who coined the phrase 'the magic number seven plus or minus two' $(7^{+/-2})$ to describe the capacity of STM. Atkinson and Shiffrin (1968) argued that the STM store had a small number of 'slots' into which information could be placed and that the limited capacity was due to the small number of slots. This view argued for structural constraints on the capacity of STM.

✗ **Other factors?** However, other factors (e.g. age and practice) have also been shown to influence STM capacity and nowadays STM limitations are more often viewed as due to processing limitations associated with attention (see the section on 'Memory improvement', pages 26–29).

How Science Works

Practical Learning Activity 1.2: Test of short-term capacity (after Jacobs, 1887)

Write out rows of random numbers, increasing the row lengths up to a maximum of ten numbers. For example:

- 3224
- 4553
- 23879
- 74561, and so on.

Read the lists out to a partner in as monotone a fashion as possible. They must repeat back the numbers in the correct order. When they can no longer correctly report back all the numbers, they have reached their digit span.

- Consider the methodological problems with this study.
- Do you think this is a realistic study of everyday memory?

Duration of STM

You'll not be surprised to learn that the duration of STM is short – that is, less than 30 seconds. Many experiments have demonstrated how long we can retain information in our STM.

The best-known experiment into the duration of STM is Peterson and Peterson's (1959) Trigram Retention Experiment, where participants were read a nonsense trigram (three consonants that have no meaning, e.g. LTB). Immediately after this, participants had to count backwards in threes starting from a very large 3-digit number (e.g. 576) for a specified time period. This time period was called the *retention interval* and varied from 3 to 18 seconds. The counting backwards task was called the *distractor task*; it was designed to prevent rehearsal of the trigrams. Approximately 90 per cent of the trigrams were recalled after a 3-second retention interval but only about 6 per cent were recalled after 18 seconds (see Practical Learning Activity 1.3). This suggests that STM duration is approximately 20–30 seconds.

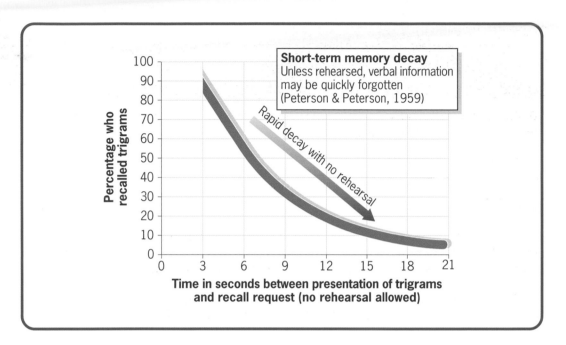

Figure 1.3: Peterson and Peterson's (1959) Trigram Retention Experiment findings

How Science Works

Practical Learning Activity 1.3:
Duration of short-term memory
(after Peterson and Peterson, 1959)

Devise some nonsense trigrams (e.g. HGU, KLD) and read one of them to a friend. Ask them to immediately count backwards in threes from a 3-digit number (e.g. 467) in order to prevent rehearsal. After a predetermined period of time (e.g. 5 seconds), ask them to repeat the trigram. Do this for varying time intervals (up to 30 seconds) and see how long they can retain the trigrams in their STM.

● What is the purpose of the counting backwards task?
● Can you think of any criticisms of this experiment (see the section on 'Validity' on pages 89–90 of Chapter 3, 'Research methods')?

Despite methodological problems, researchers agree that:

● STM has a limited duration (less than 30 seconds)

● information is rapidly lost from STM if it's not rehearsed.

Long-term memory (LTM)

Long-term memory (LTM) involves the storage of information over extended periods of time. Although it may appear surprising, storage of information for any longer than 30 seconds counts as LTM.

Encoding in LTM

With verbal material, coding in LTM appears to be mainly semantic. Baddeley (1966) investigated this using the same procedure as that described above (the 'cat/mat' STM study), except that recall of the lists wasn't immediate: there was a 20-minute retention interval, during which the 75 participants conducted another task. This ensured that recall would involve LTM. This time, those participants given List C (semantically similar) performed the worst (55 per cent recall). Recall for the other lists was comparatively good (70–85 per cent). Since List C was the least efficiently recalled, it appears there's semantic confusion in LTM. Therefore, LTM tends to be encoded on a semantic basis.

Evaluation of research into encoding in LTM

✔ **Cognitive sense:** Baddeley's (1966) acoustic/semantic LTM study is easily replicated and the findings are consistent. They also make '**cognitive sense**' in everyday life. For example, try to remember a TV programme you watched a while ago. You'll remember the overall content (meaning), but not the actual words (acoustic).

✗ **Different types of LTM:** 'knowing how' to perform various tasks (e.g. riding a bike) is called '*procedural*' memory. Autobiographical or personal memories of events or places are called '*episodic*' memories. These types of LTM are rarely examined in laboratory memory studies and are arguably not encoded in the same way. In addition, songs must be encoded acoustically, and it's hard to see how smells and tastes can be encoded on the basis of meaning. LTM coding must involve a very large, long-lasting and flexible system.

Capacity of LTM

Although it may not feel like it, the potential capacity of LTM is unlimited. No one has ever claimed that their brain is full! Anokhin (1973) estimated that the number of possible neuronal connections in the human brain is 1 followed by 10.5 million kilometres of noughts! He concluded that:

no human yet exists who can use all the potential of his/her brain. This is why we don't accept any estimates of the limits of the human brain.

How Science Works

Practical Learning Activity 1.4:
Case study of Solomon Shereshevsky

The person who is often credited with the world's best ever memory was Solomon Shereshevsky, a Latvian by birth who became a newspaper reporter in Moscow and was subsequently studied by Prof. Luria (1968) for over 30 years. It is claimed that Shereshevsky's memory was so perfect that he could remember virtually every detail of his life in the most minute detail. When Luria first met Shereshevsky and gave him long lists of numbers, words and nonsense syllables to remember, all were recalled perfectly. Over the years, Luria could find no limit to the capacity or duration of his memory. Shereshevsky started to perform his memory feats on stage; for a time earning his living as a mnemonist, demonstrating his remarkable prowess. (From Rolls, 2005.)

- What can we conclude about LTM from Solomon Shereshevsky?
- Interview your parents, friends or grandparents about their earliest memories. Can you conclude anything about the nature of memory from such research?
- Are there any methodological problems with case studies such as these (see pages 78–79, Chapter 3, 'Research methods')?

Duration of LTM

A memory can last a lifetime, so the duration of LTM just depends on how long you live. Many older people love to tell (interesting?) stories from their childhood. Material in STM that's not rehearsed is quickly forgotten, but this is *not* true of LTM. We couldn't keep repeating information over and over again in order to store it in our LTM. For example, you may not have ridden a bike for many years, but it's unlikely that you'll have forgotten how.

The duration of LTM was demonstrated by Bahrick *et al.* (1975): 400 participants ranging in age from 17–74 years were asked to remember the names of classmates from their high school (*a free recall task*). They were also shown a set of photos and a list of names, some of which were of their ex-school friends. They had to identify their ex-school friends (a *recognition task*). Those who'd left high school within the previous 15 years recalled 90 per cent of the faces and names in the recognition task. Those who'd left 48 years previously recalled 80 per cent of the names and 70 per cent of the faces. These high percentages suggest that our memories for faces last a very long time indeed.

	STM		LTM	
Encoding	Mainly acoustic (sound)	Baddeley (1966) – immediate recall study	Mainly semantic (meaning)	Baddeley (1966) – delayed recall study
Capacity	Small ($7^{+/-2}$ chunks of information) – see page 27	Jacobs (1887) – digit span	Unlimited	Luria (1968) – Solomon Shereshevsky case study
Duration	Short (<30 seconds)	Peterson and Peterson (1959) – Trigram Retention Experiment	30 seconds to a lifetime	Bahrick *et al.* (1975) – high school study

Table 1.1: Summary of STM/LTM differences*

* You *must* learn the information in this table.

The multi-store model (MSM) is shown in Figure 1.4. We've already described some of the key characteristics of the sensory, STM and LTM stores, and much of this evidence suggesting separate stores can be used to support the MSM. According to the MSM, information received through the senses (sound, sight, touch, smell) enters the sensory store. A small fraction of this information is attended to and selected for further processing in the short-term store. If it's not attended to, the sensory information is immediately for-

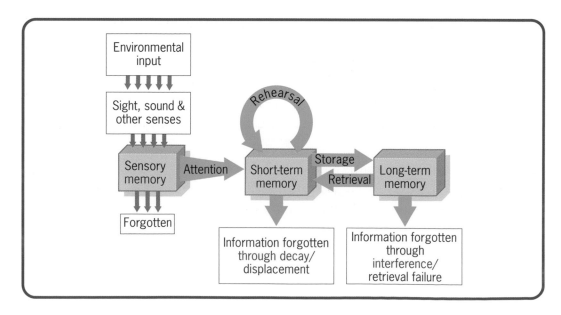

Figure 1.4: The multi-store model of memory proposed by Atkinson and Shiffrin (1968, 1971)

gotten, or not even processed in the first place. If the information now in STM is actively processed (primarily through rehearsal) then it may be transferred to LTM. The greater the amount of STM rehearsal, the greater the likelihood it will transfer to LTM for more permanent storage.

Figure 1.4 clearly shows why it's called the multi-store model. The key processes involved are attention, rehearsal and forgetting.

Evaluation and analysis of MSM

✔ **Influential, useful:** the MSM was an influential early model and psychologists still find it useful.

✔ **STM/LTM differences:** there's considerable evidence that there are distinct types of memory store – namely, sensory, STM/LTM (see research studies above).

✔ **Serial position effect:** Murdock (1962) presented participants with a list of words that they had to recall in any order (a free recall task). Murdock found that those words at the beginning and the end of the lists were recalled better than those in the middle. This is known as the *serial position effect*. Those words at the beginning of the list (the *primacy effect*) are recalled because they've been rehearsed over and over again and have been transferred to LTM. Those words from the end of the list (the *recency effect*) are recalled because they're still in STM. Thus, the primacy and recency effect provides support for the existence of the two separate memory stores (STM and LTM).

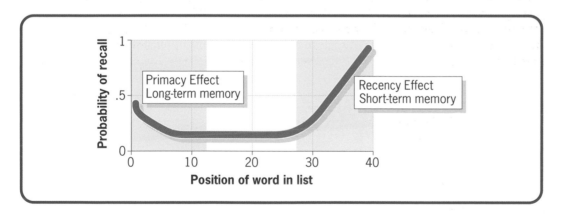

Figure 1.5: Results from free recall experiment. Probability of recall varies with an item's position in a list. Recall of the last few items (the recency effect) is based on short-term memory, whereas recall of the remaining items is based on long-term memory (the primacy effect). (After Murdock, 1962.)

How Science Works

Practical Learning Activity 1.5:
Serial position curve (after Murdock, 1962)

Simply devise ten lists of 15 words. Read out the first 15-word list fairly quickly (in order to prevent too much rehearsal). After this, ask the participants to write down as many of the 15 words as they can recall (they can do this in any order). Note down the position on the original list of the words that they recall. It is likely that they will recall more of the first words on the list and the last words on the list. Repeat this for each word list. Add up how many of the first words on the lists were recalled, how many of the second words, and so on.

- Produce a graph of your findings.
- What do the results show?
- What conclusions can be drawn from your graph?

✔ **Clinical case studies:** Shallice and Warrington (1970) reported the case of K.F. As a result of a motorbike accident, he had an extremely poor STM (only one or two digits) and a recency effect of one item. Yet his LTM for events after the accident was normal. This supports MSM. However, K.F.'s deficit in STM was only for verbal

✗ information. His STM for visual and acoustic material was normal. This suggests the existence of more than one type of STM, not incorporated in the MSM. There are other famous case studies that illustrate similar findings, such as Clive Wearing (Gross, 2005) and H.M. (see Practical Learning Activity 1.6) (Hilts, 1995).

How Science Works

Practical Learning Activity 1.6:
Case study of H.M.

One summer day in 1953, brain surgeon Bill Scoville tried an experimental technique to cure one of his patient's debilitating epilepsy. With his patient still awake, he cut a hole in his head and sucked up a part of his brain through a silver straw. As he later joked, instead of removing his epilepsy, he removed his memory. H.M., as the patient is now referred to, was destined to become the most famous neurological case in the world. Specifically, Scoville removed most of the hippocampus (a small seahorse-shaped organ), the amygdala and the entorhinal and perihinal cortexes. In a moment, H.M. had lost the ability to encode new memories. He was stuck in the past and the present but with no future to look forward to. He still had a normal short term memory (a digit span of about 7 items). He could repeat lists of numbers or letters just heard. He was aware of what had happened a minute or so before. But beyond this, or if he was distracted, he could recall nothing. He was incapable of updating his LTM. (From Rolls, 2005.)

- Explain how the H.M. case can provide support both for and against the MSM.
- Try to find more information about H.M. from the Internet and write a newspaper article outlining the importance of H.M. to the psychological study of memory.
- What problems are there in using the Internet for research?
- Does H.M. merit the title *'most famous neurological case in the world'*?

✗ **Mere rehearsal doesn't ensure transfer from STM to LTM.** Bekerian and Baddeley (1980) found that people didn't know of the changes to BBC radio wavelengths despite hearing the information, on average, well over a thousand times. This suggests that rehearsal is not the only factor in the transfer of information from STM to LTM, contradicting the model.

✗ **The multi-store model is over-simplified.** It assumes a single STM and a single LTM. It has been demonstrated that there are different types of STM (see the section about Baddeley and Hitch (1974) and working memory, below) and different types of LTM (procedural, episodic and semantic memories – see page 8).

✗ **There is an over-emphasis on the 'one-way' (linear) direction of the MSM.** There is a *two-way* flow of information between STM and LTM. Morris *et al.* (1985) demonstrated how previous knowledge and interest in football could help in the recall of fictitious football scores. Participants listened to 'made-up' football results, and then had to recall them immediately (an STM task). Participants who were interested in football recalled the most. This suggests that they'd used their greater knowledge of football (LTM) to impose meaning on the results (STM). Information thus flows from LTM to STM. This important aspect of memory is neglected too much in the MSM. Perhaps it is better to see the flow of information through the model as interactive, rather than sequential.

✗ **Over-emphasis on the amount of information.** Cohen (1990) argues that memory capacity cannot be measured purely in terms of the amount of information to be recalled, but rather the nature of the information that is to be recalled. Let's face it, some things are easier to recall than others, regardless of the amount there is to learn! The MSM does not seem to take this into account.

✔ Assessment Check 1.1

1. Define what is meant by the terms 'encoding', 'capacity' and 'duration'. (2 + 2 + 2 marks)
2. Distinguish ONE difference between STM and LTM as suggested by the MSM. (3 marks)
3. Describe the multi-store model of memory. (6 marks)
4. Explain one strength of the MSM. (2 marks)
5. Outline TWO weaknesses of the MSM. (2 + 2 marks)
6. Using the MSM, outline the processes involved in storing and retrieving material in LTM. (4 marks)
7. Outline and evaluate the MSM. (12 marks)

Working memory (WM) (Baddeley and Hitch, 1974)
Description

Baddeley and Hitch questioned the existence of a single STM store (they weren't concerned with LTM). They argued that STM was far more complex than a mere 'stopping off' point for transferring information to LTM. They saw STM as an 'active' store that holds several pieces of information while it's being worked on (hence 'working' memory). Cohen (1990) described working memory as:

the focus of consciousness – it holds the information you are consciously thinking about now.

Groome *et al.* (1999) compared working memory to a computer screen, where various operations are performed on current data. To replace the single STM, Baddeley and Hitch proposed a multi-component WM (see Figure 1.6).

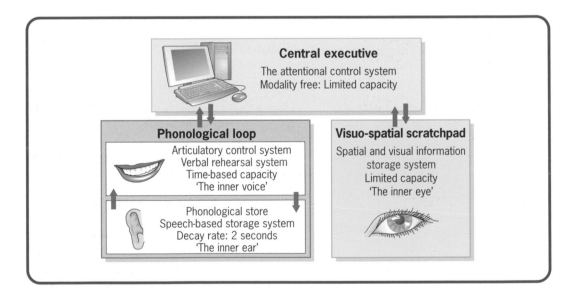

Figure 1.6: Adaptation of the working memory model

- The **central executive** is involved in higher mental processes such as decision-making. It allocates resources to the other 'slave systems' depending on the task in hand. For example, sometimes it's difficult to concentrate on driving and talking at the same time. For a difficult manoeuvre, the central executive would direct your attention to the driving task, and you'd probably have to stop talking. The central executive has a limited capacity, but it's very flexible and can process information from any of the senses.

- The **articulatory control system** is a verbal rehearsal loop that holds words we're preparing to speak. Information is represented as it would be spoken (so it's called the 'inner voice'). The capacity of the loop is about 2 seconds. This, plus the phonological store (see below), comprise the phonological loop.

- The **phonological store**, or 'inner ear', receives auditory information (the things you hear), and stores it in an acoustic code. This is important for language acquisition.

- The **visuo-spatial scratchpad** (or sketchpad) helps to rehearse visual or spatial information (what things look like). It uses a visual code, analysing features in terms of size, colour and shape (and so is called the 'inner eye'). It can process movements and actions, as well as static visual patterns.

Research to support the WM model has involved doing two tasks at once (the *dual-task method*). According to WM, it should be easier to do two tasks that use a different processing system (verbal and visual) than two tasks that use the same 'slave' system. Gathercole and Baddeley (1993) got participants to follow a moving spot of light with a pointer (a tracker task). At the same time, half the participants had to describe the angles on a 'hollow' letter F. This group found the two tasks extremely difficult, because they were using the visuo-spatial sketchpad for both. The other participants performed the tracking task along with a verbal task and had little difficulty performing both tasks simultaneously; they were using different 'slave' systems (verbal and visual).

Evaluation of the working memory (WM) model

✔ **Research support:** support comes from dual-task studies (Gathercole and Baddeley, 1993), although such laboratory studies are rather artificial. K.F. could remember visual, but not verbal stimuli in STM, so there must be at least two systems in STM.

✔ **Importance of rehearsal?** The WM model doesn't over-emphasise the importance of rehearsal for STM retention, in contrast to the MSM.

✔ **Physiological evidence:** WM is supported by studies involving brain scans. PET (positron emission tomography) scans have shown that different areas of the brain are used while undertaking verbal and visual tasks. These areas may correspond to the components of WM (Paulescu *et al.*, 1993).

✗ **Only STM:** WM concerns itself only with STM and so isn't a comprehensive model of memory.

✗ **Function of central executive?** Least is known about the most important component, namely the central executive. It isn't clear how it works or what it does. This vagueness means that it can be used to explain almost any experimental results. For example, if two tasks *cannot* be done together, then it can be argued that two processing components in the model conflict or that the tasks exceed the central executive's capacity. If the two tasks *can* be done simultaneously, then it can be argued that they don't exceed the available resources. It's a circular argument ('heads I win, tails you lose'). Eysenck (1986) claimed that a single central executive might be as inaccurate as a single STM store.

✗ **The capacity of the central executive** has never been measured.
✗ **Practice or time:** the WM model doesn't explain changes in processing ability that occur as the result of practice or time.

It's better to see STM as a number of independent components than a unitary STM store as the MSM suggests. However, there remain a number of problems with WM and even Baddeley stated.

We've a long way to go before we can be sure of the details of the model.

 Assessment Check 1.2

1. Describe key features of the working memory model. (6 marks)
2. Discuss the strengths and weaknesses of the working memory model. (6 marks)
3. Explain ONE strength of the working memory model. (2 marks)
4. Outline TWO criticisms of the working memory model. (4 marks)
5. Outline and evaluate the working memory model. (12 marks)

Memory in everyday life

Eyewitness testimony (EWT)

One of the most important practical applications of memory research involves EWT. The guilt or innocence of people is often decided on the accuracy of the memories of eyewitnesses. Juries often find EWT of overriding importance in their deliberations, even when a witness has previously been discredited!

As long ago as 1932, Frederick Bartlett stated that memory doesn't work accurately like a camera, rather it's prone to inaccuracies and interpretations based on prior experiences – that is, memories are largely *reconstructed* based on our prior expectations and experiences (or *schemas*). Schemas are our ready-made expectations, which help us to understand our world. We use schemas to interpret the world. They help us 'fill in the gaps' in our knowledge and simplify the processing of information. However, schemas can lead to memory distortions when information doesn't readily fit into existing schemas. Cultural expectations or stereotypes also influence memory. Active memory processing can lead people to inadvertently report distorted memories, and this is of particular concern with EWT.

Anxiety has been shown to affect eyewitness testimony

Factors affecting the accuracy of EWT

There are many factors that affect people's perceptions and thus interfere with the accuracy of a memory. They can be categorised into two main areas: *witness factors* such as age, race, gender and individual response to anxiety or stress; and *event factors* such as the duration of the event and the level of violence witnessed

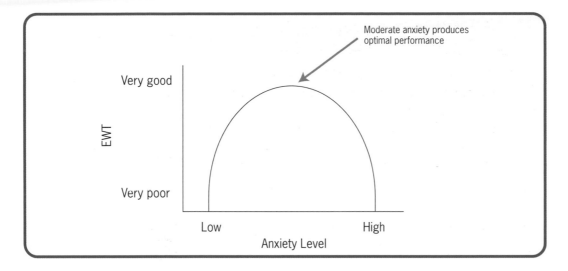

Figure 1.7: The relationship between anxiety and EWT performance

(Fruzetti *et al.*, 1992). Anxiety levels, the age of the witness and the effects of misleading information will be examined.

Anxiety and EWT

Anxiety or stress is almost always associated with witnessing a real-life crime of violence. Deffenbacher (1983) was one of the first to investigate the possible link between stress and EWT. In a review of 21 studies, he hypothesised that the stress–performance relationship follows the inverted-U function proposed by the Yerkes-Dodson law (1908) – that is, for tasks of moderate complexity (such as EWT), performance improves with increases in arousal up to an optimal point where it starts to decline (see Figure 1.7).

Evaluation of the relationship between anxiety and EWT

✔ **Research support:** support for this inverted-U model comes from research by Peters (1988). Peters tested people who were attending their local health clinic for an inoculation. During the visit, they met the nurse (who gave them an injection) and a researcher for equal periods of time. Up to a week later, participants were asked to identify the nurse and the researcher from a set of photos. Identification of the researcher was far easier than that of the nurse, suggesting that the heightened anxiety levels due to the injection led to a decrease in memory accuracy. However, a more naturalistic study of EWT does not necessarily support these results. Yuille and Cutshall (1986) (see page 22 for further details) describe a shooting where one person was killed and another wounded. Witnesses remained very accurate in their reports despite the very high levels of stress associated with the event. One weakness of this study was that those who experienced the highest levels of stress were actually closer to the events and this might have helped with their accuracy recall (Fruzetti *et al.*, 1992).

✗ **Over-simplistic explanation:** Deffenbacher (2004) has since reviewed his earlier findings and claims that they are over-simplistic. He suggests that EWT performance increases gradually up to extremely high levels of anxiety and then, at a

certain point, there is a catastrophic drop in performance. A meta-analysis (review) of 63 studies showed considerable support for the hypothesis that high levels of stress negatively impact on both accuracy of eyewitness identification and accuracy of recall of crime-related details.

Age also appears to be a moderating factor on EWT. Perhaps surprisingly, heightened stress debilitates eyewitness recall for adults, but not for children (Deffenbacher, 2004).

Age of witness

Age does seem to be a significant factor in memory for witnessed events. Dent (1988) found that children usually provide fewer details when asked to recall events without prompting and also perform significantly worse than adults when given specific questions. However, if the child is particularly interested in the topic under consideration, then she or he can match adult levels of accuracy (King and Yuille, 1987). Children also appear more willing to accept inaccurate information provided by other adults for fear of contradicting adult authority figures. A study by Roberts and Lamb (1999) investigated 161 interviews with children who had made allegations of abuse. They found that, in 68 of the interviews, investigators had sometimes misinterpreted or distorted children's reports and, of these, nearly two-thirds remained uncorrected by the child. For example, a child's response 'in private' was misconstrued as 'in the privates' (reported by Sims, 1999).

Specifically related to EWT, Ochsner *et al.* (1999) asked children to watch a staged theft. They found more accurate recall compared to children who saw the same staged event but without the theft. It was suggested that the theft had caused some of the children to consolidate their memories by telling others of the theft, or that they took the activity more seriously than the non-theft group because of the additional seriousness of the crime.

One particularly important finding with regard to children and EWT is that if the context of the original event is reinstated, then the accuracy of the recall is as good as that of adults (Gruneberg and Morris, 1992). (See also the section on 'The use of the cognitive interview', on pages 22–25.)

It's not just children who seem to be poor eyewitnesses. Older people also seem to perform worse on EWT studies than young or middle-aged adults. Elderly people are more likely to make false identifications, are poorer at recalling specific details, and elderly men in particular seem more prone to distortions through misleading post-event information (Loftus *et al.*, 1991, see page 19).

Evaluation of the relationship between age of witness and EWT

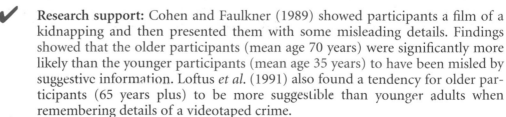

✔ **Research support:** Cohen and Faulkner (1989) showed participants a film of a kidnapping and then presented them with some misleading details. Findings showed that the older participants (mean age 70 years) were significantly more likely than the younger participants (mean age 35 years) to have been misled by suggestive information. Loftus *et al.* (1991) also found a tendency for older participants (65 years plus) to be more suggestible than younger adults when remembering details of a videotaped crime.

✗ **Conflicting research evidence:** however, a more recent study by Coxon and Valentine (1997) suggests that older witnesses may not be quite so unreliable in all respects. They compared the suggestibility of children (mean age 8 years), young adults (mean age 17 years) and older adults (mean age 70 years). All participants were asked questions after watching a videotape of a kidnapping. Half the participants were asked four questions that contained misleading information (e.g. 'Which arm was the kidnapper wearing her watch on?' when, in fact, there was no watch). The other (control) participants did not receive any misleading information. All participants were then asked 20 specific questions about the video, four of which assessed whether they had accepted the misinformation. The total number of questions answered correctly was worse in both older adults and children than in the young adults. However, on the questions testing for misinformation acceptance, not only were the older adults not more suggestible than young adults, but they were actually less suggestible. They were the only age group not to show a statistically significant misinformation effect (see Bornstein *et al.*, (2000) for a review).

✗ **Age or other factors:** it is unclear exactly why these age effects may occur. Younger adults' superior performance may be attributable to the fact that they may be more used to memory tests (e.g. exams), more motivated to achieve, or may simply be a function of associated poor physical health, which has an impact on memory. Indeed, poor health may be the important factor in memory decline rather than age in itself. Unfortunately for those of us of advancing years, age is often closely related to poorer health (Elias *et al.*, 1990).

Many laboratory-based studies that have investigated the accuracy of EWT have shown that recall can be altered by experiences that occur after the witnessed event. One key factor is the use of (mis)leading information, particularly in the form of misleading questions.

The role of (mis)leading information (Loftus)

Elizabeth Loftus's EWT research also illustrated the reconstructive nature of memory. Loftus showed that eyewitness memories can be affected by the wording of questions. This has serious implications for the judicial system.

There are two types of misleading question that appear to affect EWT.

1 *Leading questions*: questions that make it likely that a participant's schema will influence them to give a desired answer. For example, 'Did you see *the* broken headlight?' instead of 'Did you see *a* broken headlight?' The former question presupposes that there was a broken headlight.

2 *'After-the-fact information' questions*: here new misleading information is added in the question after the incident has occurred (see the text on Loftus's 1975 study in the section headed 'Evaluation of other EWT research studies', below).

Key Study 1.1: Loftus and Palmer (1974) – reconstruction of automobile destruction

Aim/hypothesis (AO1)

The study sought to investigate the influence the wording of a question has on participants' estimates of speed (how fast two cars were travelling when involved in an accident) on the actual speed estimate. It was assumed that the use of certain verbs (such as 'smashed') would result in higher speed estimates than other verbs (such as 'contacted'). The manipulation of the verb was the independent variable and the speed estimate represented the dependent variable.

Method/design (AO1)

Loftus and Palmer used a laboratory experiment involving 45 students. Short film clips of a series of traffic accidents were shown. Participants were then asked to describe the accident they had witnessed. The critical question asked about the speed of the cars involved in the collision. Nine participants were asked 'About how fast were the cars going when they smashed into one another?' whereas for others the verbs 'hit', 'bumped', 'collided', 'contacted' were used instead of 'smashed'. Loftus and Palmer found that the estimated speed was affected by the verb used in the question.

Results (AO1)

Loftus and Palmer found that witnesses were not very good at estimating how fast the cars were actually travelling. In addition, the speed estimates varied depending on the verb that was used (see Table 1.2).

Conclusions (AO1)

It seems that participants had different interpretations of the speed of the cars due to the use of the different verbs. It is unclear whether the different reported speeds were due to demand characteristics or to a genuine change in the participant's memory of the event – that is, does the use of the word 'smashed' really lead the participant into seeing the accident as more severe than it really was (Gross, 2003)?

Evaluation (AO1/AO2)

A similar follow-up study reported in the same paper involved asking participants a week later whether they had seen any broken glass on the road (in actual fact, there was none). Only 14 per cent of those who had been asked the question with the word 'hit' in it reported that they had seen glass compared to 32 per cent of those who had been questioned with the 'smashed into' phrase. It seems that post-event misleading questions can have a significant adverse effect on EWT. There are numerous studies that support such findings (e.g.

Loftus *et al*., 1978), although it has been questioned whether witnessing a video clip or slide show lacks the emotional effects of watching a real-life event (see Yuille and Cutshall (1986) on page 22).

Verb	Mean speed estimates
Smashed	40.8
Collided	39.3
Bumped	38.1
Hit	34.0
Contacted	31.8

Table 1.2: Speed estimates dependent on the verb used by Loftus and Palmer (1974)

Dr Elizabeth Loftus: the world's leading expert in EWT research

Evaluation of other EWT research studies

✔ **Other research support:** two groups of participants watched a film of a car being driven through the countryside (Loftus, 1975). Group A were asked 'How fast was the white car going when it passed the "Stop" sign while travelling along the country road?' (There was a 'Stop' sign in the film.) Group B were asked 'How fast was the white car going when it passed the barn while travelling along the country road?' (There was no barn but the question presupposes that there was one.) A week later 17 per cent of Group B reported seeing a barn, compared to

just 2 per cent of Group A. The 'after the event' question had falsely suggested to them that there had actually been a barn. The explanation for this is *source mis-attribution,* where witnesses confuse the *actual* event itself with post-event information.

✗ **Real-life eye witness testimony:** Yuille and Cutshall (1986) conducted research into a real-life crime. A thief had attempted to steal from a gun shop in Vancouver, Canada. However, the shop owner shot and killed the thief in front of 21 witnesses; 13 of the witnesses were interviewed 4 months later and they were asked misleading questions. However, witness accounts remained highly accurate and weren't adversely affected by the misleading information. Misleading information may not affect real-life memories to the same extent as laboratory-produced memories due to the emotions experienced at the time. This incident may have been encoded like a flashbulb memory, and so wasn't easily distorted.

✔ ✗ **Demand characteristics?** It has been suggested that, in many of these EWT studies, participants respond to the experimental situation and provide the answers they think they're expected to give. However, the idea that demand characteristics explain these findings has been refuted by Loftus *et al.* (1978), who incorporated rewards for correct answers into their experimental design and found similar results.

✗ **Participant expectations and consequences:** participants don't expect to be deliberately misled by university researchers and therefore the reconstructive findings should be expected since participants believe the researchers to be telling the truth. The consequences of inaccurate memories are minimal in a research setting compared to real-life crimes. Foster *et al.* (1994) showed that eyewitness identification was more accurate for a real-life crime as opposed to a simulation.

✗ **Deliberately misleading information:** memory for important events isn't easily distorted when the information is obviously misleading.

✗ **Minor aspects of memory:** misleading information affects only minor, relatively unimportant, aspects of the memory (e.g. the 'barn' details referred to above).

Does misleading information alter and replace the original memory (Loftus's view) or is the original memory merely obscured while remaining intact (McCloskey and Zaragoza, 1985)? Baddeley claimed that EWT research doesn't prove destruction of the memory trace, but merely interference with its retrieval. However, even when participants are explicitly told about misleading information, they find it hard to ignore.

The use of the cognitive interview

Much of the work into EWT has concentrated on the inaccuracy and distortion of witness accounts. There are techniques that can improve learning (see pages 26–29), but in the EWT situation the learning has already occurred, so techniques concentrate on improving recall.

One such technique involves the 'cognitive interview', developed by Fisher and Geiselman (1992). The original form of the cognitive interview was based on the theoretical idea that there are several memory retrieval paths to each memory and that information not available through one technique may be accessible through another (Tulving, 1974). Two such strategies are the 'change order' and 'change perspective' instructions, which encourage interviewees to recount events in a variety of orders and from a variety of perspectives, respectively (Memon *et al.*, 1996). These relate to the first two retrieval mnemonics summarised below (see numbers 1–4).

The second principle behind the cognitive interview involves Tulving and Thomson's Encoding Specificity theory (1973). This suggests that a memory trace is made up of several features and that, in order to enhance recall, as many retrieval cues as possible should be used. Context provides cues that increase feature overlap between initial witnessing and subsequent retrieval contexts. *Context reinstatement* involves emotional elements ('How were you feeling at the time?'), which may work via *state-dependent effects*, *perceptual features* ('Put yourself back at the scene of the crime and picture the room – how did it smell, what could you hear?'), and *sequencing elements* ('What were you doing at the time?'). This relates to the third retrieval mnemonic below (Memon *et al.*, 1996). The fourth instruction below is not actually a mnemonic in itself but is important from a forensic viewpoint since seemingly minor details may prove to be important in a court case. Additionally, sometimes trivial incidents can help to trigger more important memories.

Descriptions of the four techniques used in the interviews are read to the witnesses at the start. They can be summarised as follows:

1 *Change of narrative order:* try to recount the scene in a different chronological order – for example, from the end to the beginning.

2 *Change of perspective:* try to recount the scene from a different perspective – for example, by telling it from the point of view of another person who was involved.

3 *Mental reinstatement of context:* try to return to both the environmental (place, weather) and the emotional context (e.g. your feelings) of the scene of the crime.

4 *Report everything (hypermnesia):* recall the maximum amount of information, even if it appears to have little relevance or is accorded a lower level of confidence.

It is believed that the change of narrative order and change of perspective mnemonics aid recall because they *reduce* witnesses' use of prior knowledge, expectations or schemas. This is likely to increase witness accuracy.

How Science Works

Practical Learning Activity 1.7: Testing the effectiveness of EWT

Select a DVD (such as *Lock, Stock and Two Smoking Barrels*), which has an appropriate clip of a crime. Show this to a group of participants. Interview half the group using cognitive interviewing techniques and the other half using a standard interview technique. Devise a set of questions to reflect these two techniques.

- Compare the results of the interviews in terms of accuracy of recall.
- What do the results show?
- Select an appropriate graph to display your findings.
- Write up the results of your study.

Evaluation of the use of the cognitive interview

✔ **Research support:** support for the mental reinstatement of context comes from studies such as Godden and Baddeley (1975) (see the section on 'Memory improvement', below). There have been as many as 50 studies that have investigated the use of cognitive interviewing and it is seen as an extremely effective technique. Research has shown a significant increase in the quantity of correct information remembered by the witness without a comparable increase in the number of errors (Ginet and Py, 2001).

✔ **Enhanced cognitive interview:** the cognitive interview has been improved and now includes an attempt to build greater rapport between the witness and the interviewer. It is also made clear to the witness that the interviewer has no knowledge of the event and that the witness has to do all the work. This modified version is called the 'enhanced cognitive interview'. Bekerian and Dennett (1993) claim that *'the cognitive interview has proven to be one of the most successful areas of applied memory research'.*

✔ **Validity of cognitive interviews:** Geiselman *et al.* (1985) tested the cognitive interview procedure and found it compared favourably against a standard interview technique and a hypnosis interview. However, the use of hypnosis is controversial since it does not seem to be particularly effective (Smith, 1983). Other research supports the use of cognitive interviews with eyewitnesses (see Key Study 1.2).

Key Study 1.2: The enhanced cognitive interview (Fisher *et al.*, 1989)

Aim/hypothesis (AO1)

The aim of this study was to further test the validity of the cognitive interview technique using a field experiment. Previous research had mainly used laboratory experiments and the cognitive interview seemed highly effective in such studies.

Method/design (AO1)

Sixteen experienced police inspectors from Miami, Florida, conducted two interviews on 47 witnesses or victims of shoplifting or mugging. Between the two interviews, seven of the police officers were trained in using the cognitive interview technique. The other nine officers formed the control group. The researchers measured both the increase in facts elicited in the second interview compared to the first, and the number of facts elicited by the police officers in the cognitive interview group compared to the control group. The independent variable was the type of interview the police officers used on the second interview (cognitive or standard) and the dependent variable was the number of accurately recalled facts produced by each of these techniques.

Results (AO1)

Results provided overwhelming support for the cognitive interviewing technique. The cognitive interviewers obtained 47 per cent more facts relating to matters already examined, whereas there was no gain from the second interview for the control group.

Conclusions (AO1)

Cognitive interviews are a useful technique for improving EWT when compared to a standard interviewing technique. This seems to occur both in a laboratory and more realistic field experiments.

Evaluation (AO1/AO2)

The officers in the control group were aware that they were not being given any extra interview training and this might have affected their motivation levels. It may have been this factor rather than the cognitive interviewing training that led to the difference in recall accuracy between the experimental and control groups (adapted from Ginet and Py, 2001).

✗ **Practical problems involving application of cognitive interviewing:** some research has suggested problems with cognitive interviews. Memon *et al.* (1994) failed to find an improvement using a cognitive interview technique when used by police officers. In their study, 38 experienced police officers were trained for four hours on general interviewing principles. Half of the police officers were then trained in cognitive interviewing techniques. Immediately after this, the police officers were asked to interview witnesses of a staged event (a simulated armed robbery in the parking lot of the police training school a few hours earlier). The results showed no benefits of cognitive interviewing over standard interviewing in terms of the number of correct answers or the number of incorrect answers provided by the witnesses. Moreover, it appeared as though the cognitive interview training had little effect on the interview procedures used by the police officers, so perhaps the lack of any effect may have been due to either the training or a reluctance on the part of the officers to fully implement the training.

✗ **Limited use by the police:** there are concerns among the police that the use of the 'change of perspective' mnemonic may mislead witnesses into thinking that they are being asked to speculate on the event they witnessed. After all, no one can be certain what another person saw. Due to worries such as these, this particular mnemonic is less frequently used in practice (Memon *et al.*, 1993).

Assessment Check 1.3

1. Outline TWO factors that affect the accuracy of EWT. (4 marks)
2. Explain why research studies into EWT have been criticised as lacking validity. (5 marks)
3. Explain how the age of the witness can affect EWT. (4 marks)
4. Describe what effect anxiety has on EWT. (4 marks)
5. Outline the key features of the cognitive interview technique as you might if you were interviewing an eyewitness to a crime. (6 marks)
6. Outline and evaluate research into the use of cognitive interviews. (12 marks)
7. Outline and evaluate research into the effects of misleading information. (12 marks)

Strategies for memory improvement

One way to improve our memory is to *organise* the material to be learned. This is beyond dispute and has been shown by three kinds of evidence (Baddeley, 2005):

1 demonstrations that organised material is easier to recall than disorganised material

2 evidence that, given random material, participants spontaneously try to organise it

3 demonstrations that instructions to organise material enhance participants' recall.

There are many studies that have shown the importance of organisation for memory improvement. Many of these involve *mnemonics*, which are strategies designed to improve memory. Simply using a list to remember all your shopping would count as a simple but effective mnemonic device.

Organisation of material into categories

It has consistently been demonstrated that the more material is organised, the easier it is to learn (Tulving and Pearlstone, 1966). Deese (1959) presented 15 words in two lists. One list contained words that were all related to the given starting word. For example, *butterfly* was associated with *moth, insect, wing, bird, fly, yellow, net, pretty, flower, bug, cocoon, colour, stomach, blues, bees*. The second list consisted of totally unrelated words. Participants recalled a mean of 7.35 words from the first list and 5.50 from the unassociated list (Baddeley, 2005).

How Science Works

Practical Learning Activity 1.8: Memory improvement with the use of categories

Try to replicate the study of Deese (1959) outlined above. Think up your own category headings and groups of words and test them on your friends. Decide how long you should give them to learn the list, and the time interval for them to remember them.

- Should they undergo a distraction task in order to prevent rehearsal? Why (not)?
- Decide whether to use independent, matched or repeated measures design. Explain your choice (see pages 80–82).
- Work out the mean scores for each list and draw an appropriate graph to illustrate the means. Justify your choice of graph (see pages 96–99 for help).

Chunking

The capacity of STM can be increased if separate 'bits' of information are grouped together into larger 'chunks'. For example, the number 19391945 can be 'chunked' or organised in such a way that it is seen as the start and end dates of the Second World War. Reading involves the chunking, or organising, of letters into words and words into sentences. For Miller (1956), the capacity of STM is seven plus or minus two ($7^{+/-2}$) *chunks* rather than individual pieces of information (see Table 1.1 on page 10).

Imagery

The use of imagery is perhaps the most important mnemonic. It is believed that the visual sense is of greatest importance in memory (see Rolls, 2007). Indeed, the *method of loci* is the oldest documented mnemonic since it was mentioned in Cicero's *De Oratore*. In order to use the method of loci, you need to think of a familiar route, say your walk to college. Imagine a mental walk along this route and note various locations ('loci') along the way. Next, you need to create images to represent the material to be remembered. Concrete words such as 'desk' are easier to visualise than abstract words like 'love' (perhaps visualised as a heart?). Once you have done this, you need to visualise the route and place the images to be remembered at 'loci' on the route. The more bizarre the image, the better. To recall the list, you recreate the route in your head, noticing the desk by the bus stop and the heart in the shop window and so on until you have remembered the entire list.

Evaluation of the use of imagery

One advantage of this method is that you recall the list in the correct sequence. However, one disadvantage is that you cannot re-use the route too often, else interference between different lists can occur. It is also difficult to recall a particular item without going through the entire list in order until you reach the item you want, or to perfect this method if the information is presented too fast.

Peg word mnemonic

This mnemonic exploits the use of visual imagery and rhyme and rhythm, and uses numbers instead of places. These numbers are transformed into visual images by means of the following simple rhyme:

one is a bun
two is a shoe
three is a tree
four is a door
five is a hive
six is sticks
seven is heaven
eight is a gate
nine is a line
ten is a hen.

Having learnt this, you need to visualise the items to be remembered and imagine them interacting with the item of the appropriate number. For example, if the first word to be remembered is 'fish', you need to imagine a fish in a bun, and so on.

Evaluation of pegword mnemonic

The initial rhyme has to be learned by rote. Due to this, there is more learning than that involved with the method of loci mnemonic where the route is already known.

When there is more than one list to recall, interference between the lists often occurs. It remains a fairly slow method to use since you have to repeat the rhyme each time. It doesn't work well when abstract words (e.g. hope) are to be recalled. It is also difficult to use effectively without extensive practice.

'Non-memory' factors that improve memory

Memory improvements can also occur through the optimisation of non-memory factors such as a person's physical/emotional state or due to environmental conditions. Often these factors work by rectifying states that impair memory function (Herrmann and Palmisano, 1992).

External cues: context-dependent forgetting (or remembering)

This suggests that the context or place where material is learnt can affect recall. Godden and Baddeley (1975) got underwater divers to learn word lists either on dry land or underwater. They then had to recall the words in each of these places. Results showed that words learnt and recalled in the same context were remembered better. However, Fernandez and Glenberg (1985) have tried to replicate such studies and have never found consistent support for context-dependent effects. In practical terms, it seems useful to learn material in the same place that it will be recalled.

How Science Works

Practical Learning Activity 1.9: Context-dependent memory

Devise a list of 20 words that participants have to try to remember. Choose 20 of your classmates or friends to take part in the study. Give them all 3 minutes to try to learn the words. Then ask ten of the participants to move to another place or context to recall the words. Let the other ten stay in the same room to recall the words. Note down any differences in the average recall of the two groups.

● What can you conclude about the results?
● Did you find a 'same context' effect? (The sampling technique used involves opportunity sampling – see pages 93–94 in Chapter 3, 'Research methods'.)
● What are the advantages of the opportunity sampling method?
● Outline other sampling methods that you might have used, and explain the advantages and disadvantages associated with each.

Internal cues: state-dependent forgetting (or remembering)

This suggests that the physiological state a person is in can affect recall. Goodwin *et al.* (1969) examined this effect with alcohol. Participants who hid money while drunk were more likely to remember the hiding place when they were back in their original drunken state. Darley *et al.* (1973) found similar effects for marijuana. Studies have also investigated the effect of mood on recall but results have been inconclusive. Ucros (1989), with a meta-analysis (review) of all the research, concluded that there was a small state-dependent effect of mood.

 ## Assessment Check 1.4

Alice is visiting her doctor. She needs to remember all the information that the doctor tells her.

1. Outline TWO methods of memory improvement that might help Alice, and explain why they should improve recall. (4 marks)
2. Describe ONE memory improvement strategy that helps memory recall. (4 marks)

Conclusion

There are three characteristics central to remembering:

1 organise the material in a meaningful way

2 use as many retrieval cues as possible (particularly visual cues)

3 practise as much as possible.

It might be worth remembering that in your exams!

SUMMARY
Models of memory

CHAPTER

- There are three basic processes in memory: **encoding** (the transformation of a sensory input for it to be registered in memory), **storage** (the process of retaining information) and **retrieval** (the process of locating and extracting information).

- The **MSM (multi-store model)** of memory proposes that information flows from STM to LTM provided that rehearsal has taken place. Key elements within each of the memory stores are **capacity**, **encoding** and **duration**.

- Information encoded in **STM (short-term memory)** is mainly **acoustic** (Baddeley, 1966). STM capacity is $7^{+/-2}$ **items** (Jacobs, 1887). This can be increased by 'chunking'. STM lasts less than **30 seconds** (Peterson and Peterson, 1959).

- Information encoded in **LTM (long-term memory)** is mainly **semantic** (Baddeley, 1966). LTM capacity is **limitless**. LTM can last a **lifetime** (Bahrick *et al.*, 1975).

- Studies such as the **serial position curve** (Murdock, 1962) and **clinical case studies** (e.g. H.M.) support the existence of separate STM/LTM stores. The **primacy effect** demonstrates LTM, and the **recency effect** demonstrates STM recall.

- The **WM (working memory)** model is one alternative to the MSM and questions the idea of one unitary STM store. Instead, STM is seen as comprising a **central executive**, an **articulatory control system**, **phonological store** and **visuo-spatial scratchpad**. **Dual-task methods** provide support for this model. However, the function of the central executive remains unclear.

Memory in everyday life

- One of the most important practical applications of memory research is **EWT** (eyewitness testimony). As long ago as 1932, **Bartlett** showed that memory is prone to inaccuracies and interpretations based on prior expectations (or '**schemas**').

- **Elizabeth Loftus** applied the idea of reconstructive memory to EWT.

- **Anxiety of witness** is one factor that affects EWT accuracy. It is generally thought that the relationship between anxiety levels and performance follows an inverted-U shape (Deffenbacher, 1983), although Deffenbacher (2004) subsequently suggested that this is rather a simplistic explanation.

- **Age of witness** can also influence EWT. Children and older adults seem less reliable witnesses than middle-aged adults, although context reinstatement and the perceived seriousness of the crime can alter such findings.

- **Misleading questions ('leading' and 'after the fact information' questions)** have been shown experimentally to affect EWT (Loftus and Palmer, 1974). However, real-life studies into EWT have not demonstrated so clearly the reconstructive nature of such memories (Yuille and Cutshall, 1986). It may be that demand characteristics explain some of these research findings.

- The development of the **cognitive interview** has been an attempt to minimise the inaccuracy and distortion of EWT. Cognitive interviewing involves a **change of narrative order**, **a change of perspective** and the **mental reinstatement of the context** by the witness. Witnesses are also asked to recall all details, however trivial they may seem. There seems to be considerable support for the efficacy of cognitive interviews (Fisher *et al.*, 1989) although there appear to remain some practical problems with their use by the police.

- It is clear that the more information is organised, the easier it is to recall. Strategies that lead to memory improvement are called **mnemonics**; these include **chunking** and **the use of imagery** (including **method of loci** and **peg word system**). There are so-called non-memory factors that also aid memory recall, such as **context-dependent** and **state-dependent memory**.

AS Unit 1

Developmental psychology: early social development

What's covered in this chapter?

You need to know about:

Attachment

- Explanations of attachment, including learning theory and evolutionary perspectives, including Bowlby
- Types of attachment, including insecure and secure attachment and studies by Ainsworth
- Cultural variations in attachment
- Disruption of attachment, failure to form attachments (privation) and the effects of institutionalisation

Attachment in everyday life

- The impact of different forms of day care on children's social development, including the effects on aggression and peer relations
- Implications of research into attachment and day care for childcare practice

 Specification Hint

The order in which the material is covered within this chapter differs in places from the order shown in 'What's covered in this chapter?' on page 33 – which reproduces the exact wording of the Specification. We have chosen to deal with the topic this way because it is more logical; for example, it makes sense to know about different types of attachment before considering explanations of attachment. But this shouldn't affect your ability to answer exam questions: the content is the same, it's only the order that's different.

Attachment

What is attachment?

According to Schaffer (1996), we can formally define an attachment as:

... a long-enduring, emotionally meaningful tie to a particular individual. The object of the attachment is generally someone (most often a parent) who returns the child's feelings, creating a tie that can be extremely powerful and emotionally laden in both directions.

The first part of Schaffer's definition applies to attachments at any point in a person's life, but our earliest attachment serves as a *prototype* (model) for all later attachments. The crucial first attachment is usually taken to be with our mother.

Phases in the development of attachments

The attachment process can be divided into several phases, as described in Box 2.1.

Box 2.1: Phases in the development of attachments (based on Schaffer, 1996)

- The **pre-attachment phase** (birth to 3 months). From about six weeks, babies develop an attraction to other human beings. They prefer other people to physical objects and events, and one way of showing this preference is through smiling in response to people's faces. They direct this 'social smile' to just about anyone.

- The **indiscriminate attachment phase** (3 to 7/8 months). Babies begin to discriminate between familiar and unfamiliar people, smiling much more at people they know – the social smile has disappeared. But they'll still allow strangers to handle and look after them (they don't become visibly distressed), provided they're treated properly.

- The **discriminate attachment phase** (7/8 months onwards). Babies begin to develop specific attachments. They show this through (a) actively trying to stay close to particular people (especially the mother), and (b) becoming distressed when separated from them (separation anxiety). The baby can now consistently tell the difference between its mother and other people, but not for another few months will it also understand that she continues to exist even when she's out of sight (object permanence). Also at this time, babies avoid close contact with unfamiliar people. Some display the fear-of-strangers response, which includes crying and trying to move away. This usually occurs only if the stranger tries to make contact with them.

- The **multiple attachments phase** (9 months onwards). The baby forms strong emotional ties with (a) other major caregivers (such as the father, grandparents and older siblings), and (b) non-caregivers (similar-age siblings and other children). The fear-of-strangers response weakens, but the attachment to the mother remains the strongest.

How Science Works

Practical Learning Activity 2.1

If there are any young babies in your family, or any others that you have fairly regular contact with, observe their behaviour towards their mother, other (possible) attachment figures, and strangers. Try to identify the attachment phase they're at (preferably without knowing their age), specifying the behaviours that influenced your decision.

- Do you expect that all babies will move from phase to phase at the same age?
- Is it inevitable that the strongest attachment will always be with the mother? Give your reasons.
- Do you think that every baby's attachment to its mother is the same (for example, equally strong or secure)?

Types of attachment

Key Study 2.1: Ainsworth *et al.*'s (1971, 1978) Strange Situation Study of Attachments (SSoA)

Aim/hypothesis (AO1)

In 1971 and 1978, Ainsworth and her colleagues reported their findings from the Baltimore study of attachment. This was a replication (in Baltimore, USA) of an earlier study Ainsworth had conducted in Uganda, Africa (1967). In that earlier

study, she observed babies aged 15 weeks to two years over a nine-month period, and interviewed their mothers. Ainsworth's main interest was in *individual differences* between mother–child pairs in terms of the quality of their attachments.

Method/design (AO1)

Like the Uganda study, the Baltimore study was *longitudinal.* Ainsworth *et al.* visited 26 mother–child pairs at home every three to four weeks for the babies' first year of life, each visit lasting three to four hours. Also like the earlier study, both interviews and naturalistic observation were used (but the latter now played a much greater role).

To make sense of the vast amount of data collected for each pair, Ainsworth *et al.* needed some standard against which to compare their observations. The standard they chose was the **Strange Situation**, which comprises eight episodes (each lasting about three minutes, except for episode 1, which lasts 30 seconds), as shown in Table 2.1.

Every aspect of the participants' behaviour is observed and videotaped, but most attention is given to the baby's response to the mother's return (*reunion behaviours*). In the Baltimore study, the Strange Situation was used when the babies were 12 months old (the age group it's designed for).

Episode	Persons present	Brief description
1	Mother, baby, observer	Observer introduces mother and baby to experimental room, then leaves
2	Mother, baby	Mother is passive while the baby explores
3	Stranger, mother, baby	Stranger enters. First minute: stranger silent. Second minute: stranger converses with mother. Third minute: stranger approaches baby. After three minutes, mother leaves unobtrusively
4	Stranger, baby	First separation episode. Stranger's behaviour is geared to the baby's
5	Mother, baby	First reunion episode. Stranger leaves. Mother greets and/or comforts baby, then tries to settle baby again in play. Mother then leaves, saying 'bye-bye'
6	Baby	Second separation episode
7	Stranger, baby	Continuation of second separation. Stranger enters and gears her behaviour to the baby's
8	Mother, baby	Second reunion episode. Mother enters, greets baby, then picks up baby. Meanwhile, stranger leaves unobtrusively

Table 2.1: The eight episodes of the Strange Situation

Results (AO1)

As a group, babies explored the playroom and toys more enthusiastically when (just) the mother was present than *either* (a) after the stranger entered, *or* (b) when the mother was absent. But Ainsworth *et al.* were fascinated by the unexpected variety of reunion behaviours, and classified the babies in terms of three types of attachment, as follows.

1 15 per cent of the sample was classified as **anxious-avoidant (Type A)**. These babies typically ignored the mother, showing *indifference* towards her. Their play was hardly affected by whether she was present or absent. They showed few signs of stress when she left the room, and actively ignored or avoided her when she returned. They responded to the mother and stranger in very similar ways, and were most distressed when left on their own.

2 70 per cent were classified as **securely attached (Type B)**. They played quite happily while the mother was present (whether or not the stranger was there), but they became very upset when she left and their play was seriously disrupted. When the mother returned, they wanted immediate comfort from her; they quickly calmed down and started playing again. Overall, they treated the mother and stranger very differently.

3 15 per cent were classified as **anxious-resistant (Type C)**. These babies were fussy and wary, even when the mother was present, and they cried a lot more than Types A and B. When the mother left, they became very distressed. When she returned, they wanted contact with her, but *at the same time* showed anger and resisted contact. For example, they'd put their arms out to be picked up, but then immediately struggled to get down again. This demonstrated their *ambivalence* towards her.

Conclusions (AO1)

The Baltimore study's findings largely confirmed those of the Uganda study. The mother's *sensitivity* is the crucial factor that determines the quality of her child's attachment. Sensitive mothers see things from the baby's perspective, correctly interpret the baby's signals and respond to its needs. They're also accepting, cooperative, and accessible. Sensitive mothers tend to have babies that are *securely attached*, whereas insensitive mothers tend to have *insecurely attached* babies (either *anxious-avoidant* or *anxious-resistant*).

Evaluation (AO1/AO2)

According to Van Ijzendoorn and Schuengel (1999), the Baltimore study is the most important study in the history of attachment research (despite its rather small sample, and that of the Uganda study). They cite several more recent studies, using larger samples, which have tested and supported the original claim that parental sensitivity actually *causes* attachment security. However, most debate has focused on the Strange Situation itself.

How Science Works
Practical Learning Activity 2.2

- Draw up a list of 'fors' and 'againsts' the Strange Situation; this should include both methodological and ethical issues. Alternatively, you could hold a class debate.
- How would you describe the Strange Situation – that is, what kind of method(s) does it involve?
- Can you think of alternative ways of studying babies'/young children's attachments? What advantages/disadvantages might these have compared with the Strange Situation?

Evaluation of the Strange Situation

✔ **Established methodology:** the Strange Situation is the most widely used method for assessing attachment to a caregiver (it has become 'paradigmatic' – that is, a basic way of investigating the topic).

✗ **A stable characteristic?** Attachment type (based on the Strange Situation) is often taken to measure a *fixed characteristic* of the child. But if the family's circumstances change (such as the mother's stress levels), how the child is classified can also change. This couldn't happen if attachment style were a permanent characteristic.

✗ **Different parental relationships:** attachments to the mother and father are *independent* – that is, the same child might be securely attached to its mother but insecurely attached to its father. This shows that attachment patterns reflect *qualities of distinct relationships*, rather than characteristics of the child.

✗ **Low ecological validity:** some regard it as a highly artificial way of assessing attachment – it is a laboratory-based situation in which mother and stranger act according to a 'script', far removed from what happens in everyday, naturalistic situations. This is related to the next point.

✗ **Ethically dubious:** the Strange Situation is designed to see how young children react to an increasingly stressful situation. Although under normal circumstances mothers do leave their children for brief periods, often with strangers (such as unfamiliar babysitters or childminders), we must question the ethics of any method used in psychological research that *deliberately* exposes children to stress.

Cultural variations in attachment

The pioneering *cross-cultural study* of attachment was Ainsworth's (1967) Uganda study (see Key Study 2.1). Cross-cultural studies using the Strange Situation have shown important differences, both *within* and *between* cultures; these differences sometimes say more about the Strange Situation than about the cultures concerned, sometimes the reverse is true, and sometimes it's difficult to separate the two factors.

Key Study 2.2: Van Ijzendoorn and Kroonenberg's (1988) Review of Patterns of Attachments (RPA)

Aim/hypothesis (AO1)

Van Ijzendoorn and Kroonenberg wanted to compare the findings of studies using the Strange Situation conducted in different cultures. They were interested in *patterns* of attachment type (secure/avoidant/resistant) both between and within cultures.

Method/design (AO1)

They reviewed 32 worldwide studies involving eight countries and over 2000 children (see Table 2.2). These studies had been conducted by other researchers, and Van Ijzendoorn and Kroonenberg compared the studies, looking for any general trends.

Results (AO1)

See Table 2.2.

Country	No. of studies	Percentage of each type of attachment		
		Type B (Securely attached	Type A (Anxious–avoidant)	Type C (Anxious–resistant)
West Germany	3	57	35	8
Great Britain	1	75	22	3
Netherlands	4	67	26	7
Sweden	1	74	22	4
Israel	2	64	7	29
Japan	2	68	5	27
China	1	50	25	25
US	18	65	21	14

Table 2.2: Percentage of children displaying attachment types in eight countries

Conclusions (AO1)

The overall worldwide pattern was similar to Ainsworth *et al.*'s 'standard' pattern. This was also true of the 18 American studies as a whole, although there was considerable variation *within* these studies. The standard pattern shows Type B to be the most common and Type C the least common. However,

Type A is the least common in Israel and Japan, and Type C is relatively more common. But there were marked differences between the two Japanese studies. In one, there were *no* Type A children at all, but a high proportion of Type C; in the other, the pattern was more like that of Ainsworth *et al.* So, there are marked differences *within* cultures – as well as between some.

Evaluation (AO1/AO2)

The countries included in the review are both western and non-western (China and Japan), but only three of the 32 studies were carried out in China and Japan. The different patterns of reaction to the Strange Situation seem to reflect cultures' values and practices. For example, the greater frequency of Type A (anxious-avoidant) in Germany may reflect cultural emphasis on early independence training. Rogoff (2003) cites a study by True *et al.* (2001) involving the Dogon people of West Africa, which found a complete absence of Type A; this may stem from the community's infant care practices, which involve responsiveness, constant closeness to mothers, and immediate nursing in response to signs of stress.

The greater frequency of Type C in Japan may result from greater stress during the Strange Situation due to infants' unfamiliarity with being left with strangers. Japanese children are rarely separated from their mothers, so the separation episodes are the most upsetting for these children. In contrast, for African-American infants, who are used to being tended by several caregivers and who

Constant bodily contact with the mother would make the Strange Situation an extremely stressful way of trying to assess this baby's attachment to her

are encouraged to be friendly to the many strangers they encounter, the Strange Situation may arouse their interest in exploration (Rogoff, 2003). For children raised on Israeli *kibbutzim* (small, close-knit communities), it's the arrival of the stranger that's most distressing. This shows that the Strange Situation has a *different meaning* in different cultures; we need to know about the child-rearing practices of different cultures if we're to interpret findings based on the Strange Situation validly.

How Science Works
Practical Learning Activity 2.3

- Which countries' studies most closely match the results found by Ainsworth *et al.* (1971, 1978) in their Baltimore study?
- Which countries' studies are most different from the Baltimore findings?
- Can you think of any possible reasons for the differences between countries (especially those you identified in the previous question)? (These might reflect the child-rearing practices in those countries and/or the appropriateness of using the Strange Situation for assessing attachment in those countries.)
- What general conclusions can you draw from these results?
- Are the countries studied representative of the world's cultures?

Assessment Check 2.1

1. Define the terms 'attachment', the 'social smile', and 'separation anxiety'. (2 + 2 + 2 marks)
2. Outline the basic procedure involved in the Strange Situation. (4 marks)
3. Describe the main characteristics of anxious-avoidant (Type A), secure (Type B) and anxious-resistant (Type C) attachment. (3 + 3 + 3 marks)
4. Outline TWO weaknesses of the Strange Situation. (2 + 2 marks)
5. Describe and evaluate research into cultural variations in attachment. (12 marks)

Explanations of attachment

Learning theory

Learning theory refers to **behaviourist** attempts to explain all behaviour in terms of **conditioning** (see Chapter 6, pages 190–194). According to learning theory accounts of attachment formation, through **classical conditioning** babies learn to associate their caregivers with food, which is an **unconditioned** or **primary reinforcer**. The caregiver is a **conditioned** or **secondary reinforcer**. The baby feels secure when the caregiver is present – that is, she comes to be rewarding in her own right (without the need for food).

However, because the caregiver only becomes rewarding through her satisfying the baby's physiological needs, learning theory is known as a '**cupboard love theory**'.

Evaluation of learning theory

✗   **It's based largely on research involving non-human animals:** we cannot be sure that these findings apply to attachment in children.

✗   **Even baby monkeys need comfort more than food:** Harlow (1959) studied learning using rhesus monkeys. He separated newborns from their mothers and raised them in cages on their own, each cage containing a 'baby blanket'. The babies became extremely distressed whenever the blanket was removed for any reason, which is similar to how baby monkeys react when they're separated from their mothers. This suggested to Harlow that attachment *isn't* based on association with food.

To test this hypothesis, Harlow placed baby rhesus monkeys in cages with two surrogate (substitute) mothers. One was made from wire and had a baby bottle fitted to 'her'; the other was made from soft, cuddly terry cloth (but didn't have a bottle fitted) (see the accompanying photograph). The babies spent most of their time clinging to the cloth mother, even though she provided no milk; they'd stretch across to the wire mother to feed while still clinging to the cloth mother. Harlow concluded that monkeys have an innate (inborn), unlearned need for **contact comfort**; this is as basic as the need for food (at least in baby rhesus monkeys).

✗   **There's more to human attachment than 'cupboard love':** Schaffer and Emerson (1964) studied 60 babies every four weeks throughout their first year, then again at 18 months. Mothers were asked about the babies' protests in various separation situations, including being left alone in a room, being left with a babysitter and being put to bed. The babies were clearly attached to people who weren't involved in their physical care (notably the father). Also, in 39

A baby rhesus monkey clinging to a 'cloth mother'

per cent of cases, the mother (usually the main carer) *wasn't* the baby's main attachment figure. For Schaffer (1971), 'cupboard love' theories of attachment put things the wrong way round: babies don't 'live to eat', but 'eat to live'. They're *active seekers of stimulation*, not passive recipients of nutrition.

The evolutionary perspective: Bowlby's theory

Bowlby's attachment theory was influenced by several other theorists and researchers. As a trained psychoanalyst, he was influenced by Freud's theories, as well as drawing on his own work with children and adults (see Chapter 6, pages 187–189). In rejecting cupboard love theories, such as learning theory, he cited Harlow's research with rhesus monkeys (see above), as well as Lorenz's (1935) study of *imprinting* in goslings and other bird species. Imprinting is a form of attachment in which young birds learn to follow the first large, moving object they see during a specific time (*critical period*) after hatching; this tendency is instinctive and requires no learning.

Applying these different ideas to human infants, Bowlby claimed that their emotional tie to the mother had an evolutionary and a biological function. They evolved because, in the human species' distant past, at a time when humans were in real danger from predators, a mechanism was needed whereby offspring could keep close to their caregivers and so obtain protection and thereby increase their chances of survival. Through the course of evolution, helpless human infants have become *genetically programmed* to behave towards their mothers in ways that ensure their survival (Bowlby, 1969, 1973). These *species-specific attachment behaviours* include crying (which attracts parents' attention), looking, smiling and vocalising (which maintain parental attention and interest), and following or clinging (which gain or maintain physical closeness to the parents).

These attachment behaviours are in the baby's response repertoire from the early months on; they function in an automatic, stereotyped way to begin with and are triggered initially by a wide range of others. But, during the first year, they become focused on just one or

Lorenz being followed by goslings, which had imprinted on him after hatching

two individuals and organised into more flexible and sophisticated behaviour systems (Schaffer, 2004).

So, the *biological* function of attachment is survival, while the *psychological* function is to gain security. But this would only work, of course, if the mother responds to these attachment behaviours. Hence, during the course of evolution a maternal attachment system emerged to complement that of the baby, ensuring the mother's responsiveness to the baby's signals. However, the baby doesn't have to be her biological child: babies need adequate *mothering* (a mother-figure), rather than their birth (natural) mother.

According to Bowlby, an attachment functions like a *control system* (such as a thermostat); it's geared to maintain a particular steady state – namely, to stay close to the mother. When that state is attained, attachment behaviour is 'quiet' – the baby has no need to cry or cling, and can get on with play and exploration. But when the state is threatened (for example, the mother disappears from view or a stranger approaches), attachment behaviours are activated in order to restore it. Generally, attachment behaviours are more evident when the child is distressed, unwell, frightened or in unfamiliar surroundings, but which particular responses are produced will change as the child gets older and becomes more competent – cognitively and behaviourally (Schaffer, 2004).

Bowlby (1951) claims that there's a **critical period** for the formation of attachments: mothering must take place within a certain time period if the child is to be able to form an attachment. Mothering is useless for *most* children if delayed until after 12 months, and it's useless for *all* children if delayed until after two-and-a-half to three years. Also, babies display **monotropy**, a strong, innate tendency to become attached to one particular adult female (usually, but not necessarily, the biological mother – see above). This attachment is *unique*: it's the first to develop and is the strongest of all. For Bowlby:

Mother love in infancy is as important for mental health as vitamins and proteins for physical health.

How Science Works
Practical Learning Activity 2.4

- Bowlby seems to imply that female adults instinctively know how to respond to the attachment behaviours of babies and young children. Do you agree? Does a 'maternal instinct' exist? You could perhaps conduct a survey (try to question equal numbers of males and females and see how their answers compare); and/or hold a class debate.
- Repeat the exercise (or make it part of the first one) for the question 'Are men capable of "mothering"?'

Evaluation of Bowlby's attachment theory

✗ **The mother isn't special in the way Bowlby claimed:** babies and young children display a whole range of attachment behaviours towards various attachment figures *other than their mothers* (Rutter, 1981). In other words, there's no particular attachment behaviour that is used specifically and exclusively towards the mother.

✗ **Multiple attachments are the norm:** although Bowlby didn't deny that children form multiple attachments, Schaffer and Emerson's (1964) study (see above) showed that these are the rule (rather than the exception).

✗ **Fathers can be 'mothers' too:** for Bowlby, fathers aren't of any *direct* emotional importance to the baby – their main role is to provide emotional and financial support to the mother. But, again, Schaffer and Emerson's findings suggest that fathers can be attachment figures *in their own right*.

Bowlby's maternal deprivation hypothesis (MDH)

As we saw earlier, Bowlby claimed that there's a **critical period** for attachment formation. He combined this with his theory of **monotropy** to form his **maternal deprivation hypothesis (MDH)**, according to which the mother–infant attachment cannot be broken in the first year of life without the child's emotional and intellectual development being seriously and permanently harmed. For Bowlby (1951):

An infant and young child should experience a warm, intimate and continuous relationship with his mother (or permanent mother-figure) in which both find satisfaction and enjoyment.

Bowlby's MDH was based largely on studies (conducted in the 1930s and 1940s) of children brought up in orphanages and residential nurseries. Goldfarb (1943) studied 15 children raised in institutions (group 1) from about six months until three-and-a-half years of age; they lived in almost total social isolation during their first year. They were matched with 15 children who'd gone straight from their natural mothers to foster homes (group 2). At age three, group 1 lagged behind group 2 on measures of abstract thinking, social maturity, rule-following and sociability. Between the ages of 10 and 14, group 1 continued to perform more poorly, and their average IQs (intelligence quotients) were 72 and 95 respectively.

Spitz (1945, 1946) studied children raised in some very poor-quality South American orphanages. Staff were overworked and untrained, and rarely talked to the babies or picked them up, even for feeding; they were shown no affection and didn't have any toys. The babies displayed 'anaclitic depression' (a reaction to the loss of a love object). This includes fear, sadness, weepiness, withdrawal, loss of appetite, weight loss, inability to sleep, and developmental retardation.

Spitz and Wolf (1946) studied 91 orphanage infants in the USA and Canada; over a third died before their first birthday, despite good nutrition and medical care.

Evaluation of Bowlby's MDH

According to Bowlby, Goldfarb, Spitz and Wolf, all these institutions had one factor in common – namely, lack of maternal care. This was the crucial harmful influence on the children growing up in them (which Bowlby later called maternal deprivation). However, this interpretation fails to do the following things:

✗ **Recognise some of the methodological weaknesses of these studies:** for example, in Goldfarb's study the children weren't assigned randomly to the two 'conditions' (groups 1 and 2), as would happen in a true experiment. It's possible that group 2 children were brighter, more easy-going, sociable and healthy from a very early age, and that this is why they were fostered (rather than sent to an institution). The poorer development of the group 1 children may have been due as much to these early differences as to the time they spent in institutions.

✗ **Recognise that the institutions were extremely unstimulating environments for young children:** this lack of stimulation could have been responsible for their poor development, as opposed to (or in addition to) the absence of maternal care. In other words, a crucial variable in intellectual development is the amount of *intellectual stimulation* a child receives, *not* the amount of mothering.

✗ **Distinguish between the effects of deprivation and privation** (Rutter, 1981): *deprivation* ('de-privation') refers to the *loss through separation* of the (maternal) attachment figure; this assumes that an attachment has already developed. *Privation* refers to the *absence* of an attachment figure: there's been no opportunity to form an attachment with anyone in the first place. The studies of Goldfarb and others are most accurately seen as demonstrating the effects of *privation*, yet Bowlby's theory and his own research were mainly concerned with *deprivation*. Figure 2.1 shows that deprivation and privation refer to two very different kinds of early experience; each has very different types of effect, both short and long term. These are discussed in the next section.

Deprivation (loss/separation)

e.g. child/mother going into hospital, mother going out to work, death of mother (which may occur through suicide or murder witnessed by the child), parental separation/divorce, natural disasters. These are all examples of *acute stress* (Schaffer, 1996)

Privation (lack/absence)

e.g. being raised in an orphanage/other institution, or suffering *chronic adversity* (Schaffer, 1996), as in the case of the Czech twins (Koluchova, 1972, 1991) and the Romanian orphans (Chisolm *et al.*, 1995).

Long-term effects
Developmental retardation (e.g. affectionless psychopathy)

Short-term effects
Distress

Long-term effects
e.g. separation anxiety

Figure 2.1: Examples of the differences between deprivation and privation, including their effects

Assessment Check 2.2

1. Outline TWO weaknesses of the learning theory explanation of attachment. (2 + 2 marks)
2. Define what is meant by the terms 'cupboard love', 'contact comfort', and 'monotropy'. (2 + 2 + 2 marks)
3. Outline and evaluate Bowlby's attachment theory. (12 marks)
4. Describe Bowlby's maternal deprivation hypothesis. (6 marks)
5. Define what is meant by the terms 'anaclitic depression', 'imprinting', and a 'critical period'. (2 + 2 + 2 marks)
6. Distinguish between the terms 'deprivation' and 'privation'. (3 marks)

Disruption of attachment
The effects of deprivation/separation

One example of **short-term deprivation** (days/weeks, rather than months/years) is a child going into a nursery while its mother goes into hospital. Alternatively, the child might stay with foster parents. In addition, children sometimes have to go into hospital themselves.

Robertson and Robertson made a series of films in the 1960s documenting how young children's brief separation from their mother affected their mental state and psychological development. One of these films (1969) featured John (see the photograph on the next page). According to Robertson and Robertson (1989), 'He was a sturdy, good-looking boy

John (17 months) experienced extreme distress while spending nine days in a residential nursery when his mother was in hospital having a second baby. According to Bowlby, he was grieving for the absent mother. Robertson and Robertson (1969) (who made a series of films called Young Children in Brief Separation) found that the extreme distress was caused by a combination of factors: multiple caretakers, lack of a mother substitute, loss of the mother and strange environment and routines

who ate and slept well and said a few words. John and his mother had a quiet and harmonious relationship.' He became increasingly distressed from day three of his nine-day stay in a residential nursery (the first time he'd been separated from his mother). On day nine, when his mother arrived to take him home, he started throwing himself around and crying loudly. When she tried to put him on her lap, he struggled, screamed and ran away from her. Although he did finally lie quietly on her lap, he never once looked at her. When his father arrived, he 'escaped' into his father's arms. During the course of the nine days in the residential nursery, John displayed all the components of *distress* as described by Bowlby (1969).

Box 2.2: The components of distress (Bowlby, 1969)

- **Protest:** the immediate reaction to separation involves crying, screaming, kicking and generally struggling to escape, or clinging to the mother to prevent her from leaving. This is an *outward*, direct expression of the child's anger, fear, bitterness and confusion.

- **Despair:** the struggling and protest are eventually replaced by calmer behaviour. The child may seem apathetic, but still feels all the anger and fear etc. *inwardly*. S/he keeps these feelings 'locked up' and may no longer expect the mother to return. The child hardly reacts to other people's offers of comfort; instead, s/he prefers to comfort him/herself, by rocking or thumb-sucking.

- **Detachment:** if the separation continues, the child begins to respond to people again – but everyone is treated alike, and rather superficially. When reunited with the mother, the child may have to 'relearn' its relationship with her, possibly even 'rejecting' her as she 'rejected' him/her.

How Science Works
Practical Learning Activity 2.5

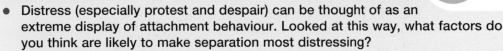

- Distress (especially protest and despair) can be thought of as an extreme display of attachment behaviour. Looked at this way, what factors do you think are likely to make separation most distressing?
- One way you could investigate this is to role play the situation, with one of you taking the role of John, and others his mother, father and nursery staff.

The description of John above provides some clues, and Bowlby's attachment theory provides others.

Factors influencing distress

Separation is likely to be most distressing:

- between the ages of 7/8 months (when attachments are beginning to develop) and three years; there's a peak at 12–18 months (Maccoby, 1980)

- for boys, although there are also individual differences *within* each gender

- if there have been any behaviour problems (such as aggressiveness) prior to the separation

- if the relationship with the mother has been too close

- if the child has never been separated from the mother before

- if there aren't other attachment figures who can provide love and care in the mother's absence.

Long-term separation includes permanent separation resulting from the death of a parent. Children are also increasingly likely to be separated from one of their parents through divorce.

The effects of divorce

According to Schaffer (1996), almost all children are adversely affected by parental divorce, at least in the short term. This is true regardless of age, but especially true of boys. However, most children are resilient enough to adapt to their parents' divorce eventually (Hetherington and Stanley-Hagan, 1999).

The nature, severity and duration of the effects are influenced by several factors. These include:

- continuity of contact with the non-custodial parent

- the financial status/lifestyle of the custodial parent

- whether the custodial parent remarries, and the nature of the resulting step-family.

The effects include: (a) lower levels of academic achievement and self-esteem; (b) higher incidence (two to three times) of anti-social and delinquent behaviour, and other problems of psychological adjustment during childhood and adolescence; (c) earlier social maturity, with certain transitions to adulthood (such as leaving home, beginning sexual relationships, cohabiting or getting married and getting pregnant) typically occurring earlier; (d) tendency in young adulthood to more job changes, lower socio-economic status, and depression, plus a greater likelihood to be divorced themselves; and (e) more distant relationships in adulthood with parents and other relatives (Hetherington and Stanley-Hagan, 1999; Richards, 1995; Schaffer, 2004).

One important effect of long-term separation is what Bowlby called **separation anxiety** – that is, the fear that separation will occur again in the future. This may express itself as:

- increased aggressive behaviour, and greater demands made on the mother

- clinging behaviour – the child won't let the mother out of its sight

- detachment – the child becomes apparently self-sufficient (s/he cannot afford to be let down again – see the case of John, above)

- psychosomatic (psychophysiological) reactions – real physical symptoms associated with/caused by stress and anxiety (see Figure 4.4, page 114).

Another example of long-term deprivation is day care, which is discussed in the final section of this chapter (pages 55–61).

Failure to form attachments (privation) and the effects of institutionalisation

As we noted earlier, privation is the failure to develop an attachment to any individual. As the child's first relationship acts as a model, or prototype, of relationships in general, failure to develop an attachment of any kind is likely to have a negative effect on all future relationships.

Affectionless psychopathy

According to Bowlby, maternal deprivation in early childhood causes **affectionless psychopathy**. This is the inability to care and have deep feelings for other people, combined with the inability to experience guilt.

Bowlby et al. (1956) studied 60 children, aged 7–13 years, who'd spent between 5 and 24 months in a tuberculosis (TB) sanatorium at various ages up to 4 years; about half had been separated from their parents before their second birthday. As far as Bowlby was concerned, these children had experienced maternal deprivation and so were likely to have developed affectionless psychopathy.

They were compared to a group of non-separated (control) children from the same school classes. Those in the sanatorium group were more likely to display signs of emotional disturbance, but they *weren't* more likely to show affectionless psychopathy. Also, it made no difference when they were separated (before or after two years). Bowlby admitted that part of their emotional disturbance was due to factors *other than separation*, such as illness and death in their families. The study provides very little evidence for a link between affectionless psychopathy and separation/deprivation, but some of the sanatorium children may have suffered *privation*.

According to Rutter (1981), privation is likely to lead to:

- an initial phase of clinging, dependent behaviour

- attention-seeking and indiscriminate friendliness

- lack of guilt, an inability to follow rules and an inability to form lasting relationships (i.e. affectionless psychopathy).

Are the effects of privation reversible?

Some of the major kinds of study which show that it's possible to undo the effects of early privation include the following:

- Studies of *late adoption*. Children raised in institutions are adopted after Bowlby's critical period for attachment (12 months for most children, up to two-and-a-half/three years for the rest). Examples include the studies of Tizard and her colleagues (see Key Study 2.3).

- Case studies of children who have endured extreme early privation, often involving almost complete isolation. Examples include the Czech twins studied by Koluchova (1972, 1991 – see page 55).

Studies of late adoption

Key Study 2.3: Hodges and Tizard's (1989) study of Teenagers Raised in Orphanages (TRIO)

Aim/hypothesis (AO1)

This is the latest in a series of reports on the development of several children who spent at least the first two years of their lives in institutions. They subsequently grew up in family situations. They were first studied at age 4 (Tizard, 1977), then at age 8 (Tizard and Hodges, 1978); this study reports on these children at age 16.

This 'progress report' is common in *longitudinal studies*, in which the same group of people is followed up over a period of time (usually several years). This

represents an overall *approach* within developmental psychology – the aim is to study *change over time*.

Method/design (AO1)

Hodges and Tizard collected their data through interviews and questionnaires, with the participants (the 16-year-olds), their parents and teachers. The children left care between the ages of 2 and 7 years, when they were either adopted or returned to their own (biological) families. The children whose environment changed (the *ex-institution group*) were compared to similar children raised from birth by their natural parents (*matched controls*).

Results (AO1)

The institutions the teenagers grew up in provided good physical care and also appeared to offer adequate intellectual stimulation. But staff turnover was high and the institutions discouraged the formation of strong attachments between staff and children. As a result, the children had little opportunity to form close, continuous relationships with adults before they left care to live with a family.

By age 8, most of the adopted children had formed close attachments to their adoptive parents, but only some of those who had returned to their biological families had done so. The ex-institution group as a whole didn't have more problems than the control group (according to their parents), but their teachers thought they were attention-seeking, restless, disobedient and had poor peer relationships.

At age 16, most of the adopted children had mutually satisfying family relationships; in this respect, they were very similar to the control group. But those who had returned to their biological families still had poor family relationships: they had difficulty showing their parents affection (as did the parents towards them), and their parents reported feeling closer to their other children. However, *outside* the family, *both* the adopted and returned children were:

- still more likely to seek adult affection and approval
- still more likely to have difficulties in their peer relationships
- less likely to have a special friend, or to see peers as a source of emotional support
- more likely to be friendly towards any peer, rather than choosing their friends.

Conclusions (AO1)

Children who don't enjoy close, lasting relationships early on in life *can* still form attachments later on. The adopted children managed to have close relationships with their adoptive parents, and they became as much part of the family as any other child. This is contrary to Bowlby's MDH. However, these attachments don't develop simply by the child being placed in a family – they depend on the adults concerned and how they nurture such attachments. Adoptive parents very much wanted a child, while many of the biological parents seemed reluctant to have their children back.

In contrast, the finding that *all* the ex-institution adolescents had difficulties in their *peer* relationships suggests that early privation does leave its mark. This is consistent with Bowlby's MDH (although remember that he didn't distinguish between deprivation and privation).

Evaluation (AO1/AO2)

The findings are 'theoretically rich'. The data both support and contradict Bowlby's MDH. For example, they suggest that there may be a critical period for the formation of attachments to peers later in life, but there may *not* be one for forming attachments to adults.

There are methodological problems: how was it decided which children would be adopted and which would return to their biological families? This could have been based on certain characteristics of the children themselves, such as the more socially responsive being chosen for adoption. If so, the participants wouldn't all have had an equal chance of being allocated to one or other of the 'conditions' of this natural experiment (see Practical Learning Activity 2.6).

'Drop-out rate' (or attrition) is a major problem associated with longitudinal studies. Of the 51 ex-institution children studied at age 8, nine were unavailable (for various reasons) at age 16. So how *representative* of the institutionally reared children was the sample of 16-year-olds?

How reliable and valid are the data? Was there any independent check on the accuracy of the answers given in the interviews and questionnaires? How objective can parents be about their children, or children about their parents? How objective could the teachers be, since they knew which pupils were ex-institutional children?

How Science Works
Practical Learning Activity 2.6

Hodges and Tizard refer to their study as a form of 'natural experiment'.

- What does this mean and how does it differ from other kinds of experiment?
- Identify the independent and dependent variables in Hodges and Tizard's study.
- Outline two advantages and two disadvantages of a natural experiment compared with other kinds of experiment.
- Name some other psychological studies that could be described as natural experiments.
- What characteristics or abilities would have been important to consider when matching the ex-institution group and the control group?
- The issue regarding selecting children for adoption or return to their biological families is similar to one that arises in one of the studies on which Bowlby based his MDH. Can you name it?

Chisolm *et al.* (1995) studied Romanian orphans adopted by Canadian families between the ages of 8 months and 5 years, 6 months. The children had been reared in extremely poor conditions in large-scale institutions, and the early privation seemed to have some negative impact on their relationships with their adoptive parents. For example, their behaviour was often described as *ambivalent*: they both wanted contact and resisted it (see Key Study 2.1). Also, they weren't easily comforted when distressed.

Schaffer (1998) believes that, based on their intellectual recovery, there are good reasons for being optimistic that they will eventually overcome these problems. However, two follow-up studies of Romanian orphans adopted by British families suggest that there's a continuing effect of their early privation.

- When studied up to the age of 6 (Rutter *et al.*, 2004), many children displayed **disinhibited attachment** (DA). In many ways, this resembles the attachment behaviour of Hodges and Tizard's ex-institution sample: a lack of close, confiding relationships, rather indiscriminate friendliness (being friendly towards anyone who's 'available'), a relative lack of differentiation in response to different adults (treating them all alike), a tendency to go off with strangers, and a lack of checking back with a parent in anxiety-provoking situations.

- Rutter (2006) believes that DA might reflect how brain structure and functioning have been affected through the child's attempt to adapt to the poor environmental conditions it faced in the orphanage at a sensitive period of development. If this was the case, we'd expect it to persist into middle childhood and early adolescence. Rutter *et al.* (2007) reported a further follow-up at age 11. This confirmed that DA persisted from ages 6 to 11, although it did become less frequent during that period. Although DA was strongly associated with institutional rearing, children adopted after six months didn't display it significantly more, as we might expect them to.

Studies of extreme privation

What happens to children who suffer extreme early privation, but are then 'rescued' and enjoy much improved conditions?

Koluchova (1972, 1991) studied identical twin boys born in 1960 in the former Czechoslovakia. Their mother died shortly after their birth. At about 18 months of age, they went to live with their father, who had remarried. Their stepmother treated them very cruelly: they spent much of the next five-and-a-half years locked in the cellar and were harshly beaten.

The twins were discovered in 1967 and were legally removed from their parents. They were very short in stature and had rickets (caused by lack of calcium), had no spontaneous speech (communicating largely by gesture), and were terrified by many aspects of their new environment. After spending time in a school for children with learning difficulties, they were adopted by two women. By age 14, they showed no signs of psychological abnormality or unusual behaviour, and they progressed onto further education.

They both had very good relationships with their adoptive mothers, their adoptive sisters, and the women's other relatives. They both later married and had children, and at age 29 were entirely stable, with no abnormalities and enjoying warm relationships. Clearly, the twins' experience of prolonged early privation didn't predestine them to a life of severe handicap (Clarke and Clarke, 2000).

Assessment Check 2.3

1. Give TWO examples of short-term deprivation. (1 + 1 mark)
2. Outline the THREE components of distress. (2 + 2 + 2 marks)
3. Outline the THREE factors that are likely to make separation most distressing. (2 + 2 + 2 marks)
4. Give TWO examples of long-term deprivation. (1 + 1 mark)
5. Describe THREE effects of divorce. (2 + 2 + 2 marks)
6. Define what is meant by the terms 'separation anxiety', 'affectionless psychopathy', and 'disinhibited attachment'. (2 + 2 + 2 marks)
7. Outline and evaluate research into the effects of being brought up in an institution. (12 marks)

Attachment in everyday life

What is day care?

Day care includes all varieties of non-maternal care of children who normally live with their parent(s) or close relatives (Scarr, 1998). So, it *excludes* foster care and institutional (residential) care.

Day care *includes*:

● crèches, day nurseries, childminders (called 'home-based day care' in the USA) and other 'out-of-home' facilities

● nannies (non-resident), grandparents and other 'in-the-home' arrangements.

How Science Works
Practical Learning Activity 2.7

● **What do you think Bowlby's attitude towards day care would be?**
● **You could hold a class debate: 'Day care – for and against'. Alternatively, stage a discussion involving a student pretending to be Bowlby, another pretending to be, say, Rutter, chaired by, say, Jeremy Paxman, with the rest of the class being the audience invited to ask questions.**
● **Did you experience day care as a child? What, if anything, do you remember about it? Ask your mother and/or father about it: what effects – positive and negative – do they consider it had on you, and on the family as a whole?**

Attitudes towards day care

Most children are cared for by their own mothers, so childcare provided by anyone other than the child's mother is *non-normative*. This view partly reflects Bowlby's theory of attachment. In the early 1950s, Bowlby was the most high-profile critic of day care, arguing that child development, maternal well-being and human progress in general depended on the mother providing continuous care. The use of day nurseries and crèches was condemned as leading to the long-term emotional damage of future generations.

Bowlby (1953) recommended that:

We must recognise that leaving any child of under three years of age is a major operation only to be undertaken for good and sufficient reasons, and, when undertaken, to be planned with great care. On no account should the child be placed with people he doesn't know.

But in most industrialised societies, such as the UK and USA, women's increased participation in the workforce and the rise of single parenthood in recent decades has meant that substantial proportions of young children (of school age or younger) now spend parts of their week in day care. So, non-maternal shared childcare is now actually a *normative* experience. Indeed, according to Scarr (1998), childcare has *always* been shared (usually among female relatives), in *all* cultures (and so is *universal*).

The demand for childcare is driven entirely by the economic need for women in the labour force. In 1997, women comprised 49.5 per cent of those in paid employment in the UK, and in 2000 they outnumbered men, although with a far higher percentage in part-time work (Kremer, 1998). Just over 52 per cent of women in the UK with children under the age of five worked in 2003 (Hinsliff, 2004). However, many people still believe that women are 'meant to be' mothers (the *motherhood mystique/mandate*), a belief that affects our attitudes about working mothers (Kremer, 1998). Whether or not working mothers have pre-school children is still a significant factor shaping these attitudes.

Non-maternal shared care is both historically and culturally normative

The impact of day care on children's social development

Attachment

In Bowlby's terms, children whose mothers go out to work suffer maternal deprivation, experiencing repeated separations from, and (in Ainsworth *et al.*'s terms) reunions with, their principal caregiver. They're confronted with adults they don't (initially) know, who are responsible for several other children all competing for their attention. If this happens *before* they've become attached to the mother (during the child's first year), s/he may fail to form an attachment at all (remember, strictly this is *privation*); if it happens *after* an attachment has formed, the child will be distressed and may experience separation anxiety (see above, pages 47–50). So, what does the research evidence tell us about the effects of day care on children's attachments?

Durkin (1995) cites studies which show that, although day care staff behave differently from mothers, and have to divide their attention between several children, children tend to relate happily to them and sometimes become attached to them. But familiar caregivers aren't forgotten as a result of these new relationships, and mothers remain the preferred attachment figure when the child is distressed.

The stability and quality of day care

The daily separations involved in day care *don't* weaken the attachment to the mother, and children suffer no ill effects provided the day care is *stable* and of a reasonable *quality*. They might even benefit from the experience (Schaffer, 1996). But how should we assess the quality of day care? According to Scarr (1998), there's widespread agreement about the criteria used to assess quality, including:

- health and safety requirements

- responsive and warm interaction between children and staff

- developmentally appropriate curriculum

- limited group size

- age-appropriate caregiver:child ratios

- adequate indoor and outdoor space

- adequate staff training

- low staff turnover (as a measure of the *stability* of care).

Studies have found that poor-quality care puts children's development at risk: they're likely to obtain lower language and cognitive scores; and they're also likely to be rated lower on social and emotional development. However, the quality of care chosen by parents is correlated with their personal characteristics or circumstances. For example, children from families with single working mothers or low incomes are more likely to experience low-quality care. As a result, we cannot be sure whether it's the quality of day care or the parental characteristics that influence(s) children's development; this confusion between the two variables has led to an *over-estimation* of the effects of day care (Scarr, 1998).

But is there any reason to believe that day care can be harmful even if it is both stable and of a reasonable quality?

Belsky and Rovine (1988) reported that day care *can* adversely affect attachments. Babies who had been in day care for at least four months before their first birthday and for more than 20 hours per week were more likely to develop *insecure attachments* than 'home-reared' babies (43 per cent and 26 per cent respectively).

In the USA, 36 per cent of babies with working mothers are classified as *insecure* (22 per cent Type A, 14 per cent Type C). This is almost identical to the overall percentages for worldwide studies, based on almost 2000 children of mainly *non-working-mothers* (Van Ijzendoorn and Kroonenberg, 1988). Several studies have shown that children who were in day care as babies are as self-confident and emotionally well adjusted as those that weren't (Clarke-Stewart, 1989).

Also, as we noted when evaluating the Strange Situation (page 38), the child's attachment reflects the relationship with that person rather than a general characteristic of the child. If the children of working mothers are more insecure with them, this doesn't necessarily mean that they're emotionally insecure in general. We need to assess their emotional health in a range of situations, with a variety of attachment figures.

Aggression and peer relations

Durkin (1995) refers to studies which have found that preschoolers who had been in day care since infancy (below 12 months) were more prone to aggressiveness, negative social adjustment, hyperactivity and anxiety, compared with those who started day care later. He cites other studies showing the opposite to be true: for example, Andersson (1992) followed up Swedish children at the ages of 8 and 13 and found evidence that those who had entered day care before 12 months were performing better in school and attained higher scores on measures of adjustment and social competence.

Ratings of some preschoolers as more aggressive may reflect the fact that their day care experiences have encouraged them to become more determined to get their own way. This may not always be as 'nice' as the behaviour of some other children, but it doesn't necessarily indicate lasting maladjustment. Parents who place their children in day care may value independence in their offspring, and this may be reflected in their parenting styles (Clarke-Stewart, 1989).

It's also possible that children who are aggressive or otherwise 'difficult' are more likely to be put in day care, because their parents need a break. Some parents may opt to go out to work because their interactions with their baby are less than satisfactory (Hock *et al.,* in Durkin, 1995).

Commonly in western societies, the main source of peer contact among preschoolers occurs in day care settings, where children face several new personal and interpersonal challenges. One of these is being expected to regulate their emotions according to the requirements of an institution (e.g. Maccoby, 1980). Much of the research into preschoolers' social development has been conducted in nurseries and childcare centres, often using observational techniques. These were initially very popular in the 1930s and 1940s, then gave way to more laboratory-based studies (such as Bandura's famous 'bobo doll' experiments in the 1960s).

But, by the late 1960s, direct observation began to make a comeback, as in Blurton Jones's (1967) observational study of the social behaviour of children in an English nursery school. Most aggressive behaviour occurred in relation to 'property rights': between ages 1 and 2 years, conflicts arise over toys and other possessions and they focus exclusively on the toy – not the other child. What we don't see is an increase in what may legitimately be called aggression: they're not tying to force another child to withdraw by hurting or frightening them, but merely trying to remove an obstacle to something they want (Maccoby, 1980). Blurton Jones drew a clear distinction between aggressive behaviour (beating or hitting another, with a frown or angry face) and rough-and-tumble play (chasing and tackling each other, often smiling and laughing). These two kinds of behaviour can be confused because they're superficially similar (Smith *et al.,* 1998).

Evaluation of research into the effects of day care

✗ **The research is culturally biased:** much of the research into the effects of day care has been conducted in the USA, and the conclusions drawn from these studies may not apply to other societies and cultures. Patterns of maternal, and paternal, employment differ between cultures, and mothers' and fathers' contribution to childcare at home may also vary. For example, daily supervision of children may be the responsibility of the whole community; in many communities, caregiving and disciplinary duties belong to anyone who happens to be near the child. Babies are usually surrounded by relatives and non-relative neighbours of many ages who take responsibility for them when the mother is away or busy (Rogoff, 2003).

Rogoff gives the example of Polynesia, where many adults and children have responsibility for a child's upbringing: children belong to the community and everyone is expected to comfort, instruct and correct them. Children are often adopted and raised by relatives other than their biological parents in a system where children are shared and help to strengthen ties among households. Similarly, in West Africa, biological parents often delegate the care of their child

to foster parents without losing parental rights, as a way of rearing children within the extended social network and cementing family and friendship bonds.

✗ **Using the Strange Situation to assess the effects of day care may be invalid:** Belsky and Rovine's findings, for example, were based on the Strange Situation and this is an *inappropriate* technique to use with children in day care. It assumes that repeated separations from the mother are stressful for the child, but day-care children are *used* to such separations and so may not find them stressful. While they might *appear* to be indifferent to the mother's return (see Key Study 2.1), this may really be independence and self-reliance. This is similar to the interpretation of a child being determined to get its own way as aggressive (see above).

✗ **Day care may not be the only difference:** again in relation to Belsky and Rovine's findings, there may be differences between mothers who choose to work and those who don't, which account for the different rates of insecure attachment (Clarke-Stewart, 1989).

Implications for childcare practices

The case of childminding

According to Smith *et al.* (1998), ideally childminding could provide an economic form of day care with high adult-to-child ratios; perhaps best of all is when care is provided by relatives such as grandparents. There's been relatively little research on childminding (or home-based day care in the USA), but what there is has mostly been carried out in the UK. Smith *et al.* (1998) cite two studies, one in London (Mayall and Petrie, 1977, 1983), the other in Oxfordshire (Bryant *et al.*, 1980). Both found that children often appeared insecure in the minder's home and scored below average on tests of language and cognitive ability. However, neither study used a proper control group, so we cannot be sure whether the outcomes were due to the day care rather than home circumstances.

However, there are certainly problems associated with some *unregistered* minders, who may provide a very poor emotional and material environment. Smith *et al.* cite Moss (1987), who argues that much can be done by improving facilities for childminders, providing training courses, and encouraging registration and resource back-up.

Putting day care research into context: to work or not to work?

As we saw above when evaluating research into the effects of day care, it's easy to draw the wrong conclusions. One reason for this is that the effects of day care on the child may be looked at in isolation from other related variables: having a job outside the house, plus parenting, as well as housework, is tiring and stressful for the mother, and may well reduce her physical and psychological availability to the infant. As Clarke-Stewart (1989) puts it, 'in other words, [it] is not that 40 hours of day care is hard on infants but that 40 hours of work is hard on mothers'.

The very stresses that lead some parents to place their children in day care in the first place may, in turn, be associated with how the child relates to his/her new circumstances – that is, negative adjustments to day care may reflect negative domestic circumstances, rather than the harmful effects of leaving the child with strangers (Durkin, 1995).

Similarly, Schaffer (2004) argues that it's not the *fact* that mothers work that affects the child. Rather, there's a whole range of factors, such as her ability to cope with her occupational and domestic duties, how much support she receives from her husband/partner and other relatives, her motives for working, and the effect on her self-esteem (as well as the day care itself), that really make a difference:

What can be safely concluded is that, where conditions are optimal, children of employed mothers may actually benefit compared with those of non-employed mothers, largely as a result of extra experiences with other adults and with peers in day-care settings . . . (Schaffer, 2004)

Even in the early years, 24-hour-a-day mothering needn't be regarded as a necessary pre-requisite for healthy psychological development (Gottfried *et al.*, 2002).

Durkin also observes that a crucial issue is the *quality* of the day care available (see above). If there's a correlation between (a) the quality of the day care and (b) what parents can afford and their overall socio-economic status, then it's an over-simplification to claim that day care (the independent variable) is invariably good or bad for children (the dependent variable); this is to single out one variable from a larger number of related variables and to give it the status of a cause.

Mooney and Munton (cited in Judd, 1997) reviewed 40 years' research. They concluded that there's *no* evidence that working mothers stunt their children's emotional or social development. Even poor-quality day care may make no difference to a child from a stable family, while good-quality care may provide real benefits.

Finally, we shouldn't be discussing the rights and wrongs of working mothers. What's important is providing enough good childcare; as Clarke-Stewart (1989) says:

Maternal employment is a reality. The issue today, therefore, is not whether infants should be in day care but how to make their experiences there and at home supportive of their development and of their parents' peace of mind.

 Assessment Check 2.4

1. Define what's meant by the terms 'day care' (giving examples of both 'out of home' and 'in the home' arrangements) and the 'motherhood mystique/mandate'. (4 + 2 marks)
2. Outline and evaluate research into the effects of childcare on the child's social development. (12 marks)
3. Give FOUR examples of criteria used to define the quality of day care. (1 + 1 + 1 + 1 mark)

CHAPTER

SUMMARY
Attachment

- **Attachments** are lasting, emotionally meaningful ties to another person. They develop through a series of **phases: pre-attachment** (birth to 3 months); **indiscriminate attachment** (3 to 7/8 months); **discriminate attachment** (7/8 months onwards); **multiple attachment** (9 months onwards).

- The **Strange Situation** is the most widely used observational method for studying attachment. It comprises eight episodes involving the baby (usually 12 months old), its mother and a female stranger, with most attention given to the baby's **reunion behaviours**.

- Ainsworth *et al.* classified 15 per cent of their sample as **anxious-avoidant (Type A)**, 70 per cent as **securely attached (Type B)** and 15 per cent as **anxious-resistant (Type C).** The baby's attachment type is related to the mother's **sensitivity**.

- There are also important **cultural variations** (both **within** and **between** cultures). But the Strange Situation may not be equally valid in western and non-western societies.

- Bowlby's **evolutionary** attachment theory rejects **cupboard love** accounts of attachment formation (such as **learning theory**). He was a psychoanalyst influenced by both Harlow's research with rhesus monkeys and Lorenz's study of **imprinting** in goslings.

- For Bowlby, the baby's attachment to the mother serves both a **biological** (survival) and a **psychological** (the need for security) function. Newborn humans are **genetically programmed** to display **attachment behaviours** towards one particular adult female (**monotropy**), which ensure their survival through the mother's instinctive responsiveness to them. The **critical period** for attachment formation lasts, for most babies, up to 12 months.

- Bowlby's **maternal deprivation hypothesis (MDH)** was based largely on studies of children raised in institutions. However, he failed to acknowledge the baby's need for other types of stimulation, as well as to distinguish between **deprivation** and **privation.**

- **Deprivation** refers to the loss, through **separation**, of an attachment figure.

- A typical response to **short-term deprivation** is **distress**. This comprises **protest**, **despair** and **detachment**, and can be influenced by a number of factors, including the child's age, gender and previous separations.

- **Divorce**, the **death** of a parent and day care are all examples of **long-term deprivation**.

- While almost all children are adversely affected by divorce, most adapt eventually. A crucial factor influencing the effects of divorce is continuity of contact with the non-custodial parent.

- One important effect of long-term deprivation is **separation anxiety**.

- **Privation** refers to the failure to form an attachment to any individual. A major effect of privation is **affectionless psychopathy**.

- **Studies of late adoption** (including studies of Romanian orphans) and **case studies of extreme early privation** (such as Koluchova's study of Czech twins) suggest that the effects of privation may be **reversible**.

- Hodges and Tizard's study of children raised in institutions supported Bowlby's MDH in relation to peer relationships, but it also showed that attachments can be formed with adults long after the critical period.

- Studies of Romanian orphans adopted by Canadian and British families have shown that the effects of an institutional upbringing may persist, in the form of **disinhibited attachment (DA)**.

Attachment in everyday life

- **Day care** includes all varieties of non-maternal care of children who normally live with their parent(s) or close relatives.

- Bowlby was an early critic of any form of day care in which the child is cared for by people it doesn't know. His views complement the **motherhood mystique/ mandate**, according to which working mothers are somehow behaving 'unnaturally'.

- However, changes in patterns of work among women make day care essential.

- As a form of maternal deprivation, day care has been studied in terms of its effects on children's **social development**, including **attachment to the mother** and **aggressiveness towards other children**.

- Research (such as Belsky and Rovine's) which claims that children in day care become **insecurely attached** to their mothers may be mistaking independence/autonomy for indifference towards the mother.

- Similarly, children rated as aggressive may be displaying a determination to get their own way not evident in 'stay at home' children.

- Also, many studies (including that of Belsky and Rovine) have used the Strange Situation to assess the child's attachment, but this may be inappropriate with children used to regular separations from their mother.

- Much of the research is US-based and so is **culturally biased**. In many non-western cultures, the concept of day care hardly exists, with the whole community sharing responsibility for childcare in a way that is completely unfamiliar in western countries.

- A crucial aspect of childcare is its **quality** (including its **stability**). When the quality is poor, it's difficult to know whether any negative effects are the result of the quality of care itself, or factors correlated with day care, such as the stress faced by working mothers, and parental characteristics and circumstances.

- The issue isn't whether or not mothers of preschool children should go out to work, but rather the provision of enough good-quality day care.

Research methods

What's covered in this chapter?

You need to know about:

Methods and techniques

- Experimental method including laboratory, field and natural experiments
- Studies using a correlational analysis
- Observational techniques
- Self-report techniques including questionnaire and interview
- Case studies

Investigation design

- Aims
- Hypotheses, including directional and non-directional
- Experimental design (independent groups, repeated measures and matched participants)
- Design of naturalistic observations including the development and use of behavioural categories
- Design of questionnaires and interviews
- Operationalisation of variables, including independent and dependent variables
- Pilot studies
- Control of extraneous variables
- Reliability and validity
- Awareness of the BPS Code of Ethics
- Ethical issues and ways in which psychologists deal with them
- Selection of participants and sampling techniques, including random, opportunity and volunteer sampling
- Demand characteristics and investigator effects

Data analysis and presentation

- Presentation and interpretation of quantitative data, including graphs, scattergrams and tables
- Analysis and interpretation of quantitative data. Measures of central tendency, including median, mean and mode
- Measures of dispersion, including ranges and standard deviation
- Analysis and interpretation of correlational data. Positive and negative correlations and the interpretation of correlation coefficients
- Presentation of qualitative data, including processes involved in content analysis

> ## ✔ Specification Hint
>
> We have made reference to research methods throughout the rest of the book, especially in the Practical Learning Activities. We hope that you will have learnt some of the material through undertaking these activities. However, since there are separate questions relating to research methods in your Unit 1 exam, we have included all the material you need to learn in this chapter as well.

Research methods and techniques

There are a number of different research methods in psychology. Like the carpenter who selects the most appropriate tool for the job, psychologists choose the most appropriate method for their research. No single method is perfect or better than another. You need to know what these methods are and what their advantages and weaknesses are.

Quantitative research methods allow the numerical measurement of *how much* there is of something (i.e. the quantity). *Qualitative research* methods allow for the measurement of *what* something is like (i.e. the quality). An example of quantitative data would be the *number* of stressful incidents per day, whereas qualitative data would involve a *description* of these incidents.

Experimental method

The experimental method refers to a research method using random assignment of participants (see pages 93–94 for information on sampling techniques) and the manipulation of variables in order to determine cause and effect. A variable is any object, characteristic or event that changes or varies in some way. Experiments are the most widely used method in psychology.

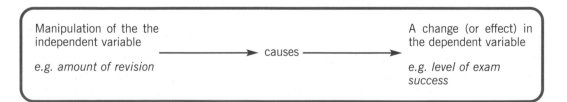

Manipulation of the the
independent variable ⎯⎯⎯⎯→ causes ⎯⎯⎯⎯→ A change (or effect) in
the dependent variable

e.g. amount of revision   *e.g. level of exam success*

Figure 3.1: The causal link between an independent variable (IV) and dependent variable (DV) in an experiment

The experimenter manipulates an independent variable (IV) to see its effect on the dependent variable (DV). The IV is the variable that's manipulated or altered by the experimenter to see its effect on the DV. The DV is the measured result of the experiment. Any change in the DV should be as a result of the manipulation of the IV. For example, alcohol consumption (IV) could be manipulated to see its effect on reaction time (the DV).

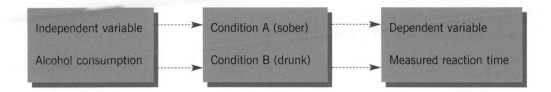

Extraneous variables are any other variables that may have an effect on the DV (see page 89). Controls are employed to prevent extraneous variables spoiling the results. Any extraneous variables that aren't controlled can become confounding variables, so called because they 'confound' (that is, confuse) the results.

There are several types of experiment, as described below.

Laboratory experiments

Here, the researcher controls as many variables as possible. There's control over the 'who, what, when, where and how'. This is *usually* done in a laboratory using standardised procedures, but can be conducted anywhere provided it's in a controlled environment. Participants should also be randomly allocated to experimental groups.

Research examples

- Bandura's (1965) bobo doll study.

- Milgram's (1963) study of destructive obedience (see pages 157–159).

Advantages of laboratory experiments

- **High degree of control:** experimenters can control all variables in the situation. For example, the IV and DV can be very precisely defined (or operationalised – see page 88) and measured. This leads to greater accuracy and objectivity.

- **Replication:** other researchers can easily repeat the experiment and check results. This is an important feature of the experimental method.

- **Cause and effect:** it should be possible to determine the cause-and-effect relationship between the IV and DV, provided that the experiment is well designed.

- **Technical equipment:** it's easier to use complicated technical equipment in a laboratory.

- **Stronger effects outside the lab?** Laboratory experiments are often criticised for being artificial, but it may be the case that some laboratory effects are even stronger outside the lab than those recorded within it. For example, Milgram's study of destructive obedience (1963) demonstrated high levels of obedience in the lab situation, but it is likely that the effects are even stronger outside of the laboratory where obedience is associated with social pressure and a likelihood of painful sanctions from authority figures (Coolican, 2004).

Weaknesses of laboratory experiments

- **Experimenter bias:** sometimes an experimenter's expectations about the study can affect the results. Participants may be influenced by these expectations (see page 95).

- **Problems operationalising the IV and DV:** sometimes, in order to gain a precise measure of behaviour, the measure itself becomes too specific and doesn't relate to wider

behaviour. For example, Bandura's measures of aggression involved only a very narrow range of the kind of hostile behaviour of which children are capable (Coolican, 2004).

- **Low external (ecological) validity:** the high degree of control can make the experimental situation artificial and unlike real life. As such, it may be difficult to generalise results to other settings. A laboratory setting can be a strange and intimidating place. As such, people may be overly worried by the surroundings and not act in a way that is representative of their normal everyday behaviour.

- **Demand characteristics (Orne, 1962):** sometimes participants try to guess the purpose of the experiment and then act according to the 'demands' of the experiment. In contrast, the 'screw you' effect refers to situations where participants guess the purpose of an experiment and act in a deliberately contradictory way (see page 94).

How Science Works
Practical Learning Activity 3.1:
A laboratory experiment into the effects of caffeine on reaction times

It's generally believed that caffeine decreases reaction times (i.e. makes people react faster). Some studies indicate that the effect is most marked at lower doses – for example, one or two cups of coffee per day.

- Devise a laboratory experiment to test this.
- Carry out this study and write up the experiment. Include sections such as 'Introduction', 'Method' ('design', 'sample', 'procedure', 'ethical issues'), 'Results' and 'Conclusion'.

Field experiments

A field experiment is an experiment performed in the 'real world' rather than the laboratory. The IV is still manipulated by the experimenter and as many other variables as possible are controlled.

Research example
- Piliavin *et al.*'s (1969) New York Subway study.

Natural experiments

Here, the IV occurs naturally, it's not manipulated by the experimenter. The experimenter merely records the effect on the DV. An advantage here is that the effect of an IV can be studied where it would be unethical to deliberately manipulate it (e.g. create family stress). Strictly speaking, this is a *quasi-experiment* since the random allocation of participants is not possible.

Research example
- Hodges and Tizard's (1989) study of teenagers raised in orphanages.

Advantages (can apply to both field and natural experiments)

- **High ecological validity:** due to the 'real world' environment, or naturally occurring environment, results are more likely to relate to everyday behaviour and can be generalised to other settings.

- **No demand characteristics:** often, participants are unaware of the experiment, and so there are no demand characteristics.

Weaknesses (can apply to both field and natural experiments)

- **Less control:** it's far more difficult to control extraneous variables, either 'in the field' or in naturally occurring situations.

- **Replication:** it's difficult to *precisely* replicate field or natural experiments since the conditions will never be exactly the same again.

- **Ethics:** there are ethical issues (e.g. informed consent, deception) when participants aren't aware that they are taking part in the experiment. This applies more to field experiments, since in natural experiments the independent variable occurs naturally and isn't manipulated by the experimenter.

- **Sample bias:** since participants aren't randomly allocated to groups, there may be some sample bias.

- **Time-consuming and expensive:** experiments in the real world can often take more time and involve more costs than those in the laboratory. Researchers often have to consider many other aspects of the design and how it may affect other people in the vicinity of the experiment, which they don't have to do in the comfort of their laboratory.

Type of experiment	Variable details	Environment
Laboratory	Manipulation of IV Measure DV	Controlled
Field	Manipulation of IV Measure DV	Real life
Natural	IV occurs naturally Measure DV	Real life

Table 3.1: Summary of experimental research methods

Studies using correlational analysis

This isn't a research method as such, but a method of data analysis. It involves measuring the strength of the relationship between two or more variables (co-variables) to see if a trend or pattern exists between them.

- A **positive correlation** is where one variable increases as the other variable increases (e.g. ice cream sales increase as temperature increases).

- A **negative correlation** is where one variable increases while the other variable decreases (e.g. raincoat sales decrease as temperature increases).

- A **correlation co-efficient** is a number that expresses the degree to which the two variables are related. The measurement ranges from $+1$ (perfect positive correlation) to -1 (perfect negative correlation). The closer the correlation to a perfect correlation, the stronger the relationship between the two variables. If there's no correlation, the result will be near to zero (0.0) (see Figure 3.8, page 103).

Research example

- Anderson's (2004) study into violent video game playing found a positive correlation with real-life violence.

How Science Works
Practical Learning Activity 3.2:
Positive and negative correlations

Examine the following made-up statements.

1 Older people are more forgetful.
2 Beautiful people are more successful in their careers.
3 Poorer people have a lower level of education.
4 The longer you spend revising, the less worried you become.
5 The better the teaching, the fewer the number of failures.

- Decide which of these statements are positive or negative correlations.
- Think up some other examples of positive and negative correlations.
- Try to think of some examples from research you have studied previously.

Now, imagine that a local head teacher has found research evidence in her school which suggests that larger class sizes are positively correlated to exam success.

- Try to criticise this research and think of the arguments you might give to support the claim that smaller class sizes are actually of greater benefit to schoolchildren.
- Consider any extraneous or confounding variables that might have affected the head teacher's research.

Advantages of correlational analysis

- **Allows predictions to be made:** once a correlation has been found, we can make predictions about one variable from the other (e.g. we can predict the number of ice creams sold on hot days).

- **Allows quantification of relationships:** correlations can show the strength of the relationship between two co-variables. A correlation of $+0.9$ means a high positive correlation; a correlation of -0.3 indicates a fairly weak negative correlation.

- **No manipulation:** correlations don't require the manipulation of behaviour, and so can be a quick and ethical method of data collection and analysis.

Weaknesses of correlational analysis

- **Quantification problem:** it is worth noting that sometimes correlations that appear to be quite low (e.g. +0.28) can be meaningful or significant if the number of scores recorded is quite high. Conversely, with a large number of recorded scores, correlations that are quite high (e.g. +0.76) are not always statistically significant or meaningful. You must be aware of this when interpreting correlation co-efficient scores.

- **Cause and effect:** it cannot be assumed that one variable caused the other. Interpretation of results is made difficult since there's no cause and effect in a correlation (see Practical Learning Activity 3.3). It could be that both co-variables are influenced by some other variable(s).

- **Extraneous relationships:** other variables may influence both measured variables (e.g. most holidays are taken in the (hot?) summer and people eat ice creams on holiday). Therefore, the variable 'holiday' is related to both temperature and ice cream sales.

- **Only works for linear relationships:** correlations measure only *linear* (straight-line) relationships. The relationship between temperature and aggression is a *curvilinear* relationship. This would be a zero correlation, and yet there's an obvious relationship or pattern between these two variables.

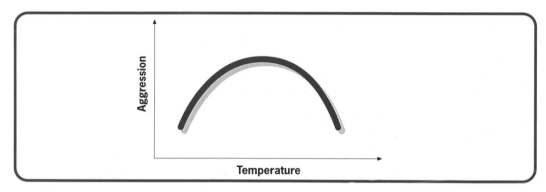

Figure 3.2: The curvilinear relationship between temperature and aggression

How Science Works

Practical Learning Activity 3.3:
Causation in a correlation

We have already stated that we cannot assume that one variable caused the second variable in a correlation and that other variables may have played a part. Think up some extraneous variables that might account for these correlations:

- lower-income parents have more children
- older people make poorer eyewitnesses
- sales of running shoes have increased at the same rate as sales of personal computers.

Think up some hypothetical correlations and try to think of other variables that might be able to explain the link between them.

Observational techniques

To some extent, most psychological studies involve some observation of behaviour, whether it be observing children playing in a school playground or observing the speed of a person's reaction in a laboratory. Observation can occur as part of a laboratory study, as in Milgram's (1963) study of destructive obedience and Bandura's (1965) study of aggression through imitation. However, when one talks of observational techniques this usually refers to a study where observation is the main research method involving the precise (objective) measurement of naturally occurring and relatively unconstrained behaviour. Moreover, the observation usually occurs in the participant's own natural environment.

There are two main types of observation.

1 **Participant observation** involves the observer becoming actively involved in the activities of the people being studied. Instead of merely observing, the psychologist can experience a more 'hands on' perspective on the people and the behaviour being observed. S/he becomes a 'participant' in the research. Participant observation can either be disclosed (people are told they are being observed) or undisclosed (participants remain unaware of being observed).

2 **Non-participant observation** involves the researcher observing the behaviour from a distance; they do not become actively involved in the behaviour to be studied.

Research examples

- Participant observation: Rosenhan's (1973) study entitled 'On being sane in insane places' (see pages 184–186).

- Non-participant observation: Griffiths and Parke's (2005) observational study of the effect of music in gambling environments such as casinos and amusement arcades.

The distinction between participant and non-participant observation is not always clear-cut since it may be difficult for an observer to participate fully in some behaviours (e.g. criminal activities); conversely, a non-participant observer is unlikely to have *no* impact whatsoever on a situation. Think of the example of a football referee. Are they a non-participant or participant observer of the match?

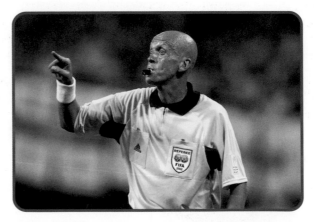

A football referee: participant or non-participant observer?

Specification Hint

Although there are differences between the advantages and weaknesses of participant and non-participant observation, the examiner cannot ask specifically about these types in an exam. This is because they are not specifically named in the Specification. The examiner can only ask about observational techniques in general and, for this reason, we have dealt with advantages and weaknesses common to both types.

Advantages of observational techniques

- **High external validity:** since observed behaviour takes place in the natural environment, participants tend to behave naturally and results can usually be generalised to other settings.

- **Practical method:** can be used in situations where deliberate manipulation would be unethical or impractical (e.g. a study of soccer hooliganism). It is useful where cooperation from those being observed is unlikely and where the full social context for behaviour is needed. It's particularly useful for studying animals or children (Coolican, 2004).

- **Few demand characteristics:** participants are often unaware of the observation and so there are few demand characteristics (see page 94).

Weaknesses of observational techniques

- **Cause and effect:** this cannot be inferred, since the variables are only observed, not manipulated. There is also little control of extraneous variables (see page 89).

- **Observer bias:** if observers know the purpose of the study, they may see what they want to see. Observers need to produce reliable results. Where there is more than one observer, the observational records of one observer can be checked or correlated against another to see if they are observing in the same way. A comparison such as this is called *inter-rater reliability (inter = between)*. Sometimes one observer changes their method of observation over time. For example, the behavioural categories that they were using to do the observation at the beginning of the study may alter by the end of the study. A comparison from the start of the observation to the end of the observation would check this; this is called *intra-rater reliability (intra = within)*.

- **Replication:** despite the possibility of checking for both inter- and intra-rater reliability, in practice it's often difficult to accurately check the reliability and validity (see pages 89–90) of observations, since a lack of control means conditions can never be repeated accurately.

- **Ethics:** if participants are unaware of being observed, issues of invasion of privacy and informed consent arise (see pages 90–92). If participants are informed of the study, then there is a possibility of demand characteristics.

● **Practical problems:** sometimes it is difficult to remain unobserved and there are practical problems making recordings (e.g. video/audio) of some behaviours. Furthermore, it is often difficult to categorise the observed behaviours accurately (see Practical Learning Activity 3.4).

How Science Works

Practical Learning Activity 3.4: Classroom observation

Imagine you are a government inspector of psychology classes. You decide to use a non-participant observation technique.

● Outline exactly how you would observe a psychology lesson.
● Decide on the behavioural categories that you might use to measure a successful lesson. You might consider the number of times students contribute to the lesson, how frequently they take notes, their levels of engagement. How would you record these behaviours?
● Ask to observe a psychology lesson and write up your experiences.
● How successful were you at assessing a lesson?
● What would you do differently next time?

Self-report techniques including questionnaires and interviews

Questionnaires

Questionnaires are a written method of data collection where respondents record their own answers to a pre-set list of questions. They're usually concerned with people's behaviour, opinions and attitudes. Two main types of question are used.

1 **Closed (fixed) questions:** responses are fixed by the researcher. They usually involve 'tick boxes' (e.g. 'yes' or 'no') or a range of fixed responses (e.g. 'always', 'usually', 'sometimes', 'never'). Such answers are easy to quantify, but restrict participants' answers.

2 **Open questions:** these allow participants to answer in their own words. They're more difficult to analyse, but allow freedom of expression and obtain greater depth.

Box 3.1: Examples of closed and open questions

● **Closed question:** Do you enjoy Psychology? YES/NO* (*delete as appropriate).

● **Open question:** Which aspects of Psychology do you enjoy and why?

....

....

Specification Hint

Although there are differences between the advantages and weaknesses of closed and open-ended questions, the examiner cannot ask specifically about these types in an exam. This is because they are not named in the Specification. The examiner can ask only about questionnaires in general and, for this reason, we have dealt with advantages and weaknesses common to both types of question.

Advantages of questionnaires

- **Quick and cheap:** a large amount of information can be gathered in a relatively short period of time. As such, they're quick and cheap in comparison to other methods.

- **Large samples:** questionnaires can be completed without the researcher present. Postal questionnaires can be used to gain very large samples for the cost of a stamp.

- **Quantitative and qualitative analysis:** it's easy to statistically analyse 'closed' questions. Answers can be pre-coded on questionnaires for computer input and instant analysis. Open-ended questions provide richer, fuller detail and the respondent does not feel constrained in his or her answers.

- **Replication:** since questionnaires use standardised questions, it's fairly easy to replicate studies. This is particularly true of questionnaires that use closed questions.

Weaknesses of questionnaires

- **Misunderstanding:** designing a questionnaire is a highly skilled job. Participants may misunderstand or misinterpret questions. For example, what do you mean when you say you 'usually' do your homework? There are problems with the use of complex technical terms, emotive language and leading questions (see Key Study 1.1, pages 20–21).

- **Biased samples:** questionnaires are suitable only for people who are literate, and willing and able to spend time filling them in. It may be that certain groups of people are more willing to find the time to fill in questionnaires.

- **Low response rates:** some questionnaires have been known to obtain as little as a 5 per cent return rate. Might these 5 per cent of people differ from the other 95 per cent of the population who do not fill in the questionnaire?

- **Superficial issues:** questionnaires, particularly those that predominantly use closed questions, aren't suitable for more sensitive issues that require detailed understanding.

- **Social desirability:** participants may present themselves in a positive light. Indeed, they may lie on particularly sensitive issues (e.g. to do with sexual behaviour).

Interviews

Interviews involve researchers asking questions in a face-to-face situation. They can be very different but there are two broad types.

1 **Structured (or formal) interviews:** a questionnaire is read to participants and the interviewer writes down their responses. These interviews are identical for all participants and tend to involve more simple, quantitative questions. Interviewers don't need a lot of training, since they are fairly easy to conduct.

2 **Unstructured (or informal) interviews:** these are less controlled and involve an informal discussion on a particular topic. However, while the topic is predetermined the direction of the interview isn't. This allows the interviewer to explore the areas of greatest interest. Friendly rapport between the interviewer and respondent is important in order to gain the required level of detail and understanding. Interviewers need considerable training and expertise to conduct such interviews.

Interviews can combine these two types in **semi-structured interviews.**

Social desirability: in the 1980s, voters were reluctant to admit that they supported the Conservative Party, but the Tories kept on winning!

✔ Specification Hint

Although there are differences between the advantages and weaknesses of structured and unstructured interviews, the examiner cannot ask specifically about these types in an exam. This is because they are not named in the Specification. The examiner can ask only about interviews in general and, for this reason, we have dealt with advantages and weaknesses common to both types of question.

Advantages of interviews

● **Complex issues:** complicated or sensitive issues are best dealt with in face-to-face interviews. This is particularly true of unstructured interviews, where a natural flow of conversation is likely to make the respondent feel more relaxed and will thus enhance the quality of the answers.

● **Ease misunderstandings:** any ambiguity or misunderstanding can be clarified within the interview. Interviewers can follow up on any interesting answers and explore them more tully. Questions can be adapted to the individual needs of the respondents, and this should make the interview process more productive for all concerned.

- **Data analysis:** the variety and flexibility of interviews allows for the analysis of both quantitative and qualitative data. Structured interviews in particular produce data that can be analysed in quantitative form fairly easily.

- **Replication:** the more standardised or structured the interview, the easier it is to replicate. Unstructured interviews are less easy to replicate but it should still be possible for other researchers to review the data produced.

Weaknesses of interviews

- **Interviewer effects:** interviewers may inadvertently bias the respondent's answers. This could even occur because of the interviewer's appearance. For example, would a white person be less willing to admit to being racist to a black interviewer? Interviews are subject to demand characteristics and social desirability bias.

- **Interview training:** with structured interviews there is less training required. However, a great deal of skill is required to carry out unstructured interviews, particularly those concerned with sensitive issues. It is not always easy to obtain highly trained interviewers.

- **Ethical issues:** these can arise when participants don't know the true purpose of the interview. There is also a danger that participants may reveal more than they wish to.

- **Respondent answers:** respondents may be unable to put into words their true feelings about a particular topic. For obvious reasons, this applies mainly to structured interviews.

Victoria Beckham inadvertently revealed her husband's nickname, 'Golden Balls', in an interview on TV chat show Parkinson

How Science Works
Practical Learning Activity 3.5:
Questionnaire or interview?

Choose a topic to research. For example, you might want to investigate people's views on the monarchy, or the use of animals in psychological research.

● Half the class could investigate the topic using a questionnaire, with the other half using interviews. Compare the results of the two groups.
● Discuss the advantages and weaknesses of each method for that particular research topic.

Case studies

A case study is the in-depth, detailed investigation of an individual or group. It would usually include biographical details as well as details of behaviour or experiences of interest. Case studies allow a researcher to examine a particular individual in far greater depth than experimental methods of investigation. So-called qualitative methods tend to be followed that are not easily quantified through the use of statistics. Explanations of behaviour are outlined in written descriptive ways. Subjective reports are often used. These outline what the person feels or believes about a particular issue. Bromley (1986) has argued that case studies are 'the bedrock of scientific investigation' and that psychologists' preoccupation with experimental procedures has led to a neglect of this area. Coolican (2004) cites a clever example in defence of individual case studies, or the single participant design as he terms it. If only one rock was collected from the moon for study, would scientists discard it claiming that it would be unlikely to be representative of other rocks that exist on the moon?

Research examples

● S.B. (Gregory and Wallace, 1963), who was blind almost from birth but recovered his sight at the age of 52.

● Phineas Gage, who blew a 6-foot metal bar through his head and yet lived to tell the tale.

For more details of these and other cases, see Rolls (2005).

Advantages of case studies

● **Rich detail:** case studies can help to shed light on both specific and general psychological issues. For example, Freud developed his psychoanalytic theory of human development based on his own patients' case histories. Case studies have the advantage of providing greater depth and understanding about an individual, and acknowledge and celebrate human diversity. Because case studies are about 'real, genuine people' they have a special feeling of truth about them.

● **The only possible method to use:** case studies allow psychologists to study behaviours or experiences that are so unique that they could not have been studied in any other way. These case studies allow the researcher to explore possibilities in human behaviour that may not previously have been considered or thought possible.

- **Useful for theory contradiction:** one case study may be enough to contradict a theory. The case study of Genie (Curtiss, 1977) helped to question the evidence regarding critical stages of language development.

Weaknesses of case studies

- **Unreliable:** case studies are criticised for being unreliable (no two case studies are alike) and therefore results cannot easily be generalised to other people. The question arises as to whether we do always *have* to find out universal truths of behaviour.

- **Researcher bias:** a further criticism levelled at case studies is that sometimes the researcher conducting the study may be biased in their interpretations or reporting method. This 'subjectivity' means that it could be difficult to determine factual information from researcher inference. An awareness of this does not detract from the stories that emerge. Indeed, much of the rich detail from first-hand accounts would not have been possible had the researcher(s) not formed warm and friendly relationships with the main people involved.

Assessment Check 3.1

1. **Discuss ONE advantage and ONE weakness of field experiments. (3 + 3 marks)**
2. **Outline ONE difference between a laboratory and natural experiment. (2 marks)**
3. **Give ONE criticism of studies that use correlational analysis. (2 marks)**
4. **Explain ONE weakness of using a questionnaire to collect data. (2 marks)**
5. **Explain ONE advantage of using a case study research method. (2 marks)**

Investigation design

Aims

An **aim** is a reasonably precise statement of *why* a study is taking place (e.g. to investigate the effect of alcohol on reaction times). It should include what's being studied and what the study is trying to achieve.

Hypotheses, including directional and non-directional

A **hypothesis** is much more precise than an aim and predicts what's expected to happen (e.g. alcohol consumption will significantly affect reaction times). Hypotheses are testable statements.

There are two types of hypotheses:

1 **Experimental (or alternative) hypothesis:** this predicts significant differences in the dependent variable (the variable that is measured) as a result of manipulation of the independent variable (the variable that the experimenter alters). It predicts that any difference or effect found will not be due to chance (e.g. there will be a significant difference in reaction times as a result of alcohol consumption). (Note: the term 'experimental hypothesis' should be used only with the experimental method. For all other research methods, 'alternative hypothesis' should be used.)

2 **Null hypothesis:** this is the 'hypothesis of no differences'. It predicts that the IV will not affect the DV. It predicts that results will simply be due to chance (e.g. there will be no (significant) difference in reaction times as a result of alcohol consumption). (Note: the inclusion of the word 'significant' in the null hypothesis is still being argued about by psychologists.)

One of these hypotheses will be supported by the findings.

 Specification Hint

The term 'null hypothesis' is not actually mentioned in the AS Specification, so the examiner could not ask a question asking you to identify the null hypothesis. However, it plays an important part in scientific research and therefore we felt it was important to include it here.

There are also two types of experimental (or alternative) hypotheses.

1 **Directional (also called 'one-tailed'):** this states the direction of the results (e.g. there will be a significant *slowing* in the speed of reaction times as a result of alcohol consumption). It is called directional because it states one direction in which the results can go.

2 **Non-directional (also called 'two-tailed'):** this states that there will be a difference, but doesn't state the direction of the results (e.g. there will be a significant *difference* in the speed of reaction times as a result of alcohol consumption); in this example, reaction times could either get quicker or slower, and so they are referred to as 'non-directional' hypotheses.

Directional hypotheses are used when previous research evidence suggests that it's possible to make a clear prediction, or when you're replicating a previous study that has also used a directional hypothesis.

Experimental design

There are three main types of experimental design, each of which is described below.

Repeated measures design

The same participants are tested in the two (or more) conditions. Each participant *repeats* the study in each condition.

Advantages

- **Group differences:** the same person is measured in both conditions; there are *no* individual differences between the groups. Extraneous variables are kept constant (controlled) between the conditions.

- **Fewer participants:** half as many participants are needed with repeated measures when compared to independent measures design. If you need 20 scores, then 10 participants undertaking both conditions will suffice with repeated measures. With independent groups design, you'd need 20 participants, 10 for each condition. It's not always that easy to get participants for psychology experiments and finding more participants is always time-consuming.

Weaknesses

- **Order effects:** when participants repeat a task, results can be affected by **order effects**. On the second task, participants either:

  (a) do worse due to fatigue or boredom

  (b) improve through practice in the first condition.

This can be controlled by *counterbalancing,* where half the participants do Condition A followed by Condition B, and the other half do Condition B and then Condition A. This counterbalancing procedure is known as 'ABBA', for obvious reasons.

- **Lost participants:** if a participant drops out of the study, they are 'lost' from both conditions.

- **Guess aim of study:** by participating in all conditions of the experiment, it's far more likely that the participant may guess the purpose of the study. This may make demand characteristics more common.

- **Takes more time:** a gap may need to be given between conditions, perhaps to try to counter the effects of fatigue or boredom. If participants are taking part in both conditions of the experiment, different materials need to be produced for each condition. In a memory test, for example, you could not simply use the same list of words for both conditions. Inevitably these issues involve more time and money.

Independent groups design

Different participants are used in each of the conditions. Each group of participants is *independent* of the other. Participants are usually **randomly allocated** to each condition to try to balance out any differences (see the section on 'Sampling' on page 93).

Advantages

- **Order effects:** there are *no* order effects.

- **Demand characteristics:** participants take part in one condition only. This means there's less chance of participants guessing the purpose of the study.

- **Time saved:** both sets of participants can be tested at the same time. This saves time and money.

Weaknesses

- **More participants:** with participants in only one condition, you need twice as many participants as for repeated measures design.

- **Group differences:** any differences between the groups may be due to individual differences that are distinct from the IV. This can be minimised by the random allocation of participants to each group.

Matched pairs design

Different, but similar, participants are used in each of the conditions. Participants are matched across the groups on any characteristics judged to be important for that particular study. These are typically age, gender and ethnicity. Identical (monozygotic) twins are the perfect matched pair at birth since they share identical genetic characteristics. Later in life, identical twins are still likely to be closely matched on many important characteristics, even in cases where they have been reared apart.

Advantages (see also independent groups design)

- **Group differences:** participant variables are more closely matched between conditions than in independent groups design.

Weaknesses (see also independent groups design)

- **Matching is difficult:** it's impossible to match *all* variables between participants. The one variable missed might be vitally important.

- **Time-consuming:** it takes a long time to accurately match participants on *all* variables. This task can become almost a research study in itself!

 Specification Hint

You'll notice that many of the weaknesses of one sort of experimental design are advantages of other experimental designs. For example, a weakness of independent groups design is likely to be an advantage of repeated measures design.

Experimental design summary

Repeated measures: same participants

Independent measures: different participants

Matched pairs: matched participants

How Science Works

Practical Learning Activity 3.6:
Summary of the advantages and
weaknesses of experimental designs

Devise a table (using the template below for guidance) and complete it as thoroughly as you can. In the final column, consider alternative designs or techniques you might use to overcome some of the weaknesses noted in the previous column.

Design	Advantages	Weaknesses	Possible remedy?
Independent groups			
Repeated measures			
Matched pairs			

Once completed, you *must* learn this table.

Design of naturalistic observations including the development and use of behavioural categories

We have already noted what we mean by naturalistic observation, and the advantages and weaknesses of this research method (see pages 72–74). One difficulty with naturalistic observations involves the development and use of appropriate behavioural categories. There are several ways that data can be gathered in a naturalistic observation. These include the use of visual recordings (video or still), audio recordings or 'on-the-spot' note-taking using previously agreed rating scales or coding categories. The use of video or audio recordings tends to result in later analysis back in the 'lab' using coding categories.

Behavioural categories

Observers have to agree on a grid or coding sheet on which to record the behaviour they wish to study. The behavioural categories chosen will depend on the subject matter under study. For example, if observers are interested in the effect of age and sex on the speed of car driving, they might want to develop behavioural categories such as those shown in the table below.

Driver	Sex?	Age? (estimate)	Number of passengers?	Observed behaviour	Type of car?	Speed? (estimate km per hour)	Safe driving rating? 1 = very unsafe 5 = very safe
A	M	55	0	M-P	Saloon	40	2
B	F	21	2	T	Hatch	30	5
C							
D etc.							

Observed behaviour code:
D = Distracted
T = Talking
M-P = Using mobile phone
... and so on

Rather than writing a detailed description of all behaviour observed, it is often easier to code or rate behaviour according to a previously agreed scale. Coding might simply involve numbers (such as age of driver) or letters to describe participant characteristics (such as M = male) or observed behaviours (such as T = talking, M-P = using mobile phone). Observed behaviour can also be rated on a structured scale (such as 1–5 on a scale of 'safe driving').

In practice, it is difficult to achieve standardisation between the different observers, and considerable training is required before the actual observational sessions occur. Checks that all observers are coding behaviour in the same way ensure inter-observer reliability. One way to assess inter-observer reliability is to conduct a correlation of all the observers' scores. If there is a high agreement (or correlation) between observers, then it is clear that they are observing and categorising the behaviours in the same way. We cannot be sure that they are observing behaviour *correctly*, but we can be sure they are doing it *consistently* as a group (Coolican, 2004).

How Science Works

Practical Learning Activity 3.7: Investigating flirting behaviour

Let's assume you wish to investigate whether people flirt with other people of roughly the same level of attractiveness as themselves.

- Devise an observational study using appropriate behavioural categories to examine this. You would need to have some categories to operationalise flirting behaviour and some way of assessing levels of attractiveness.
- Should you consider 'non-verbal' or only 'verbal' flirting?
- You could conduct the observation in any place where you consider flirting occurs – at a café, a party, the canteen, the classroom, and so on.
- Always ensure that you do not breach any ethical guidelines associated with psychological research and check that the research method is appropriate with a friend or your teacher. The first rule of observations is to stay safe and follow the ethical guidelines.
- Record your results and feed them back to the rest of the class.

The UK Social Issues Research Centre at Oxford has a fascinating website on the subject of flirting, which is worth a look: http://www.sirc.org/publik/flirt.html.

Design of questionnaires

With some questionnaires suffering from a response rate of as little as 5 per cent, it is essential that a questionnaire is well designed. There are a number of essential factors in questionnaire design.

- **Aims:** knowing exactly what the aim of the research is should help the questionnaire design. Determining the use of any information gained will ensure that only questions that address these aims are asked.

- **Length:** the longer the questionnaire, the more likely people will not complete it. Questionnaires should be short and to the point. Any superfluous questions must be deleted.

- **Advice:** when designing a questionnaire, advice should be sought from experts in the field. Examples of questionnaires that have proved successful in the past should be used as a basis for the questionnaire design.

- **Statistical analysis:** even at the design stage, the statistical analysis of the questionnaire responses should be considered. If a question is not going to be analysed, then it should be omitted.

- **Presentation:** looks matter! Questionnaires should look professional, include clear and concise instructions and, if sent through the post, should be in an envelope that doesn't immediately signify 'junk mail'! Spaces should be left in the design of each page for respondents to include comments to questions as they see fit.

- **Question order:** it is useful to start with some simple factual biographical questions before moving on to more probing questions. However, the first questions also need to be interesting enough to keep the respondents engaged while completing the rest of the questionnaire. It is usually best to put the essential questions in the first half of the questionnaire since respondents often send them back half completed.

- **Question formulation:** questions should be simple, to the point and easily understood. In order to avoid ambiguity, complicated terms should be avoided. Questions must probe only one dimension. For example, a question that asks 'Do you like the content and design of this book?' is poorly phrased. If a respondent answers 'yes', we cannot be sure if they like the content, the design or both.

- **Incentives:** offering an incentive for questionnaire completion can help to provide additional motivation to respondents. It should also be extremely convenient for respondents to return the questionnaire. A pre-paid envelope is often used to achieve this.

- **Pilot study:** a test of the questionnaire should be done on people who can provide detailed and honest feedback on all aspects of the questionnaire design.

- **Measurement scales:** some questionnaires use measurement scales in order to assess psychological characteristics or attitudes. These often involve statements on which respondents rate their level of agreement (or disagreement). For example:

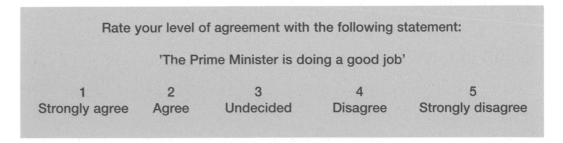

Usually, there are a number of statements on a particular topic and the answers to all these statements would be combined to determine a single score of attitude strength. There are a few problems with this approach. First, it isn't always easy for respondents to judge their answer and many respondents choose the middle score (in this case 'undecided'). When this happens it is impossible to know whether they have no opinion on the subject or cannot decide between their attitudes in both directions. Perhaps the best known of these attitude scales is the Likert scale.

How Science Works
Practical Learning Activity 3.8:
Questionnaire design

With a partner, decide on a topic that you wish to investigate. Perhaps you might research people's views of the fox-hunting ban, car choice preferences, favourite advertising campaigns or an assessment of government performance.

- Devise two versions of a questionnaire that investigates your chosen topic. One version should include examples of poor questionnaire design and the other should encompass good design.
- Annotate on the questionnaires the reasons why one version is superior to the other.

Design of interviews

The first decision when designing an interview is whether to choose a structured interview (where every participant answers the same questions) or an unstructured interview (where different questions on the general topic are asked) or indeed some combination of both. We have already discussed the relative merits of these approaches (see pages 74–78). There is also the decision regarding the use of 'open' and 'closed' questions.

An important factor in the design of interviews is to consider who will be the interviewer. Decisions as to the most appropriate type of interviewer can depend on what type of person is being interviewed, but there are a number of general interpersonal variables that might be considered. These include the following.

- **Gender and age:** several studies have demonstrated that the sex and age of the interviewer affect the answers of respondents when the topic is of a sensitive sexual nature (Wilson *et al.*, 2002), but these effects are less obvious with less personal topics.

- **Ethnicity:** perhaps due to cultural upbringing, sometimes interviewers have more difficulty interviewing people drawn from a different ethnic group to themselves. Word *et al.* (1974) found white participants spent 25 per cent less time interviewing black job applicants than they did white applicants.

- **Personal characteristics and adopted role:** some people are just easier to get on with than others! Interviewers can also adopt different roles within the interview setting. Use of formal language, accent and appearance (e.g. clothing) can also affect how someone comes across to the interviewee.

Interviewer training is an essential factor in successful interviewing. Interviewers need to listen appropriately and learn when and when not to speak. Non-verbal communication is also important in helping to relax the interviewee so that they will give more natural answers. More difficult or probing questions about feelings or emotions are usually best left to the end of the interview, whereas initial questions are better for ascertaining factual information.

How Science Works
Practical Learning Activity 3.9:
The preferred interviewer?

- Try to make a list of various factors that you believe might alter an interviewee's response to questions.
- Imagine that you are carrying out research into the following topics and describe the kind of interviewer that you would want to conduct the interviews. State whether you would favour structured or unstructured interviews and explain your choice:
  (a) post-natal depression
  (b) football fan rivalry
  (c) men's role in the upbringing of children
  (d) children's experiences of primary school
  (e) drivers' views of speed cameras
  (f) chocolate bar preferences.

Operationalisation of variables, including independent (IV) and dependent variables (DV)

The term 'operationalisation' means being able to define variables simply and easily in order to manipulate them (IV) and measure them (DV). Sometimes, this is very easily done. For example, if we were investigating the effect of alcohol consumption on reaction times we could 'operationalise' the IV as the number of alcohol units consumed and the DV could be the speed of response to a flashing light. However, on other occasions this is more difficult. For example, how would you 'operationalise' anger or stress levels? There isn't always a 'best way' of operationalising complex variables. The researcher has to make a judgement as to whether they're actually measuring the variables they hope to be measuring, and present their arguments to support their decision. A major problem with the operationalisation of complex variables is that they often only measure *one* aspect of the variable.

Both IV and DV need to be 'operationalised' accurately and objectively to maintain the integrity of any research study. Without accurate operationalisation, results may not be reliable or valid, and certainly cannot be checked or replicated.

Pilot studies

These are small-scale 'practice' investigations, where researchers can check all aspects of their research. Changes to the design, method, analysis and so on can be made in the light of this. Pilot studies should improve the quality of the research, help avoid unnecessary work, and save time and money. Participants may be able to suggest appropriate changes for the real study. For example, participants may admit that they guessed the purpose of the study and acted accordingly (demand characteristics).

The control of extraneous variables

In any experiment, the IV is manipulated and the DV is measured. It's assumed that the IV causes any change or effect in the DV. However, there can be other variables that may affect the DV. These are called **extraneous variables.**

Extraneous variables must be carefully and systematically controlled so they don't vary across any of the experimental conditions or, indeed, between participants. When designing an experiment, researchers should consider three main areas where extraneous variables may arise.

1 **Participant variables:** participants' age, intelligence, personality and so on should be controlled across the different groups taking part.

2 **Situational variables:** the experimental setting and surrounding environment must be controlled. This may even include the temperature or noise effects.

3 **Experimenter variables:** the personality, appearance and conduct of the researcher. Any change in these across conditions might affect the results. For example, would a female experimenter have recorded lower levels of obedience in Milgram's obedience to authority studies (see pages 157–159)?

Extraneous variables aren't a problem unless they're not controlled. If they aren't carefully controlled then they may adversely affect or confound the results. They may systematically vary from one condition to another. If this happens we can no longer be sure whether any change in the DV is solely due to the manipulation of the IV or due to the presence of these other 'changing variables'. If this happens, they're called **confounding variables.** The presence of confounding variables minimises the value of any results and are a serious problem.

For example, if researchers wished to investigate the effect of background music (Condition 1) or silence (Condition 2) on homework performance using two classes, they'd have to control a number of possible extraneous variables. These might include: age, homework difficulty and so on. If these were all successfully controlled, then the results would probably be worthwhile. However, if the researchers discovered that those in Condition 1 were considerably brighter than those in Condition 2, then intelligence might be acting as a confounding variable. The researchers could no longer be sure whether any differences in homework performance were due to the presence of the music or due to intelligence levels. Results would be confounded and worthless.

Reliability and validity

Researchers try to produce results that are both reliable and valid. If results are reliable, they're said to be *consistent*. If a study was repeated using the same method, design and measurements, you'd expect to get similar results. If this occurs, the results can be described as reliable.

Reliability in science is essential. If results are unreliable, they cannot be trusted and so will be ignored. However, results can be reliable (i.e. consistent) but still not be accurate. Sometimes measuring instruments may be reliably producing inaccurate results. You may feel this is the case when you consistently get poor marks for your psychology homework: the teacher marks reliably but inaccurately.

Research results must also measure what they're supposed to be measuring (i.e. **validity**). If they do this and they're accurate, they're said to be valid. In effect, the measures can be described as 'true'. For example, is your teacher measuring your work according to exam board guidelines? If not, then their marking may be reliable (consistent) but not valid (accurate).

It's possible to test both reliability and validity, as described below.

- **Internal reliability:** whether a test is consistent within itself. For example, a set of scales should measure the same weight between 50 and 100 grams as between 150 and 200 grams.

- **External reliability:** whether a test measures consistently over time. An IQ (intelligence) test should produce roughly the same measure for the same participant at different time intervals. This is called the **test–retest method**. Obviously, you'd have to ensure that participants don't remember the answers from their previous test.

- **Internal validity:** whether the results are valid (see above) and can be directly attributed to the manipulation of the IV. Results are internally valid if they've not been affected by any confounding variables. Are the results valid *within* the confines of the experimental setting? Various characteristics are required in order for an experiment to be internally valid. These are:

  (a) no investigator effects (see page 95)

  (b) no demand characteristics (see page 94)

  (c) use of standardised instructions

  (d) use of a random sample (see pages 93–94).

- **External (or ecological) validity:** whether the results are valid *beyond* the confines of the experimental setting. Can the results be generalised to the wider population or to different settings or different historical times? It's difficult to test whether a study has high external validity. It often only becomes clear when research findings are found to either apply or not apply to different situations. Field and natural experiments, and naturalistic observations, are usually regarded as being high in external validity. This is because the results can more easily be generalised to other real-life settings. Milgram's obedience experiments have low external validity on all three counts outlined above. The sample was predominantly male (cannot be generalised to females); it involved an artificial setting (Yale University laboratory), and it took place in a different historical time (1960s) to today. Bearing this in mind, we can question whether the results are still valid today (see pages 157–159).

Awareness of the BPS Code of Ethics and the ways in which psychologists deal with ethics

High-quality research should involve good ethical practice. Ethics should be of paramount importance and before any psychological work is conducted its ethical implications should be considered. In addition to formal professional ethical guidelines, most research institutions, such as universities, have their own ethical committees, which meet to consider all research projects before they commence. The British Psychological Society (BPS) publishes a Code of Ethics that all psychologists should follow (BPS, 2007). The informal basis of the code is 'do unto others as you would be done by'. The Code includes the following information.

- **Informed consent:** whenever possible, the investigator should inform all participants of the objectives of the investigation. Parental consent should be obtained in the case of children (under 16 years). In addition, consent should also be obtained from children who are old enough to understand the study.

- **Avoidance of deception:** the withholding of information or the misleading of participants is unacceptable if the participants are likely to object or show unease once debriefed. Intentional deception of the participants over the purpose and general nature of the investigation should be avoided whenever possible. Participants should never be deliberately misled without extremely strong scientific or medical justification. However, there may be occasions where some deception is unavoidable. There are a number of possible ways to try to deal with the problem of deception.

  (a) **Presumptive consent:** this could be gained from people of a similar background to the participants in the study. If they state that they'd have been willing to participate, it's likely that you'll not upset the actual participants (too much).

  (b) **Prior general consent:** this involves participants agreeing to being deceived without knowing how they will be deceived. This can be done some time before the start of the research. Of course participants might suspect deception and this might affect the results, but at least they would have given a form of consent to participate in the study.

  (c) **Retrospective consent:** this involves asking participants for consent after they have participated in the study. Of course, a major problem here is that they may not agree to it and yet they have already taken part!

If deception is used, participants should be told immediately afterwards and given the chance to withhold their data from the study. Before conducting such a study, the investigator has a special responsibility to:

  (a) determine that alternative procedures avoiding deception are not available

  (b) ensure that the participants are provided with sufficient information at the earliest stage

  (c) consult appropriately about the way that the withholding of information or deliberate deception will be received.

- **Adequate briefing/debriefing:** all relevant details of the study should be explained to participants both before and after the study. The debrief is particularly important if deception has been used. Participants should leave the study feeling the same (or better) about themselves as when they started the study. Debriefing does not provide a justification for any unethical aspects of the procedure.

- **Protection of participants:** investigators have a primary responsibility to protect participants from physical and mental harm during the investigation. Normally, the risk of harm must be no greater than in ordinary life (i.e. participants should not be exposed to risks greater than, or in addition to, those encountered in their normal lifestyles).

- **Right to withdraw:** participants should always be aware that they can leave the study at any time, regardless of whether or not any payment or inducement has been offered. This can be particularly difficult to implement during observations. Participants should also be aware that they can withdraw their data at any point in the future.

- **Confidentiality:** participants' data should be treated as confidential and not disclosed to anyone, unless a different arrangement has been agreed in advance. Numbers should be allocated immediately, and used instead of names, and these should be used throughout by the research team and in any subsequent published articles. It's easy to confuse confidentiality with anonymity. Confidentiality means that data can be traced back to names, whereas anonymous data cannot, since no names are collected by the research team. Confidential data collection is preferable in cases where participants might be followed up later.

- **Observational research:** observations should only be made in public places where people might expect to be seen by strangers.

- **Giving advice:** during research, an investigator may obtain evidence of psychological or physical problems of which a participant is, apparently, unaware. In such a case, the investigator has a responsibility to inform the participant if s/he believes that by not doing so the participant's future well-being may be endangered.

- **Colleagues:** investigators share responsibility for the ethical treatment of research participants with their collaborators, assistants, students and employees. A psychologist who believes that another psychologist or investigator may be conducting research that is not in accordance with the ethical principles should encourage that investigator to re-evaluate the research.

Before any research is conducted, psychologists must seek peer guidance, consult likely participants for their views, follow the BPS Code of Ethics, consider alternative research methodologies, establish a cost/benefit analysis of both short-term and long-term consequences, assume responsibility for the research, and gain approval from any ethical committees that monitor their research. If, during the research process, it becomes clear that there are negative consequences as a result of the research, the research should be stopped and every effort should be made to correct for these adverse consequences. Any researcher that has ethical concerns about a colleague should contact them in the first instance, and if their concerns are not allayed they should then contact the BPS (British Psychological Society).

How Science Works

Practical Learning Activity 3.10: Milgram and ethical issues

Review Milgram's (1963) Study of Destructive Obedience and consider his procedure in the light of the ethical issues in the BPS Guidelines.

- Which guidelines did Milgram break? (See pages 163–166.)
- Could he have conducted the study in a different way? Outline some suggestions.
- Why couldn't he have actually broken the BPS Guidelines at the time of his research?

Take a look at http://www.sbg.ac.at/kriterion/documents/14/14patry.pdf for more details on the ethical issues concerned with Milgram (Patry, 2001).

Research method	Key ethical issues
Laboratory experiments	• Participants feel pressure to act in a particular way • Reluctance of participants to exercise their right to withdraw • Experimental situation can be stressful
Field/natural experiments	• Informed consent is difficult to obtain • Participants are unlikely to know of the right to withdraw • Debriefing is difficult
Observations	• If participants do not know they are being observed, there are issues of informed consent, confidentiality and invasion of privacy
Correlational analysis	• Interpretation of results: the public may interpret correlations incorrectly
Questionnaires/ interviews	• Confidentiality must be maintained • Right to withhold information on embarrassing topics
Case studies	• Issues of confidentiality and invasion of privacy

Table 3.2: Summary of ethical issues with different research methods

The selection of participants, and sampling techniques

Psychological studies usually involve **samples** drawn from larger **populations**. Sampling is essential to avoid the need to study entire populations. The selected sample should be **representative** of this wider population. Representative samples *represent* the target population and should share (some of) the same important characteristics. It's called a **target population** because this is the group of people whom the researcher is hoping to *target* or generalise the results to. In general, the larger the sample, the better it is. However, the larger the sample, the more costly or time-consuming it is, too. Psychologists use a number of sampling techniques to try to obtain unbiased samples; some of these are described below.

• **Random sampling:** this is the best-known method. It's where every member of the population has an equal chance of being selected. The easiest way to do this is to place all names from the target population in a hat and draw out the required sample number. Computer programs can also generate random lists. This will result in a sample selected in an unbiased way. However, it can still result in a biased sample. For example, if ten boys' and ten girls' names were placed in a hat, there is a (small) chance that the first ten drawn from the hat could be boys' names. Selection would have been unbiased, but the sample would still be biased. A special form of random sampling involves the random allocation of participants to different conditions in independent groups design (see pages 81–82).

Evaluation of random sampling

✔ The sample is likely to be representative and therefore results can be generalised to the wider population.

✗ It's sometimes difficult to get details of the wider population in order to select the sample.

● **Opportunity sampling:** involves selecting participants who are readily available and willing to take part. This could simply involve asking anybody who's passing. A surprising number of university research studies (75 per cent) use undergraduates as participants simply for the sake of convenience (Sears, 1986).

● **Volunteer sampling:** involves people volunteering to participate. They select themselves as participants, often by replying to adverts. This sampling method was used by Milgram (1963) in his Destructive Obedience Study.

Evaluation of opportunity and volunteer sampling

✔ The easiest, most practical and cheapest methods to ensure large samples.

✗ The sample is likely to be biased in some (important) way. Thus the findings may be less easily generalised to the wider population. Volunteers may be more motivated and thus perform differently than randomly selected participants. Bauman (1973) found different results on reported sexual knowledge, attitudes and behaviour of undergraduate students dependent on whether they were willing or non-willing volunteers.

Demand characteristics

Any social interaction affects people's behaviour. Conducting research is no different. It doesn't take place in a 'social vacuum', and involves some interaction between the researcher and the participant. Such interaction can therefore affect the research findings.

Orne (1962) believed that there are many features in research studies that enable the participants to guess what the study is about and what is expected of them. These **demand characteristics** can involve participants:

● guessing the purpose of the research and trying to please the researcher by giving the 'right' results

● guessing the purpose of the research and trying to annoy the researcher by giving them the wrong results; this is called the '**screw you' effect** (for obvious reasons!)

● acting unnaturally out of nervousness for fear of being thought 'abnormal'

● acting unnaturally in order to 'look good' (**social desirability bias**).

We've already noted the effect of demand characteristics in different research methods (see pages 66–79).

A technique that reduces demand characteristics is the **single blind procedure**. This is where participants have no idea which condition of the study they're in. In drug trials, they wouldn't know whether they're being given the real drug or the placebo drug ('sugar pill').

Investigator effects

Investigators may inadvertently influence the results in their research. This can occur in a number of ways, some of which are described below.

- Certain physical characteristics of the investigator may influence results. Such factors might include age, ethnicity, appearance, attractiveness and so on. For example, male participants may be unwilling to admit their sexist views to a female researcher.

- Other less obvious personal characteristics of the investigator, such as accent, tone of voice or non-verbal communication (eye contact, smiling), can influence results. Participants may pick up on this and not act as they normally would.

- The investigator may also be biased in their interpretation of the data. This, of course, should never be deliberate. It is claimed that Burt (1955) made up some of his evidence on the influence of heredity on intelligence.

A technique that reduces investigator effects is the **double blind procedure**. This is where neither the participant nor the investigator knows which condition the participant is in. They are both 'blind' to this knowledge. This prevents the investigator from inadvertently giving the participant clues as to which condition they are in and therefore reduces demand characteristics. (Obviously, there is an investigator in overall charge who is aware of the allocation to conditions.)

Assessment Check 3.2

1. A researcher wanted to investigate if age affects forgetting. Write a suitable directional hypothesis for such a study. (2 marks)
2. Explain why a directional hypothesis might be chosen. (2 marks)
3. Outline ONE advantage and ONE weakness of using a repeated measures design. (2 + 2 marks)
4. Identify and explain how ONE weakness of independent groups design could be dealt with. (2 + 2 marks)
5. Outline any TWO factors that researchers need to consider in the design of a questionnaire. (2 + 2 marks)
6. A researcher wished to investigate the effect of diet on intelligence. Outline ONE possible extraneous variable that she should consider when designing such a study. (2 marks)
7. What is meant by the term 'reliability'? (2 marks)
8. Outline ONE way of assessing reliability. (2 marks)
9. Outline the purpose of a pilot study. (3 marks)
10. Describe ONE ethical issue in psychological research and outline ONE possible way that psychologists have attempted to deal with this issue. (2 + 2 marks)

11. **Describe ONE way that psychologists might select a random sample. (2 marks)**
12. **What is meant by the term 'demand characteristics'? (2 marks)**
13. **Give an example of investigator effects in an interview situation. (3 marks)**

Data analysis and presentation

Research involves the collection of data. Data can be analysed both quantitatively and qualitatively. Psychologists are still debating the merits of each approach. Generally, qualitative studies produce subjective, detailed, less reliable data, whereas quantitative studies produce objective, less detailed, more reliable data.

Qualitative data	Quantitative data
Subjective	Objective
Imprecise measures used	Precise measures used
Rich and detailed	Lacks detail
Low in reliability	High in reliability
Used for attitudes, opinions, beliefs	Used for behaviour
Collected in 'real life' setting	Collected in 'artificial' setting

Table 3.3: General summary of quantitative and qualitative data

Analysis and interpretation of quantitative data, including graphs, scattergrams and tables

Psychological data can be presented in a number of ways. Although psychology as a science places the emphasis on statistical analysis, data should also be presented in a visually meaningful way. Graphs and charts enable the reader to '**eyeball**' the data and help to illustrate any patterns in the data. The use and interpretation of scattergrams are dealt with below (see page 103). Other types of graphs include those described below.

Bar charts

These show data in the form of categories that the researcher wishes to compare (e.g. males, females) (see Figure 3.3). These categories should be placed on the x axis ('x is across'). The columns of bar charts should all be of the same width and separated by a space. The use of a space illustrates that the variable on the x axis is not continuous. It is 'discrete' data such as the mean score of several groups. It can also involve percentages, totals, ratios, and so on. A bar chart can display two values together – for example, if the male and female groups shown in Figure 3.3 were divided into a further two groups: under and over 20 years of age (see Figure 3.4). Notice that the different y axis scale gives a different impression of the results. This is something to be aware of when designing a bar chart.

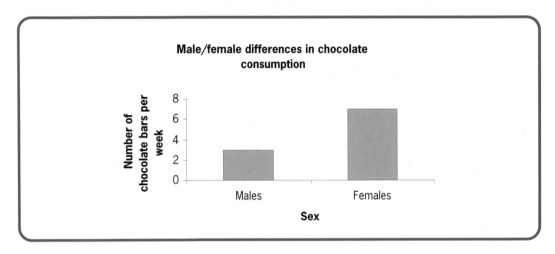

Figure 3.3: Example of a bar chart

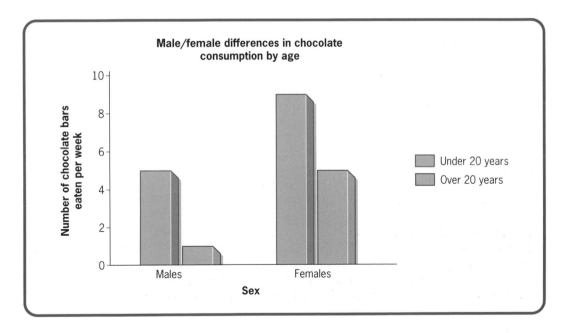

Figure 3.4: A bar chart can display two values together

How Science Works
Practical Learning Activity 3.11: Misleading bar charts

Imagine you are a supporter of either Political Party A or Political Party Z and you are presented with the following data table.

Percentage increase in crime, year on year, during Party A and Party Z governments
Party A: 1983: +10% Party Z: 1997: +3%
Party A: 1987: +5% Party Z: 2002: +14%
Party A: 1992: +3% Party Z: 2007: +1%

- Choose an appropriate graph to illustrate these figures. Draw up a graph (or two graphs) that you would use if you were a Party A or Party Z supporter.
- How might you explain such figures?
- Consider in your answers issues such as policing funding and the public's willingness to report minor crimes.

Histograms

Students often confuse histograms and bar charts. The main difference is that histograms are used for continuous data (e.g. test scores) like the example in Figure 3.5. These continuous scores or values should ascend along the x axis. The frequency of these values is shown on the y axis. There should be no spaces between the bars since the data are con-

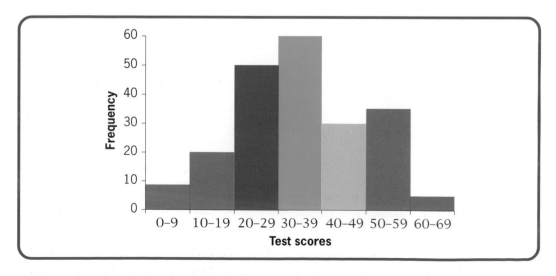

Figure 3.5: Example of a histogram

tinuous. The column width for each value on the x axis should be the same width per equal category interval. Thus the area of each column is proportional to the number of cases it represents throughout the histogram.

Frequency polygon (or line graph)

This is very similar to a histogram in that the data on the x axes must be continuous. A frequency polygon can be produced by drawing a line from the midpoint top of each bar in a histogram. The one real advantage of a frequency polygon is that two or more frequency distributions can be displayed on the same graph for comparison (see Figure 3.6).

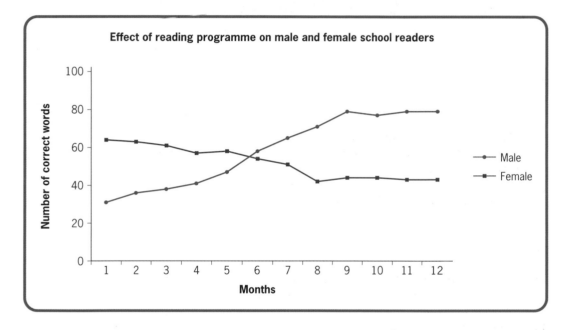

Figure 3.6: Example of a frequency polygon

General points to consider with presentation of graphs and charts

- All graphs and charts must be fully labelled with an appropriate title, and the x and y axes should be labelled accurately.

- Graphs and charts generally look best if the y axis height is three-quarters the x axis width.

- Only one graph or chart should be used to illustrate a set of data. (Many students produce different graphs or charts of the same data.)

- Use an appropriate scale on the axes. Do not mislead people by using an inappropriate scale. Political parties often do this and it's best not to follow their example.

- Do not draw the raw data. A chart or graph should be a summary of the data. Do not be tempted to include each individual score. The raw data table will already have shown this.

Analysis and interpretation of quantitative data

Measures of central tendency are used to summarise large amounts of data into a typical value or average. They are ways of estimating the midpoint of scores. There are three averages: the median, the mean and the mode.

The median

This is the central score in a list of rank-ordered scores. With an odd number of scores, the median is the middle number. With an even number of scores, the median is the midpoint between the two middle scores and therefore may not be one of the original scores.

The advantages of this measure are that:

- it is not affected by extreme 'freak' scores
- it is usually easier to calculate than the mean.

The weaknesses are that:

- it is not as sensitive as the mean, because the raw scores are not used in the calculation
- it can be unrepresentative in a small data set. For example:

  1 1 2 3 4 5 6 7 8 – the median is 4

  2 3 4 6 8 9 12 13 – the median is 7

The mean

This is where all the scores are added up and divided by the total number of scores. It is the exact midpoint of all the combined values.

The advantages of this measure are that:

- it is a very sensitive measure and the most accurate of the measures of central tendency outlined here because it works at the interval level of measurement
- it includes all the information from the raw scores.

The weaknesses are that:

- it is less useful if some of the scores are skewed – that is, if there are very large or small scores in the distribution of scores
- often, the mean score is not one of the original scores.

The mode

This is the most common, or 'popular', number in a set of scores.

The advantages of this measure are that:

- it is not affected by extreme scores in one direction

- it sometimes makes more sense than the other measures of central tendency – for example, the average number of children in a British family is better described as 2 (the mode) rather than 2.4 children (mean).

The weaknesses are that:

- there can be more than one mode in a set of data (e.g. 2 3 6 7 7 7 9 15 16 16 16 20 – modes are 7 and 16)

- it doesn't take into account the exact distances between all the values.

Measures of dispersion, including ranges and standard deviation

Measures of dispersion are measures of the variability or spread of scores. They include the range, semi-interquartile range and standard deviation.

The range

This is calculated by taking away the lowest value from the highest value in a set of scores and then adding 1.

The advantages of this measure are that:

- it is fairly easy and quick to work out

- it includes extreme values, but does not incorporate individual values.

The weaknesses are that:

- it can be distorted by extreme 'freak' values and does not show whether data are clustered or spread evenly around the mean (e.g. 2 3 4 5 5 6 7 8 9 21 and 2 5 8 9 10 12 13 15 16 18 21 – the range of these two sets of data is the same, despite the data being very different).

Semi-interquartile range

This shows the middle 50 per cent of a set of scores. When the scores are in rank order, the first 'quartile' (Q1) is the first 25 per cent of scores. The third quartile (Q3) includes the first 75 per cent of scores. The inter-quartile range is half the distance between Q1 and Q3. To obtain this, you subtract Q1 from Q3 and divide by two. For example:

$$1 \quad 2 \quad 4 \quad 6 \quad 7 \quad 8 \quad 9 \quad 12 \quad 14 \quad 16 \quad 19$$

Q1 – this is the inter-quartile range – Q3

Q3 – Q1 = 14 – 4 = 10. 10 divided by 2 = 5 = semi-interquartile range.

The advantages of this measure are that:

- it is fairly easy to calculate

- it is not affected by extreme scores.

The weaknesses are that:

- it doesn't take into account extreme scores

- it is inaccurate if there are large intervals between the scores.

Standard deviation

This is a measure of the spread or variability of a set of scores from the mean. The larger the standard deviation, the larger the spread of scores.

The advantages of this measure are that:

- it is a more sensitive dispersion measure than the range since all scores are used in its calculation

- it allows for the interpretation of an individual's score; thus in Figure 3.7, anybody with an IQ of 131 is in the top 5 per cent of the population (between +2 and +3 standard deviations of the mean).

The weaknesses are that:

- it is more complicated to calculate

- it is less meaningful if data are not normally distributed (Figure 3.7 shows a normal distribution).

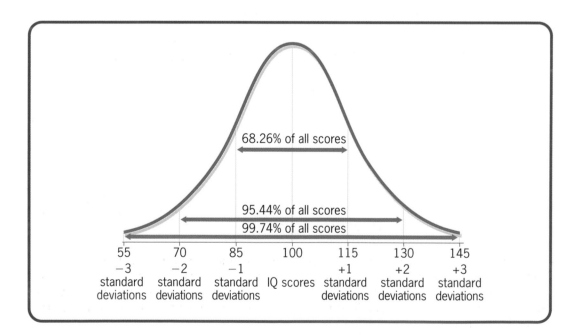

Figure 3.7: Standard deviation: IQ scores

Specification Hint

You do not need to know how to calculate any of the measures of central tendency or dispersion for the AS exam.

Analysis and interpretation of correlational data

Positive and negative correlations and the interpretation of correlation coefficients

Correlational methods have been mentioned above (see pages 69–71). Correlations can be either positive or negative, or show no correlation. The stronger the correlation, the nearer it is to +1 or −1. Scattergrams (or scattergraphs) are useful techniques that show at a glance how two variables are correlated. However, a statistical test or correlation coefficient has to be calculated to determine the exact nature of the correlation. Given a scattergram or a correlational coefficient (e.g. +0.7), you should be able to determine the strength and direction of the correlation (see Figure 3.8).

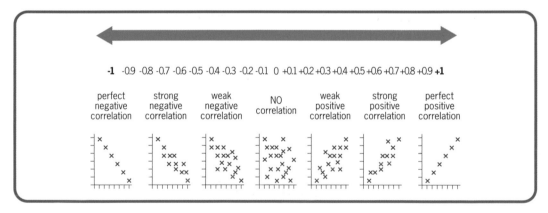

Figure 3.8: Scattergrams and correlational strength

Analysis and presentation of qualitative data, including processes involved in content analysis

Qualitative data involves people's meanings, experiences and descriptions. It is particularly good for researching attitudes, opinions and beliefs. Data usually consist of verbal or written descriptions. The qualitative approach suggests that information about human events and experience loses much of its meaning and value when reduced to numerical form (Coolican, 2004).

There is no one agreed way to analyse qualitative data. Each researcher has his or her own ideas for the best way to do it. The analysis of qualitative data is a fairly new field and new methods are emerging and developing. Some of the ways to analyse qualitative data include those described below.

Content analysis

This is most commonly done within media research. Strictly speaking, it actually involves the quantification of qualitative material – that is, it analyses in a numerical way written, verbal or visual communication. It can involve the analysis of speeches, graffiti, newspapers, TV adverts and so on. Waynforth and Dunbar (1995) analysed the content of 'lonely hearts' columns to see if men and women were looking for the same things in life.

Content analysis requires coding units to be developed where analysed material can be categorised. For instance, the number of times women appear as housewives in TV adverts. Analysis can involve words, themes, characters or time and space. The number of times these things do not occur can also be important.

Unit	Examples
Word	Count the number of slang words used
Theme	The amount of violence on TV
Character	The number of female bosses there are in TV programmes
Time and space	The amount of time (on TV) and space (in newspapers) dedicated to famine in Africa

Table 3.4: Coding units for content analysis

Categorising

This involves the grouping of common items together. For example, it might be possible to group students' perceptions of their Psychology course into: resources (books, DVDs), peer/teacher relationships, teacher knowledge, delivery, and so forth. It's often difficult to decide on the categories to use. Once the categories have been selected, quantitative graphical techniques, such as bar charts, can be used to present the data.

Quotations

Word-for-word quotations are often used to bring the research findings to life. The quotes should 'tell it like it is'. They should typify what others have said during the research.

Qualitative data and naturalistic observations

Observers typically give a running commentary into a tape recorder as they observe behaviour. This produces qualitative data. Such data can be coded or categorised (see above) and can help to add detail to quantitative data. The **diary method** is another technique where observers can take notes on behaviour. This can be self-reported behaviour. The diary method has the advantage of providing genuine information in the participants' own surroundings. However, participants often find it difficult to complete on a long-term basis.

Qualitative data and questionnaire surveys

Qualitative data are mainly collected from open-ended questions where participants are invited to give an answer using their own words. Such data are less likely to be biased by the interviewers' preconceived ideas. Analysis of this data can involve content analysis, categorisation or the use of quotations, as described above.

Qualitative data and interviews

Interviews are likely to be transcribed and can then be analysed using many of the qualitative techniques described above. Unstructured interviews are most suitable for qualitative analysis. The interpretation of interview data is open to subjective interpretation. However, this lack of objectivity may be overcome by the detail that such a method allows.

Evaluation of qualitative data analysis

Qualitative data analysis tends to be subjective, although there are methods for checking both reliability (through replication) and validity (through the use of other methods). In any case, many qualitative researchers argue that subjectivity and the personal opinion of a participant are extremely valuable and strengthen any research study. Qualitative data analysis can, however, be extremely time-consuming.

Assessment Check 3.3

1. **Name ONE measure of central tendency and give ONE reason why it might be used. (2 + 3 marks)**
2. **Outline ONE weakness of the 'mode'. (2 marks)**
3. **Explain what standard deviation tells us about a set of data. (3 marks)**
4. **Describe the type of correlation that you would have if the correlation coefficient was +0.87. (2 marks)**

CHAPTER

SUMMARY
Methods and techniques

- There is a range of different research methods that psychologists use. Each has its own strengths and weaknesses.

- A **laboratory experiment** takes place in a controlled environment where the IV is manipulated and the DV is measured.

- A **field experiment** takes place in a real-life setting where the IV is manipulated and the DV is measured.

- A **natural experiment** takes place in a real-life setting where the IV occurs naturally and the DV is measured.

- **Correlational analysis** allows the strength of the relationship between two variables to be measured.

- **Observational techniques** involve the precise (objective) measuring of naturally occurring behaviour. They tend to take place in a natural setting and can involve **participant or non-participant** observation.

- **Questionnaires** involve the systematic large-scale collection of data. A questionnaire is a pre-set list of questions and can include **open and closed questions**.

- **Interviews** involve researchers asking questions in a face-to-face way. They range from **unstructured** to **fully structured interviews.**

- **Case studies** involve the in-depth, detailed investigation of an individual or group.

- Each of the research methods has different **ethical problems** associated with it.

Investigation design

- **Aims** give an indication of why a study is taking place.

- A **hypothesis** is a testable statement and predicts what might happen. An **alternative or experimental** hypothesis predicts significant differences in the DV as a result of manipulation of the IV. It can be **directional or non-directional**. A **null hypothesis** predicts that any results will simply occur as a result of chance.

- There are **three types of experimental design**:
  1 **independent groups design** is where different participants are used in each condition of the study
  2 **matched participants design** is where similar, matched pairs of participants are allocated to each of the conditions
  3 **repeated measures design** is where the same participants take part in all the conditions.

- There are advantages and weaknesses of each of the designs. **Counterbalancing** can help to overcome the problem of **order effects** with repeated measures design.

- The **operationalisation of variables** refers to the need to define and measure the variables (IV and DV) being studied simply and easily.

- **Pilot studies** are small-scale 'practice' investigations. They are carried out prior to the actual research and help to identify potential problems.

- **Extraneous variables** are variables other than the IV that might affect the DV. They must be controlled in any study. If they are not controlled, they will adversely affect the results. They are then called **confounding variables** because they 'confound' the results.

- Results should be checked for **reliability** (i.e. consistency) and **validity** (i.e. accuracy). There are a number of ways to test this, including **internal reliability** and **external reliability**, and **internal validity** and **external (ecological) validity**. External (ecological) validity refers to whether or not the results can be generalised beyond the confines of the experimental setting.

- All psychological research must be carried out **ethically** according to BPS guidelines. The main issues involve: **informed consent**, **protection from harm**, **avoidance of deception** and the **right to withdraw**.

- The selection of participants for psychological research can be done in many ways. These include **random**, **opportunity** and **volunteer sampling**. **Random sampling** is the best known way in which every member of the **target population** has an equal chance of being selected. It is important to try to obtain a *representative* sample. **Opportunity sampling** involves asking anybody who is passing to participate. **Volunteer sampling** involves advertising for participants to come forward.

- The **relationship between researchers and participants** can affect the results obtained. **Demand characteristics** occur when participants try to guess the purpose of the study and then try to give the 'right' results/answers.

- **Investigator effects** occur when some aspects of the investigator (e.g.

appearance, gender, ethnicity) influence participants' answers. **Single and double blind procedures** can help to overcome these problems.

Data analysis and presentation

- **Quantitative data** involve the numerical analysis of data.

- **Graphs and charts** illustrate patterns in data at a glance. The strength and direction of a correlation can be seen in a **scattergram**. A perfect positive correlation is +1 with a perfect negative correlation being −1. **Bar charts**, **histograms** and **frequency polygons** are other graphical techniques used for quantitative data.

- **Measures of central tendency** are used to illustrate the **average values** of data. These include the **mean** (all scores added and divided by the number of scores), the **mode** (the most common score) and the **median** (the middle score).

- **Measures of dispersion** show the **variability** of a spread of scores. These include the **range**, the **semi-interquartile range** and **standard deviation.**

- **Qualitative data** involve people's meanings, experiences and descriptions. They are subjective, but rich and detailed. There is no agreed way to code qualitative data but it often involves the **categorisation of common themes** and the use of direct, illustrative **quotations**. **Content analysis** involves the quantification of qualitative written material.

Biological psychology: stress

4 Chapter

What's covered in this chapter?

You need to know about:

Stress as a bodily response

- The body's response to stress, including the pituitary–adrenal system and the sympathomedullary pathway in outline
- Stress-related illness and the immune system

Stress in everyday life

- Life changes and daily hassles
- Workplace stress
- Personality factors, including Type A
- Distinction between emotion-focused and problem-focused approaches to coping with stress
- Psychological and physiological methods of stress management, including cognitive behavioural therapy and drugs

Stress as a bodily response

What do we mean by stress?

How Science Works
Practical Learning Activity 4.1

- What do you understand by the term 'stress'?
- What makes you feel stressed?
- Ask a sample of your friends and family the same two questions.
- Can you identify any patterns in the answers (relating to age or gender, for example)?

Stress can be defined in three main ways.

1 Stress as a **stimulus:** this refers to the characteristics of an environmental event or situation, and is basically something that happens *to* us. *Sources of stress* ('stressors') include life changes and workplace stressors.

2 Stress as a **response:** this refers to what happens *within* us as a result of environmental events or situations. In particular, it refers to the physiological/bodily responses, such as the General Adaptation Syndrome (Selye, 1956). This relates to stress as a *bodily response.*

3 Stress as **interaction** between an individual and his/her environment: we experience stress when we believe we don't have what's needed to meet the demands of a particular situation. But people differ in what makes them feel stressed, how much stress they feel and how they try to deal with it. This relates to *stress management.*

According to Selye (1956):

Stress is the non-specific response of the body to any demand made upon it.

Selye observed that all hospital patients display the same pattern of symptoms (or *syndrome*), regardless of their particular illness. These symptoms included:

- loss of appetite

- an associated loss of weight and strength

- loss of ambition

- a characteristic facial expression.

After examining extreme cases in more detail, Selye concluded that this non-specific response in turn reflected the **General Adaptation Syndrome (GAS):** the body responds in the *same* way to *any* stressor, whether it's environmental or arises within the body itself. Environmental stressors may include insulin, excessive heat or cold, X-rays, sleep and water deprivation, and electric shock. Another of Selye's definitions of stress is:

the individual's psychophysiological response, mediated largely by their autonomic nervous system and the endocrine system, to any demand made on the individual.

In order to understand GAS, we must have a working knowledge of the **nervous system** and the **endocrine system.** We also need to understand how they *interact* with each other. This is summarised in Figure 4.1.

How Science Works

Practical Learning Activity 4.2

Before looking at Figure 4.1, find out about the general characteristics of the *nervous system* and the *endocrine system.* Most Psychology textbooks will provide sufficient information.

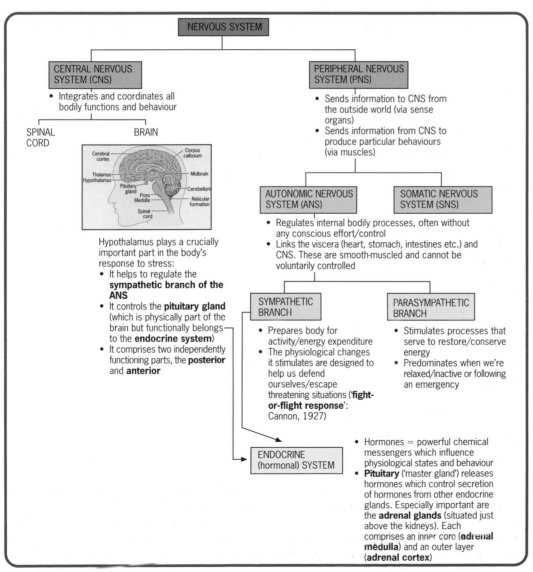

Figure 4.1: Major sub-divisions of the nervous system and their interactions with the endocrine system

The three stages/phases of GAS

Alarm reaction

When a stimulus is perceived as a stressor, there's a brief, initial *shock phase*. Blood pressure (BP) and muscle tension drop, and resistance to the stressor is reduced. However, this is quickly followed by the *countershock phase*: the hypothalamus activates the sympathetic branch of the ANS, which, in turn, stimulates the *adrenal medulla* to secrete increased levels of adrenaline and noradrenaline (*catecholamines*, or 'stress hormones'). The catecholamines:

- mimic the activity of the sympathetic branch of the ANS (and so are called *sympathomimetics*), and

- trigger and maintain increased levels of physiological activity, which are collectively called the *fight-or-flight response* (FOFR) (Cannon, 1927). These changes are summarised in Table 4.1 (see also Figure 4.2).

For all these reasons, the alarm reaction is associated with the *sympatho-adrenomedullary axis* (SAA).

Organ or function involved	Sympathetic reaction
Heart rate	Increases
Blood pressure	Increases
Secretion of saliva	Suppressed (dry mouth)
Pupils of eye	Dilate (to aid vision)
Limbs (and trunk)	Dilation of blood vessels of voluntary muscles (e.g. to help us run faster)
Peristalsis (contraction of stomach and intestines)	Slows down (we don't feel hungry in an emergency)
Galvanic skin response (GSR) (measure of skin's electrical resistance)	Decreases (due to increased sweating associated with increased anxiety)
Bladder muscles	Relax (there may be temporary loss of bladder control)
Breathing rate	Increases (through dilation of bronchial tubes)
Liver	Glucose (stored as energy) released into bloodstream to increase energy
Emotion	Experience of strong emotion (e.g. fear)

Table 4.1: Major sympathetic reactions associated with the 'fight-or-flight response' (FOFR)

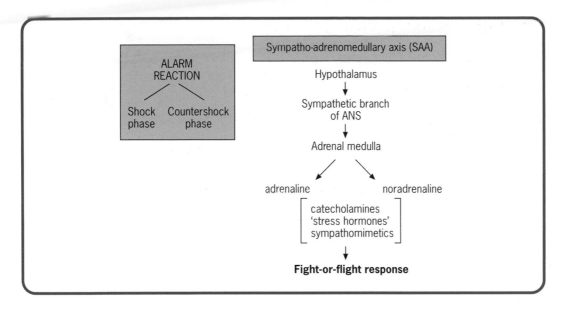

Figure 4.2: The alarm reaction of the GAS and the associated sympatho-adrenomedullary axis (SAA)

Resistance

If the stressor isn't removed, sympathetic activity *decreases*. But output from the other part of the adrenal gland (the *adrenal cortex*) *increases*. The adrenal cortex is essential for the maintenance of life, and its removal causes death. It's controlled by how much *adrenocorticotrophic hormone* (ACTH) there is in the blood. ACTH is released from the *anterior pituitary*. In turn, the anterior pituitary is controlled by the hypothalamus.

ACTH stimulates the adrenal cortex to release *corticosteroids* (or *adrenocorticoid hormones*). One group of adrenocorticoid hormones are the *glucocorticoid hormones*, which include corticosterone, cortisol and hydrocortisone. These regulate the amount of glucose in the blood (*glucogenesis*), which helps to resist all kinds of stress. The glucocorticoids:

● convert protein into glucose

● make fats available for energy

● increase blood flow, and

● generally stimulate behavioural responsiveness.

In this way, the *hypothalamic–pituitary–adrenal axis* (HPAA) contributes to the fight-or-flight response.

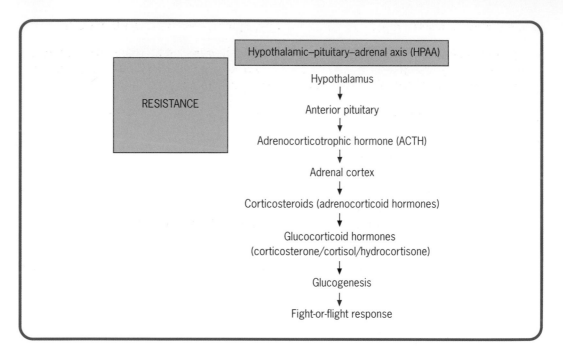

Figure 4.3: The resistance stage of the GAS and the associated hypothalamic–pituitary–adrenal axis (HPAA)

Exhaustion

Once ACTH and corticosteroids are circulating in the bloodstream, they tend to inhibit more ACTH being released from the pituitary. If the stressor is removed during the resistance stage, blood sugar levels will gradually return to normal. But if the stressful situation continues, so will the pituitary–adrenal excitation. By this time:

● the body's resources are becoming depleted

● the adrenals can no longer function properly

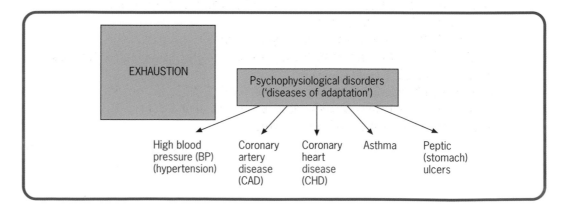

Figure 4.4: The exhaustion stage of the GAS and the associated psychophysiological disorders ('diseases of adaptation')

- blood glucose levels drop; in extreme cases, hypoglycaemia could result in death

- *psychophysiological disorders* develop; these include high blood pressure (BP) (hypertension), coronary artery disease (CAD), coronary heart disease (CHD), asthma and peptic (stomach) ulcers. Selye called these the *diseases of adaptation.*

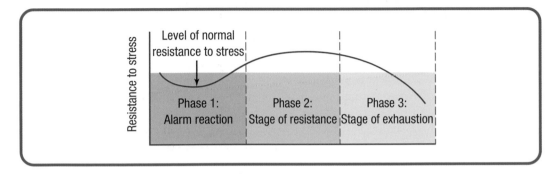

Figure 4.5: The three stages of the GAS

Evaluation of the GAS

✔ It helps account for the physiology of stress.
✘ Not all stressors produce the same pattern of physiological activity.
✘ Research into the GAS involved mainly rats' responses to stressors.
✘ Selye largely ignored the *psychological* aspects of stress: a stressor must first be *perceived* as a stressor before any physiological changes occur. It's almost as though Selye left the person out of the picture by focusing on the body's responses.

 Assessment Check 4.1

1. Define what is meant by 'stress as a stimulus'. (2 marks)
2. Describe the THREE stages of Selye's General Adaptation Syndrome (GAS). (6 marks)
3. Outline TWO weaknesses of Selye's GAS. (2 + 2 marks)
4. Outline the TWO main functions of the catecholamines (or 'stress hormones'). (2 + 2 marks)
5. Define the term 'fight-or-flight response' (FOFR). (2 marks)
6. Give TWO examples of psychophysiological disorders (or 'diseases of adaptation'). (1 + 1 mark)

How does stress make us ill?
Cardiovascular disorders

The GAS provides us with a general answer to the question 'Why does stress make us ill?' For more specific, detailed answers, we need to consider other research.

An evolutionary perspective

Like the GAS, this represents a general way of trying to understand why stress is bad for us, but it also provides some important links with research into the cardiovascular effects of stress (such as heart disease and circulatory disorders).

Box 4.1: The evolutionary explanation of how stress makes us ill

The sympathetic branch of the ANS responds as a unit. This causes a state of generalised arousal, which is pretty much the same whatever the stressor might be. This was probably crucial in our evolutionary past, when our ancestors were commonly faced with life-threatening dangers. This is exactly what the FOFR is for.

For example, an increased heart rate supplied blood to the muscles, which is a good idea when faced with a hungry sabre-toothed tiger. Although most everyday stressors involve a much greater *psychological* element and *aren't* life-threatening, our nervous and endocrine systems have evolved in such a way that we typically react to everyday stressors *as if they were.* What may have been *adaptive*, advantageous, responses for our ancestors may have become *maladaptive* today.

So, what happens to all that internal, physiological activity?

- Chronic (long-term, ongoing) stress involves repeated episodes of increased heart rate and BP; this, in turn, increases plaque formation within the cardiovascular system.

- Adrenaline and noradrenaline contribute to increases in blood cholesterol levels. Cholesterol particles clump together, leading to clots in the blood and artery walls: the arteries become thickened.

- Raised heart rate is linked to more rapid build-up of cholesterol walls, and high BP causes small lesions to form on the artery walls, where cholesterol gets trapped.

Friedman and Rosenman's research

Friedman and Rosenman (two American cardiologists) concluded that some men are more prone to coronary heart disease (CHD) because they typically respond to stressful situations in a particular way. So, their research is just as relevant to understanding the factors that affect stress as it is to how stress makes us ill.

In the late 1950s, Friedman and Rosenman found that American men, compared with American women, were far more susceptible to CHD – despite the similarity of their diets. A subsequent questionnaire study suggested that job-related stress may have been the crucial factor. They followed this up by monitoring the *blood-clotting speed* and *serum cholesterol levels* (two warning signs of CHD) of 40 tax accountants over a period of several months. As the deadline for submitting tax returns approached (an especially stressful time for them), the two measures rose alarmingly; but they soon returned to normal levels once the deadline had passed.

A modern stressor

Key Study 4.1: Friedman and Rosenman's (1974) Study of Type A Behaviour (STAB)

Aim/hypothesis (AO1)

Friedman and Rosenman wanted to find evidence for the role of *non-physiological factors* in CHD. In particular, they were interested in the role of *individual differences* in men's ways of dealing with stressful situations.

Method/design (AO1)

Starting in 1960–61, 3000 American men, aged 39–59, were followed for a period of over eight years. They were all well when the study began. How they dealt with stressful situations was assessed in two ways:

1 a *structured interview*, which involved predetermined, open-ended questions
2 a pencil-and-paper *self-assessment* test, consisting of several multiple-choice questions.

Based on these two measures, the men were classified as displaying either Type A behaviour (TAB) or Type B (non-Type A) behaviour (TBB).

- *TAB* involves a chronic sense of time urgency, excessive competitiveness, and a generalised (but well controlled) hostility. These men are always setting themselves deadlines, suffer from 'hurry sickness', cannot bear waiting their turn (in queues) and have to do several things at once. They're also insecure about their status, and need to be admired by their peers in order to feel good about themselves.
- *TBB* may involve the same degree of ambition, but these men seem to be steadied by it. They're much more self-confident, relaxed and easy-going, not driven to achieve perfection, and much less hostile.

Results (AO1)

Type A men were more likely to develop CHD than Type B men. After taking risk factors into account (e.g. age, smoking, blood cholesterol, BP, family history of heart disease), they were still *twice* as likely to suffer from heart attacks.

Conclusions (AO1)

A man's personality can make it more likely that he will develop CHD, over and above the effects of smoking and other ('traditional') risk factors: personality, therefore, can be regarded as a risk factor. This shows that *psychological* factors can have *physiological effects* (an example of *mind–body interaction*). It might be more accurate to say that the harmful effects of stressors can be *mediated* through psychological factors. In other words, stressors aren't harmful in themselves: it's how people perceive and react to them that's (potentially) dangerous for health (see below, pages 134–135).

Evaluation (AO1/AO2)

Friedman and Rosenman's basic findings have been replicated in several countries (including European countries, Canada and New Zealand). However, the men's scores on the two measures of personality didn't always match, which means that they might have been measuring *different things*. Also, the fact that their participants were all male means that we cannot generalise the results to women. While Type A men may be more at risk of developing CHD, the risk is only *relative*: the vast majority of Type As *don't* develop CHD, while many Type Bs *do*. Most studies have found that TAB assessed immediately following a heart attack doesn't predict future attacks, which suggests that it's not a distinct risk for CHD in those already at risk (Penny, 1996).

How Science Works
Practical Learning Activity 4.3

- What's another name for a 'follow-up' study?
- What is meant by (a) open-ended and (b) closed questions? Give an example of each.
- What kind of data are involved when participants are classified as belonging to one category or another?
- Can you think of any famous people (male or female) who seem to display TAB? What is it about them that makes you categorise them in this way?
- What's another term for 'taking risk factors into account'? Why was this necessary?
- Friedman and Rosenman see personality as playing a *causal* role in CHD. Do their data allow them to draw such a conclusion? How else might you interpret their findings?

The effects of stress on the immune system
What is the immune system?

The **immune system** is a collection of billions of cells that travel through the bloodstream. These cells are produced mainly in the spleen, lymph nodes, thymus and bone marrow. They move in and out of tissues and organs, defending the body against foreign bodies, or *antigens* (such as bacteria, viruses and cancerous cells). The major type of cell are white blood cells (*leucocytes*), of which there are many types. Some immune cells produce and secrete *antibodies*, which bind to antigens and destroy them. (See Figure 4.6 on the next page.)

What happens to the immune system when we're stressed?

When we're stressed, the immune system's ability to fight off antigens is reduced. This is why we're much more likely to pick up infections when we're 'under stress' (we often talk of being 'run down'). But this doesn't mean that stress actually *causes* infections. Stress makes us more susceptible to infectious agents by temporarily suppressing immune function (the **immunosuppressive effects** of stress). Stressors that seem to have this effect include exams (e.g. Kiecolt-Glaser *et al.,* 1984, see Key Study 4.2) and the death of a spouse (e.g. Schliefer *et al.,* 1983, see page 121).

While intermittent production of corticosteroids doesn't do the immune system much harm, if they're produced *continuously* (as in GAS), they can interfere with leucocyte activity and the production of antibodies. Stressful events have been linked to various infectious illnesses, including influenza, herpes and the Epstein-Barr virus (associated with extreme fatigue).

Research that demonstrates the immunosuppressive effects of stress

Riley (1981) created stress by placing mice on a turntable rotating at 45 rpm. He found a marked decrease in their lymphocyte count over a five-hour period. In other words, their immune response was suppressed. In a later study, Riley studied the link between stress

and tumour growth. He implanted cancer cells in two groups of mice: Group 1 had 10 minutes of rotation per hour (on the turntable) for three days (*high-stress condition*), while Group 2 had no rotation at all (*no-stress control condition*). As expected, the mice in Group 1 developed large tumours, while those in Group 2 showed no tumour growth.

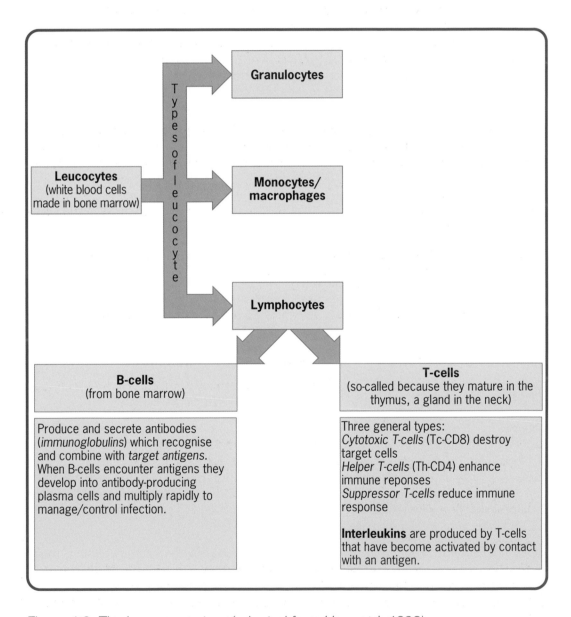

Figure 4.6: The immune system (adapted from Hayward, 1998)

How Science Works
Practical Learning Activity 4.4

- Do you consider Riley's experiments to be ethically acceptable?
  (You might like to arrange a class debate, in which the objections to and
  justifications for such research are considered.)
- What can studies of mice tell us about the immunosuppressive effects of stress
  in humans? (Note that this is a *scientific* issue, rather than an ethical one.
  Again, a class debate might be useful.)

Studies involving humans that support Riley's findings include that of Schliefer *et al.* (1983), who found that the immune system of men whose wives had died from breast cancer functioned less well after their wives had died than before. Cohen *et al.* (1991) gave participants nasal drops containing cold viruses. Stress was defined as (a) the number of life changes an individual had recently experienced; and (b) how 'out of control' they felt. Those participants with the highest stress levels were almost *twice* as likely to develop colds as those with the lowest levels.

Interleukin-b (see Figure 4.6) is produced soon after tissue damage, helping to remodel connective tissue in wounds and to form collagen (scar tissue). Kiecolt-Glaser *et al.* (1995) compared the rate of wound healing in two groups:

- Group A – a group of 'high-stress' women, caring for relatives with Alzheimer's disease, and

- Group B – a 'stress-free' matched control group.

On average, it took nine days longer for the wounds of those in Group A to heal than those in Group B.

Key Study 4.2: Kiecolt-Glaser *et al.*'s (1984) study of immunosuppression in medical students (ISMS)

Aim/hypothesis (AO1)

Kiecolt-Glaser *et al.* wanted to study the 'competence' of the immune system in people facing stressful situations (medical students facing important exams). They predicted that immunosuppression – as measured by the amount of natural killer cell activity – would be greatly reduced when stress levels were at their highest.

Method/design (AO1)

The researchers took blood samples from 75 first-year medical students (49 males, 26 females), all volunteers. The samples were taken one month before their final exams, and then again on the first day of their exams (after they'd sat two papers). The blood samples were analysed for the amount of leucocyte activity – specifically, for the amount of *natural killer cell* activity (involved in fighting off viruses and tumours).

Results (AO1)

As predicted, natural killer cell activity was greatly reduced in the second sample compared to the first.

The students were also given questionnaires to assess psychiatric symptoms, loneliness and life events – all potential sources of stress (see pages 123–125). Immune responses were weakest of all in those students who reported feeling most lonely. They were also weakest for those experiencing other stressful life events and psychiatric symptoms (such as depression and anxiety).

Conclusions (AO1)

Stress is associated with reduced immune function: Kiecolt-Glaser *et al.* found evidence for the immunosuppressive effects of stress. They also showed that these effects can be increased when individuals are exposed to particular kinds of stressor.

Evaluation (AO1/AO2)

The study was a *natural experiment* – that is, the researchers didn't decide what stressors the students should be exposed to; the exams would have happened anyway and the researchers took the opportunity to measure the students' immune function in response to these 'natural' stressors.

The students were being compared *to themselves* on the two occasions the blood samples were taken. This controls for important *participant variables*, such as personality. However, strictly, we cannot be sure that it was the stressors (and only the stressors) that caused the change in immune function: other (situational) variables that *weren't* controlled (as would happen in a true experiment) might have played a part.

4

How Science Works
Practical Learning Activity 4.5

- What other kinds of experiment are used by psychologists?
- What are the advantages and disadvantages of natural experiments compared to other kinds of experiment?
- Give some other examples of participant variables that may have been relevant in this particular study (apart from personality).
- Give some examples of situational variables that weren't controlled and may have had an effect on the medical students' immune function.

✔ Assessment Check 4.2

1. Outline the evolutionary explanation of how stress makes us ill. (4 marks)
2. Define what is meant by the terms 'immune system', 'antigens', and 'leucocytes'. (2 + 2 + 2 marks)
3. Describe the main characteristics of Type A behaviour. (4 marks)
4. Explain why we cannot be sure that Type A behaviour actually causes coronary heart disease (CHD). (3 marks)
5. Outline and evaluate research into how stress makes us ill. (12 marks)

Stress in everyday life

In the previous section, we mentioned a number of different **stressors**, including insulin, electric shock, excessive heat or cold, exams and the death of a spouse. The last of these is an example of a major **life change**. In the first part of this section, we concentrate on life changes and **workplace stressors**.

Life changes

Key Study 4.3: Holmes and Rahe's (1967) Social Readjustment Rating Scale (SRRS)

Aim/hypothesis (AO1)

The main aim of Holmes and Rahe's pioneering study was to construct an instrument for measuring stress. They defined stress as the amount of *change* an individual has had to deal with during a particular period of time, and

predicted that the degree of stress is related to both physical and psychological illness. People are more likely to show symptoms following periods of stress: the greater the stress, the more serious the illness.

Method/design (AO1)

Holmes and Rahe examined the medical records of 5000 patients. They also compiled a list of 43 life events, which seemed to cluster in the months prior to the onset of the patients' illness. They then told 100 people ('judges') that 'marriage' had been assigned an arbitrary value of 500. The judges had to assign a number to each of the other life events, indicating how much *readjustment* they'd involve *relative to marriage.*

Death of spouse was judged (on average) to require *twice* as much readjustment as marriage. The average (mean) of the numbers assigned to each event was then divided by 10, and the resulting values became the weighting (numerical value) of each life event. For example, the weighting for death of spouse was 100 (1000 divided by 10). A sample of the 43 life events and their weightings is shown in Table 4.2.

The amount of life stress a person has experienced in a given period (say, 12 months) is measured by the total number of **life change units** (LCUs). These units are calculated by adding the mean values (in the right-hand column of Table 4.2) associated with the events the person has experienced during that time (the middle column).

Results (AO1)

Most life events were judged to be *less* stressful than getting married. But six (including death of spouse, divorce, and personal injury or illness) were rated as *more* stressful.

Holmes and Rahe found that people with high LCU scores for the preceding year were more likely to experience some sort of physical illness the following year. For example, someone scoring over 300 LCUs had an 80 per cent chance of becoming ill; health problems included sudden cardiac death, non-fatal heart attacks, tuberculosis (TB), diabetes, leukaemia, accidents and sports injuries.

Conclusions (AO1)

Holmes and Rahe concluded that stress could be measured objectively as an LCU score; this, in turn, predicts the person's chances of becoming ill (physically and/or mentally) following the period of stress. They argue that stress and illness aren't just correlated: stress actually makes us ill.

Evaluation (AO1/AO2)

While the SRRS assumes that *any* change is, by definition, stressful, the *undesirable* aspects of events are at least as important as the fact that they change people's lives. Table 4.2 suggests that life changes have a largely *negative* feel about them (especially those with the highest LCU scores), so the SRRS may be confusing 'change' with 'negativity'. Also, some of the life events are *ambiguous*; for example, those that refer to 'change in ...' could be positive or negative.

It may not be change as such that's stressful, but rather change that's *unexpected* and, in this sense, *uncontrollable*. When people are asked to classify the undesirable life events on the SRRS as either 'controllable' or 'uncontrollable', only the latter are correlated with later illness (Brown, 1986).

Rank	Life event	Mean value
1.	Death of spouse	100
2.	Divorce	73
3.	Marital separation	65
4.	Jail term	63
5.	Death of close family member	63
6.	Personal injury or illness	53
7.	Marriage	50
8.	Fired at work	47
10.	Retirement	45
11.	Change in health of family member	44
12.	Pregnancy	40
13.	Sex difficulties	39
16.	Change in financial state	38
17.	Death of close friend	37
18.	Change to different line of work	36
23.	Son or daughter leaving home	29
27.	Begin or end school	26
38.	Change in sleeping habits	16
42.	Christmas	12
43.	Minor violations of the law	11

Table 4.2: A selection of life events from the Social Readjustment Rating Scale (SRRS)

How Science Works
Practical Learning Activity 4.6

- What do the ranks in the left-hand column of Table 4.2 denote?
- What kind of measure is the mean?
- Why might the mean not be the most appropriate/accurate measure to use with certain sets of scores?
- Taking the example of death of spouse, do you think that the mean was the appropriate measure to use to calculate the weightings for the various life events?
- When participants are given the SRRS, they're presented *only* with the list of life events (without the weightings) and are asked simply to tick the ones that apply to them. Why do you think it's done this way (i.e. without the weightings)?
- Show Table 4.2 to friends and relatives and ask them if they think there any important life changes that are *missing*. Do you think the list is *complete*?
- What would a *negative correlation* between LCU score and physical/mental illness mean?

Evaluation of studies using the SRRS

✔ **Support using a large sample:** 2500 naval personnel from three US navy cruisers completed the SRRS before they left for a six-month tour of duty. While they were away, a health record was kept for each participant by the ships' doctors. As predicted, LCUs were positively correlated with illness (Rahe *et al.,* 1970).

✔ **Results are open to interpretation:** instead of life events causing illness, it could be the other way round. Some life events (such as 8, 13 and 38 in Table 4.2) might
✗ be early signs of an illness that's already developing (Penny, 1996). Since the data from studies like Rahe *et al.*'s are *correlational*, we cannot be sure which variable causes the other – or whether one causes the other at all!

✗ **The data are unreliable:** many studies are *retrospective* – people are asked to *recall* both their illnesses and the stressful life events that occurred during, say, the previous 12 months. This is likely to produce unreliable data. For example, if you're under stress (for whatever reason) you may focus on minor physiological sensations and report them as 'symptoms of illness' (Davison and Neale, 2001).

✗ **Life events may mean different things to different people:** on the SRRS, particular events give a predetermined LCU score, but individuals may experience the 'same' life event very differently. For example, divorce may mean release from an unhappy, stressful situation, and so may be a very *positive* event. Also, what's a hassle one day may not be the next, and vice versa (see below).

✗ **Hassles are more stressful:** by definition, most of the 43 life changes included in the SRRS aren't everyday occurrences. Kanner *et al.* (1981) designed a *hassles scale* (comprising 117 items) and an *uplifts scale* (135 items).
Kanner *et al.* define hassles as:

the irritating, frustrating, distressing demands that to some degree characterise everyday transactions with the environment. They include annoying practical problems, such as losing things or traffic jams and fortuitous occurrences, such as inclement weather, as well as arguments, disappointments, and financial and family concerns.

Daily uplifts are:

positive experiences such as the joy derived from manifestations of love, relief at hearing good news, the pleasure of a good night's rest, and so on.

In a study of 100 men and women, aged 45–64, over a 12-month period, Kanner *et al.* confirmed their prediction that hassles are correlated with undesirable psychological symptoms. However, the effect of uplifts was unclear, and research interest waned (Bartlett, 1998). Kanner *et al.* also found that hassles were a more powerful predictor of symptoms than life events (as measured by the SRRS). 'Divorce', for example, may exert stress by any number of component hassles, such as cooking for oneself, handling money matters and having to tell people about it. So, daily hassles may intervene between major life events and health: it's the *cumulative* impact of these day-to-day problems that may prove detrimental to health.

According to Lazarus (1999), life events (as measured by the SRRS) are *distal* (remote) causes of stress. We need to know the *psychological meaning* a person attaches to an environmental event, the personal significance of what's happening (the *proximal* or immediate cause). This is what makes Kanner *et al.*'s scale a more valid approach. According to Lazarus:

Although daily hassles are far less dramatic than major life changes ... and what constitutes a hassle varies greatly from person to person, our research has suggested that, especially when they pile up or touch on special areas of vulnerability ... they can be very stressful for some people and very important for their subjective well-being and physical health ...

DeLongis *et al.* (1982) compared the hassles scale and a life events scale as predictors of later health problems. They also wanted to study the effects of 'uplifts'. A total of 100 participants, aged 45–64, completed questionnaires once a month over a 12-month period. Both the frequency and intensity of hassles were significantly correlated with overall health status and physical symptoms. While there was *no* relationship between life events and health during the course of the study itself, there had been for the two to three years *prior* to the study. Daily uplifts had little effect on health.

How Science Works
Practical Learning Activity 4.7

- Can you think of some third variable that could be the cause of *both* a particular life event *and* some physical or mental illness?
- Based on Kanner *et al.*'s definition of hassles, above, and the examples given, have a go at constructing a hassles scale.
- Repeat the exercise for an uplifts scale.
- Rewrite the following sentence: 'Both the frequency and intensity of hassles were significantly correlated with overall health status and physical symptoms.' (Assume that the correlation was *positive*.)
- What conclusions can you draw from DeLongis *et al.*'s finding that there was a relationship between life events and health for the two to three years prior to the study (but not during the study itself)? How do they relate to Kanner *et al.*'s results?
- Both Kanner *et al.* and DeLongis *et al.* used 100 participants aged 45–64. Do you consider these to be representative samples?

✔ Assessment Check 4.3

1. Define 'stress' as measured by the Social Readjustment Rating Scale (SRRS). (1 mark)
2. Give TWO examples of an *ambiguous* life event from the SRRS. (1 + 1 mark)
3. Outline TWO limitations of the SRRS (not including the ambiguity of the life events). (2 + 2 marks)
4. Outline TWO weaknesses of studies using the SRRS to investigate the relationship between life events and health. (2 + 2 marks)
5. Define what's meant by the terms 'hassles' and 'uplifts'. (2 + 2 marks)

Workplace stressors
Are some occupations more stressful than others?

Four of the most stressful occupations are nursing, social work, teaching and the emergency services (police, ambulance, fire service, etc.). In *nursing*, for example, certain sources of stress are part and parcel of the job. These include constantly dealing with patients' pain, anxiety and deaths, giving emotional support to relatives, having to maintain high levels of concentration for long periods (as in intensive care/ITU), and being in the 'front line' when major disasters occur (such as the 7/7 London bombings). In recent years, nurses and other health professionals have increasingly become the victims of violence.

The emergency services, like other occupations such as nursing, are inherently stressful

The effects of being in control: good or bad?

Executives (in industry and business organisations) are another occupational group that face above-average stress levels. They constantly have to make important decisions and are responsible for the consequences: this is very stressful ('executive stress').

In a famous – and ethically very dubious – series of experiments, Brady (1958) placed monkeys in 'restraining chairs' and conditioned them to press a lever. They'd receive an electric shock every 20 seconds unless they pressed the lever within that interval. But many of the monkeys died suddenly and the experiment had to be abandoned. Post-mortem examinations showed that the monkeys had raised levels of gastrointestinal hormones: the cause of death was ulcers. Other monkeys had been restrained for up to six months without any ill effects. So, the ulcers had been caused *either* by the electric shocks *or* by the stress of having to press the lever to avoid them.

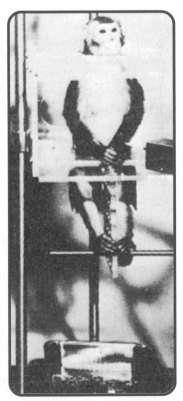

In a follow-up study, Brady tested the relationship between (a) high stress levels, and (b) increased hormone production and the development of ulcers. He was primarily interested in the effects of stress in business executives, which is why he called his subjects 'executive monkeys'. They were tested in *pairs*: the experimental 'executive' was responsible for pressing the lever, while a 'yoked control' received the shocks (but couldn't control the lever). This occurred at 20-second intervals, for six hours at a time, over a three-week period.

The executive monkeys developed severe ulcers and eventually died; their stomach acidity was greatest during the rest period. The yoked controls showed no apparent ill effects. Brady thus concluded that it was stress – not the shocks – that caused the ulcers.

An 'executive monkey'

How Science Works
Practical Learning Activity 4.8

- Conduct a survey in which you ask people about the stressful aspects of their jobs. This should include housewives/homemakers. Look for any recurring stressors in different occupations.
- Organise a class debate about the ethical acceptability of Brady's executive monkey experiment.
- How do you explain Brady's results: would you have expected the executive monkeys to have been *less* stressed than the controls, given that they could prevent the shocks by pressing the lever?

Research evidence involving people in various occupations suggests that those low down on the occupational ladder (who *lack* control) are most susceptible.

Key Study 4.4: Marmot *et al.*'s (1997) study of Stressed Civil Servants (SCS)

Aim/hypothesis (AO1)

This was a follow-up to an earlier study of British civil servants: the Whitehall I study (Marmot and Theorell, 1988). This clearly showed an *inverse* relationship between mortality from coronary heart disease (CHD) and grade of employment. About 25 per cent of this relationship could be explained by social differences in smoking, plasma cholesterol, blood pressure, obesity and physical activity. The Whitehall II study (Marmot *et al.*, 1997) involved a new cohort (generation) of male and female civil servants, and was conducted to test the hypothesis that low control in one's job makes an important contribution to the risk of developing CHD, over and above these well-established risk factors.

Method/design (AO1)

All male and female civil servants aged 35–55 in 20 London-based Civil Service departments were sent an introductory letter and screening questionnaire, and offered a screening examination for cardiovascular disease (1985–88: phase 1). There was a 73 per cent response rate and over 10,000 people were examined (almost 7000 men and over 3000 women). This represented a baseline.

They were approached again during 1989–90 (sent a postal questionnaire: phase 2) and then again in 1991–93 (another postal questionnaire and a screening examination: phase 3). The participation rates were 79 per cent and 83 per cent for phases 2 and 3 respectively; 72 per cent (over 7000 people) participated in all three phases. The average length of follow-up was 5.3 years (range of 3.7–7.6 years).

Employment grades were grouped into three categories: administrators, executive officers and clerical/office support staff. *Job control* was measured by a self-completed questionnaire at phase 1, which asked about decision authority and skill discretion. These were combined to give an index of *decision latitude or control.*

CHD was measured as: (i) doctor-diagnosed ischaemia (diagnosed or suspected heart attack or angina pectoris); (ii) angina pectoris identified on the basis of a questionnaire; and (iii) severe chest pain that lasted 30 minutes or more.

Results (AO1)

After taking age into account, men in the lowest grades (clerical/office support staff) were *three times* more likely to develop CHD compared with men in the highest grade (administrators). The largest difference was for doctor-diagnosed ischaemia. Women in the lowest grades were almost three times more likely to develop CHD than those in the highest grade, regardless of how CHD was measured.

Conclusions (AO1)

As predicted, for both men and women, *low control* at work represented the largest contributor to the development of CHD compared with established risk factors (smoking, etc.); the latter seem to account for less than half the overall risk difference between the different grades (confirming the results of Whitehall I). Low control is related to employment grade and appears to account for much of the grade difference in frequency of CHD in both sexes.

Evaluation (AO1/AO2)

The study shows that having too little stress (in the sense of too little control/responsibility) can damage your health. The common-sense view would be that it's *too much* stress that's (potentially) harmful (see below). So, the SCS study provides evidence for an important *counter-intuitive* insight into a major source of stress.

The study involved an unusually large sample of both men and women, studied over a period of years. The crucial measure was the number of people of different grades who developed CHD for the first time during the course of the study (as determined at phase 1: the baseline). Because the same people were being compared to themselves, we can be reasonably sure that individual differences (such as personality, intelligence, ethnic background) didn't affect the outcome: employment grade was the crucial independent variable. Also, the original response rate (in phase 1) of 73 per cent is extremely high for any kind of postal questionnaire, and the participation rates at phases 2 and 3 (79 and 83 per cent respectively) are even higher.

As Marmot *et al*. themselves recognise, two of the three measures of CHD were based either on self-reported symptoms or a questionnaire. These aren't as reliable or valid as doctor diagnosis based on physical examination. Also, angina diagnosed by questionnaire may be a less reliable indicator of CHD in women compared with men.

The very large sample of British civil servants may not be typical of either non-British civil servants or other groups of British (and non-British) workers. It's possible that 'decision latitude or control' is more relevant as a risk factor in the Civil Service compared with alternative occupations, where other aspects of the work itself and the work situation may have a greater influence on CHD. We saw above how inherently stressful the work of nurses and those in the emergency services is, and (consistent with Brady's monkey experiments) air traffic controllers experience high stress levels and high rates of CHD. However, Marmot *et al*. cite a study of men in the Czech Republic, which used the job control questionnaire used in Whitehall II: low control was related to acute myocardial infarction (heart attack) in middle age, and the combination of low control and coronary risk factors accounted for the higher risk of heart attacks in men with lower education.

How Science Works
Practical Learning Activity 4.9

- Explain what's meant by an *inverse* relationship between mortality from CHD and grade of employment.
- What kind of sample were the original civil servants who were sent the screening questionnaire and the invitation to have a screening examination?
- What kind of sample were the 10,000 who responded and were examined in phase 1?
- Explain how the 10,000 who were examined represented a baseline. What is the purpose of a baseline?
- What kind of a measure is the range?
- Choose a different occupational group and decide how you'd categorise employment grades if you were going to replicate Marmot *et al*.'s study.
- What terms are given to describe a study in which participants are followed up over a period of years? (One is a more technical term for 'follow-up'; the other denotes that they are studied 'into the future' as opposed to looking back at their past (i.e. *retrospective*).)
- Was employment grade a manipulated independent variable?
- Name the method used by Marmot *et al*.
- What was the dependent variable?

Other sources of workplace stress

Table 4.3 shows a number of other sources of stress related to the workplace.

Source of stress	Associated effects
Quantitative overload: too much to do; having to be excessively quick or productive	Anxiety and frustration
Quantitative underload: not having enough to do	Boredom, frustration, low job satisfaction, lack of commitment
Qualitative overload: the work is too difficult or demands excessive attention	Anxiety and frustration
Qualitative underload: under-using your skills and abilities	Boredom, frustration, low job satisfaction, lack of commitment
Role ambiguity: confusion about one's role in an organisation ('What exactly is my job?')	Frustration and anxiety
Role conflict: being asked to perform two incompatible roles or tasks	Cardiovascular disorders, peptic ulcers
Job insecurity/redundancy	Anxiety
Lack of career structure: poor promotion opportunities	Poor physical health
Poor interpersonal relations/support	Anxiety, low job satisfaction
Bullying/violence at work	Absenteeism, poor mental health

Table 4.3: Sources of workplace stress and their associated effects

Assessment Check 4.4

1. Give TWO examples of stressors that are associated with nursing (and that are unlikely to be found in most other occupations). (1 + 1 mark)
2. Describe Brady's 'executive monkey' experiments. (6 marks)
3. For Marmot *et al.*'s study of civil servants:
   (a) name the independent variable (1 mark)
   (b) name the dependent variable (1 mark)

> (c) outline TWO ways in which the dependent variable was
>   measured (1 + 1 mark)
> (d) explain what's meant by 'decision latitude or control' (2 marks)
> (e) outline ONE strength of the study (2 marks)
> (f) outline TWO weaknesses of the study. (2 + 2 marks)
> 4. Define what's meant by the terms 'quantitative overload',
>   'qualitative underload', and 'role ambiguity'. (2 + 2 + 2 marks)

Personality factors

Type A behaviour (TAB)

When discussing Friedman and Rosenman's (1974) STAB earlier in the chapter (see Key Study 4.1), several important points emerged.

- Stressors don't exist objectively: something qualifies as a stressor only if an individual *perceives* it as a stressor.

- So, we must take psychological (and other non-physiological) factors into account if we're to understand properly what stressors are and how they affect people. (One criticism of Selye's GAS is that he focused exclusively on physiological factors; see page 115.)

- One major kind of psychological factor is personality, or characteristic patterns of behaviour.

- TAB describes a typical way of reacting to life in general, and work-related situations in particular. According to Friedman and Rosenman, people who display TAB have a greater chance of developing CHD than other types.

Recent research has focused on *specific Type A characteristics*. In particular, *hostility* seems to be the best single predictor of CHD – and is a better predictor than TAB as a whole. But this *doesn't* mean that hostility *causes* CHD (just as we cannot claim that TAB as a whole does so). Hostility refers to the non-specific dislike of others, the tendency to see the worst in others, anger and envy, and a lack of compassion. The behavioural aspect involves aggressiveness and possible bullying (Forshaw, 2002).

Type C personality

Type C personalities are cancer-prone (Temoshok, 1987). They have difficulty expressing emotion and tend to suppress or inhibit emotions (especially negative ones, such as anger). It seems likely that these personality characteristics influence the progression of cancer and patients' survival time (Weinman, 1995). Women diagnosed with breast cancer showed significantly more emotional suppression than those with non-life-threatening breast disease (Greer and Morris, 1975).

Hardiness

Just as TAB (specifically, hostility) and Type C personality can make it more likely that certain individuals will develop life-threatening diseases, *hardiness* is a *protective* factor, helping to explain individual differences in the ability to resist stress. According to Kobasa (1979, 1986), 'hardy' and 'non-hardy' individuals differ in three main ways, as described in Box 4.2.

Box 4.2: The 'three Cs' of hardiness

Hardy people:

- are highly **committed** – they're deeply involved in whatever they do, and approach life with a sense of curiosity and meaningfulness

- view change as a **challenge** – they regard change, rather than stability, as normal; change is an opportunity for personal growth and development, rather than a threat to security

- have a strong sense of being in **control** – in Rotter's (1966) terms, they have a *high internal locus of control* (LOC); this means that they believe they can affect their environment (including other people) and that what they do makes a difference. (By contrast, those with a *high external* LOC believe they are *controlled* by their environment.)

How Science Works
Practical Learning Activity 4.10

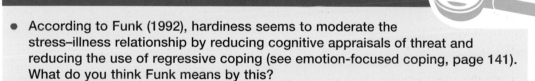

- According to Funk (1992), hardiness seems to moderate the stress–illness relationship by reducing cognitive appraisals of threat and reducing the use of regressive coping (see emotion-focused coping, page 141). What do you think Funk means by this?
- Draw a diagram to represent the relationship between stressors, personality and the effects of stress. Remember that stressors don't exist objectively, which relates to the definition of stress as an interaction between individual and environment (see page 110).

 ### Assessment Check 4.5

1. Outline the major characteristics of the Type A behaviour pattern. (4 marks)
2. Define the term 'hostility' in relation to the Type A behaviour pattern. (2 marks)

3. Explain TWO weaknesses of Freidman and Rosenman's study of the Type A behaviour pattern and its link to CHD. (2 + 2 marks)
4. Outline the 'three Cs' of hardiness. (2 + 2 + 2 marks)
5. Explain what it means to say that hardiness is a protective factor. (2 marks)

Stress management

The term **stress management** (SM) has two main meanings, as follows.

1 In a *formal* sense, SM refers to a range of techniques (both physiological and psychological) used deliberately, by professionals, to help people reduce their stress levels. These can be used singly or in combination. Major examples include *anxiolytic drugs, biofeedback, cognitive behavioural therapy* (such as Meichenbaum's *stress inoculation training*/SIT), and Kobasa's attempts to increase *hardiness*. Others include progressive muscle relaxation, meditation and hypnosis (all designed to induce a state of relaxation). These will be discussed in the first part of this section.

2 In an *informal* sense, SM refers to what we all do, quite spontaneously (and often unconsciously), on a day-to-day basis. In this sense, we all manage our stress more or less effectively. A major way of achieving this is through the use of **coping strategies/mechanisms** – that is, conscious attempts to adapt to stress in a positive and constructive way. These involve cognitive and behavioural efforts to meet those external and/or internal demands that stretch our capacities and resources. They will be discussed in the second part of this section.

Formal techniques

Physiological approaches

Psychotherapeutic drugs

Psychotherapeutic drugs act directly on the ANS, and *anxiolytic* (anxiety-reducing) drugs are commonly used in cases of chronic stress. The *benzodiazepine* group of anxiolytics include *chlordiazepoxide* (*Librium*) and *diazepam* (*Valium*). Anxiolytic drugs usually succeed in reducing the physiological effects of stress, but they may produce *side-effects* (including drowsiness and lethargy) as well as *physical dependence*. So, if the drug is stopped, the person may experience insomnia, tremors and convulsions (symptoms of *withdrawal* or *abstinence syndrome*).

Anxiolytics are also associated with *tolerance* – that is, an increasing amount of the drug is needed to produce the same, original effect. Physical dependence and tolerance together constitute *drug addiction*.

Biofeedback

Patients are given information (usually via a monitor) about BP, heart rate, muscle tension or other *autonomic functions*. These are automatically regulated by the ANS, so we're usually unaware of them and unable to control them; but the feedback provided by the monitor allows the patient to bring them under voluntary control. For example, a line on a television monitor swings to the left or right depending on changes in heart rate, and the patient is taught *meditation* or *progressive muscle relaxation*, which allows them to change the movement of the line towards some predetermined point.

College students suffering from muscle contraction headaches were given seven 50-minute sessions, twice weekly, in which they were given feedback about muscle tension (*electromyograph* (EMG) feedback). They also had to practise their newly learned skills at home when free of headaches and at the first sign of one. A *waiting-list control group* received treatment only when the study was over. In the *placebo condition*, participants engaged in 'pseudo-meditation'. Compared to both these groups, the EMG biofeedback produced significant reductions in EMG activity and tension headaches (in Bradley, 1995).

Biofeedback requires the use of specialised equipment, which is clearly a disadvantage compared with alternative techniques (such as progressive muscle relaxation), which don't. It's also unclear exactly how biofeedback works: it may not be biofeedback itself that helps in stress reduction, but other factors, such as the patient's determination to beat stress. Biofeedback is designed to treat the *symptoms* of stress, *not* to tackle the stressor itself.

Biofeedback

Psychological approaches
Cognitive behavioural therapy (CBT)

A major example of CBT is **stress inoculation training** (SIT) (Meichenbaum, 1977) (see pages 194–195 and 208–210). This is a form of **cognitive restructuring**, which refers to various methods of changing the way people think about themselves and their lives, aimed at changing their emotional responses and behaviour. SIT is an attempt to reduce stress through changing cognitions. It assumes that people sometimes find things stressful because they think about them in *catastrophising ways* – that is, they *misperceive* them in a way that makes them seem far more threatening and distressing than they 'really' are.

Underlying SIT is the analogy with biological immunisation: a small, harmless dose of the infectious disease is given as a vaccine, which then wards off any later infection the individual may be exposed to. So, a way of enabling an individual to become resistant to a stressor is to expose him/her to a 'small dose' of it (that is, having appropriate prior experience with the stressor). As Orne (1965) put it:

If an individual is given the opportunity to deal with a stimulus that is mildly stressful and he is able to do so successfully (mastering it in a psychological sense) he will tend to be able to tolerate a similar stimulus of somewhat greater intensity in the future ...

According to Meichenbaum (1977), SIT involves three stages or phases.

- The first is educational in content and is designed to provide the client with a conceptual framework for understanding the nature of his/her stressful reactions. The exact content varies according to the nature of the presenting problem (such as phobic reactions, anger control and pain tolerance).

- The second involves a number of behavioural and cognitive coping skills for the client to rehearse.

- In the third, the client is given an opportunity to practise these coping skills during exposure to a variety of stressors.

These are described in more detail in Box 4.3.

Box 4.3: The three stages of SIT

Stage 1: cognitive preparation (or conceptualisation)

The therapist explores with the client how he or she thinks about and deals with stressful situations. They also discuss how successful these strategies have been. A common response to stressful situations is to make *negative self-statements* (such as 'I can't handle this'). This is a *self-defeating internal dialogue*, which makes a stressful situation even more stressful.

Stage 2: skill acquisition and rehearsal

The therapist helps the client to develop a variety of coping techniques, both direct actions and cognitive coping. *Direct action* might include arranging for escape routes and learning physical relaxation exercises that would help physiological arousal. *Cognitive coping* might involve the use of *preparation statements* (such as 'Maybe what you think is anxiety is eagerness to confront it'). These are positive, coping statements that are incompatible with the negative self-statements. The client practises these preparation statements.

Stage 3: application and follow-through

Once the client has mastered these behavioural and cognitive skills, the therapist guides her/him through increasingly threatening situations. These are actual stress-producing situations (*not* role plays). Once the client can cope with a relatively non-threatening situation, a more threatening one is presented and the process is repeated.

Meichenbaum (1997) believes that the 'power-of-positive-thinking' approach advocated by SIT can successfully change people's behaviour. It has proved particularly successful in reducing exam nerves and the anxiety associated with severe pain.

Increasing hardiness

Based on what we said earlier about the differences between 'hardy' and 'non-hardy' people, we can predict that stress could be reduced if hardiness could be increased. So, can people learn to become more hardy? Kobasa (1979, 1986) believes they can (see Box 4.4).

Box 4.4: Three ways of increasing hardiness

1 **Teaching** people to identify the physical signs of stress (e.g. tensing of the muscles, increased heart rate and breathing rate). We cannot deal with a stressor unless we first identify it (what Kobasa calls *focusing*). But identifying a stressor doesn't by itself guarantee that we'll deal with it in an appropriate or beneficial way.

2 **Reconstructing stressful situations** is an attempt to make a more realistic assessment of different stressors. This involves considering how a past stressful experience could have been dealt with more or less effectively.

3 **Compensation through self-improvement** is related to Kobasa's claim that what we believe about our abilities to bring about change has important effects on our capacity to withstand stress. When we cannot avoid a stressor's effects, or deal with it in some other way, we should take on some other challenge that we *can* meet. In this way, we experience the *positive* aspects of coping with a stressor. This allows us to 'bounce back' more easily after things have gone wrong. As a result, we'll experience future stressors as less stressful.

How Science Works
Practical Learning Activity 4.11

- How does the use of anxiolytic drugs relate to the use of biological therapies in the treatment of psychopathology? (See Chapter 6, pages 183–187.)
- How does stress inoculation training (SIT) relate to the use of cognitive therapies in the treatment of psychopathology? (See Chapter 6, pages 194–196.)
- How might you use EMG feedback with patients who are blind?
- Try to think of some other examples of negative self-statements that a client might make during SIT.
- Repeat the exercise for preparation statements.

Coping strategies/mechanisms

These are all *psychological* and several attempts have been made to classify them. Lazarus and Folkman (1984) define coping as 'constantly changing cognitive and behavioural efforts to manage external and/or internal demands that are appraised as taxing the resources of the person'.

According to Roger and Nash (1995), the term 'coping' conjures up ideas about being able to handle any situation that comes our way. But, in relation to stress, they distinguish between *maladative* and *adapative* coping styles (see also Table 4.4).

- *Maladaptive* styles involve failing to adjust appropriately to our environment, and experiencing misery and unhappiness as a result. They can take the form of *emotional* and *avoidance* coping styles.

● *Adaptive* styles involve an appropriate adjustment to the environment and gaining from the experience. These can be either *detached* or *rational*.

Maladaptive and adaptive coping overlap with Cohen and Lazarus's (1979) *five Categories of Coping* (see Box 4.5) and Lazarus and Folkman's (1984) *Problem-focused Coping* and *Emotion-focused Coping* (see Box 4.6).

Maladaptive coping

Emotional
Feeling overpowered and helpless
Becoming miserable, depressed, angry
Taking frustrations out on other people
Preparing for the worst possible outcome and seeking sympathy from others
Short-term benefits: expression of emotion
Long-term consequences: increasingly overwhelmed by problem

Avoidance
Sitting tight and hoping it all goes away
Pretending there's nothing the matter if people ask
Thinking about something else and talking about it as little as possible
Trusting in fate and believing things will sort themselves out
Short-term benefits: temporary relief as problem blocked out
Long-term consequences: blocking out cannot be sustained

Adaptive coping

Detached
Not seeing the problem or situation as a threat
Keeping a sense of humour
Taking nothing personally and seeing the problem as separate from yourself
Resolving the issues by getting things into proportion
Short-term benefits: able to stand back and take stock of problem
Long-term consequences: prevents over-identification with problem

Rational
Using past experience to work out how to deal with the situation
Taking action to change things
Taking one step at a time and approaching the problem with logic
Giving the situation full attention and treating it as a challenge to be met
Short-term benefits: logic determines resolution of problem
Long-term consequences: problems put into perspective

Table 4.4: Maladaptive and adaptive coping, and their short- and long-term consequences (adapted from Roger and Nash, 1995)

> ## Box 4.5: Cohen and Lazarus's (1979) five Categories of Coping (COC)
>
> 1 **Direct action response:** we try to change or manipulate our relationship to the stressful situation. For example, we try to escape from it or remove it.
>
> 2 **Information seeking:** we try to understand the situation better, and to predict future events associated with the stressor.
>
> 3 **Inhibition of action:** we do nothing. This may be the best course of action if the stressor looks like being temporary.
>
> 4 **Intrapsychic (palliative) coping:** we reassess the situation (for example, through the use of defence mechanisms) or change the 'internal environment' (through drugs, alcohol or relaxation).
>
> 5 **Turning to others:** for help and emotional support.

> ## Box 4.6 Lazarus and Folkman's (1984) Problem-focused Coping (PFC) and Emotion-focused Coping (EFC)
>
> - **Problem-focused coping:** taking direct action in order to solve a problem, or seeking information that's relevant to a solution.
>
> - **Emotion-focused coping:** trying to reduce the negative emotions that are part of the experience of stress.

Evaluation of different methods of coping

Many researchers simply assume that EFC, and avoidant coping, are a less adaptive way of dealing with stress (de Ridder, 2000). But, as Lazarus and Folkman (1984) say, the effectiveness of coping depends on the situation. For example, a situation that is controllable calls for more problem-focused efforts because the individual is in a position to do something about it. In contrast, situations that don't allow for control require management of the emotions triggered by such situations (Folkman, 1984).

Effectiveness must also take into account how long the stressor lasts. With short-term stressors, avoidant strategies are preferable, while long-term stressors require more focused attention. This implies that men would be better at coping with short-term problems (because of their predominant use of avoidant coping), and that women would adjust better to less frequent but more extreme events (such as the death of spouse; see Stroebe, 1998) because of their more frequent use of attentional strategies, which provides them with timely warning signs to take action.

Sometimes, using *both kinds* may offer the 'best solution'.

Although many studies report that women engage more often in EFC than men, the majority of female coping is PFC: the observation that women are emotion-orientated copers is a *relative* one and doesn't support the stereotype of all women as emotional copers (de Ridder, 2000).

Stanton *et al.* (1994) have questioned the very concept of EFC. They found that women more often worked through their emotions than men and that this greater effort to understand and express their emotions was *more adaptive for them*. Similarly, Stroebe (1998) has suggested that widowers may be more vulnerable to physical illness and depression than widows because widowers find it easier to avoid confrontation with feelings and to deal with the problems that are created by their wife's death, rather than dealing with their grief. Widows can access their emotions and express them more easily.

How Science Works
Practical Learning Activity 4.12

- Lazarus and Folkman's definition of coping mirrors another definition made earlier in the chapter. What is this other definition?
- Conduct a survey in which you ask people about how they cope with stressful situations. You could present them with a hypothetical situation that you describe as 'making demands beyond your capacity to deal with it'. Try to identify different strategies/mechanisms, as well as any age or gender differences.
- How do you cope with stressful situations? How does this relate to the classifications described above?
- Is the term 'maladaptive coping' a contradiction in terms?
- In relation to Cohen and Lazarus's fourth category (intrapsychic (palliative) coping), give some examples of defence mechanisms that may be used (see Chapter 6, page 188).
- Try to think of three stressful situations, in one of which you used PFC, in another of which you used EFC, and in the third of which you used both.

Assessment Check 4.6

1. Distinguish between the formal and informal senses of the term 'stress management'. (4 marks)
2. Give ONE example of a formal physiological technique of stress management and ONE formal psychological technique. (1 + 1 mark)
3. Define the terms 'anxiolytic drugs' and 'cognitive restructuring'. (2 + 2 marks)
4. Explain ONE weakness of the use of anxiolytic drugs. (2 marks)
5. Describe the basic procedures involved in biofeedback. (5 marks)
6. Outline the three stages involved in stress inoculation therapy (SIT). (6 marks)
7. Outline and evaluate Lazarus and Folkman's Problem-focused and Emotion-focused Coping. (12 marks)

CHAPTER

SUMMARY

Stress as a bodily response

- **Stress** can be defined as a **stimulus**, a **response**, or as an **interaction** between an individual and the environment.

- According to Selye, the **General Adaptation Syndrome (GAS)** is the body's defence against stress. It comprises the **alarm reaction**, **resistance** and **exhaustion**.

- In the alarm reaction, **catecholamines** trigger and maintain the **fight-or-flight response (FOFR).** This is associated with the **sympatho-adrenomedullary axis (SAA)**.

- The **hypothalamic–pituitary–adrenal axis (HPAA)**, which is also associated with resistance, also contributes to the FOFR.

- **Psychophysiological disorders ('diseases of adaptation')** develop during exhaustion. These include **coronary heart disease (CHD)**.

- An **evolutionary** explanation of how stress makes us ill maintains that the FOFR is a **maladaptive response** to most stressors faced by modern human beings.

- Friedman and Rosenman identified **Type A behaviour (TAB)** as a major risk factor for developing CHD.

- Stress also makes us ill through its **immunosuppressive effects**.

Stress in everyday life

- Holmes and Rahe's **Social Readjustment Rating Scale (SRRS)** measures stress in terms of **life change units (LCUs)**.

- They claimed that a person's LCU score predicts his/her chances of becoming physically and/or mentally ill following a period of stress.

- Evidence also exists that **daily hassles** (Kanner *et al.*) are a more powerful predictor of symptoms than **life events**.

- Some occupations, such as nursing, seem to be **inherently** more stressful than others.

- Brady's **'executive monkey' experiments** suggest that it's having to be **constantly vigilant** that's stressful. This may explain why human executives and air-traffic controllers have the highest peptic (stomach) ulcer rates.

- Marmot *et al.*'s study of civil servants shows that those in positions of **low status/responsibility** are at greatest risk of CHD.

- Other **workplace stressors** include **work overload** and **underload, role ambiguity and conflict**, and **lack of career structure**.

- The effects of stressors can be mediated by **personality factors** (such as **TAB, Type C** and **hardiness**).

- **Formal stress management (SM)** refers to **physiological** and **psychological** techniques used by professionals to reduce people's stress.

- Physiological techniques include the use of **anxiolytic drugs** (side-effects of which can include **physical dependence** and **tolerance**), and **biofeedback**.

- Biofeedback is based on the principle that stress can be reduced by gaining control over **autonomic functions** about which we normally have little knowledge, let alone control. The use of monitors to reveal this autonomic activity allows the person to bring them under voluntary control.

- Psychological techniques include **cognitive behavioural therapy** (CBT), such as Meichenbaum's **stress inoculation training (SIT)** (a form of **cognitive restructuring**) and **increasing hardiness** (Kobasa).

- **Informal** SM refers to the spontaneous use of **coping strategies/mechanisms**, all of which are psychological.

- These have been classified in several different, overlapping ways, including **maladaptive** (emotional and avoidance) and **adaptive** (detached and rational) (Roger and Nash), **direct action response/information seeking/inhibition of action/intrapsychic (palliative)/turning to others** (Cohen and Lazarus), and **Problem-focused Coping (PFC) and Emotion-focused Coping (EFC)** (Lazarus and Folkman).

Social psychology: social influence

5

What's covered in this chapter?

You need to know about:

Social influence

- Types of conformity, including internalisation and compliance
- Explanations of why people conform, including informational social influence and normative social influence
- Obedience, including Milgram's work and explanations of why people obey

Social influence in everyday life

- Explanations of independent behaviour, including how people resist pressures to conform and pressures to obey authority
- The influence of individual differences on independent behaviour, including locus of control
- Implications of research into conformity, obedience and independence for social change

Conformity

How Science Works
Practical Learning Activity 5.1

- What do you understand by the term 'conformity'?
- Try to observe some examples of conformity (a) in your Psychology class, (b) in a shop, (c) in the street, (d) at home, and (e) among your friends.
- Is there anything that all these different examples have in common?

Conformity can be defined as yielding to group pressure. It's the influence a group has over an individual, which is why it's often referred to as **majority influence**. How you dress, and the type of music you listen to, are probably influenced by your peer group ('age mates'), but this influence isn't always obvious. While authority figures might *request* or *demand* that you act in a certain way, your peers (who are your equals) *expect* certain behaviour of you – but you may not realise it at the time.

Experimental studies of conformity

Probably the best known and most influential study of conformity is Asch's experiment, which is described in Key Study 5.1.

Key Study 5.1: Asch's (1951) Comparison-Of-Lines Experiment (COLE)

Aim/hypothesis (AO1)

Asch criticised an earlier study by Sherif (1935), who claimed that when people are unsure about the answer to a question, they use others' answers to guide them. In what Sherif claimed was a demonstration of conformity, he gave his participants an *ambiguous task* (estimating how far a light moved that actually didn't move at all – as when you look at a lighted cigarette in a completely dark room). Consequently, there couldn't be any correct or incorrect answers.

Asch argued that Sherif hadn't demonstrated conformity at all. The true test of conformity is to see if people will agree with others when the experimental task is *unambiguous*, so that there's an obvious correct answer.

Method/design (AO1)

Asch showed participants two cards (as in Figure 5.1).

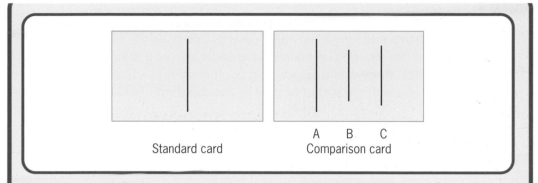

Figure 5.1: Stimulus cards used in Asch's experiment

He then asked them to say which of the comparison lines was the same length as the standard line. This was repeated 17 times (making 18 trials altogether). On every trial, the correct answer was obvious to anyone with normal eyesight. This happened in groups of between seven and nine people, but only *one* participant was naive; the others were *stooges* (or accomplices of Asch). The stooges had been briefed beforehand about what answers to give on particular trials. The stooges gave their answers in turn, out loud, and the naive participant was the last (or last but one) to answer.

On the first two trials, the stooges gave the *correct* answer (*neutral trials*), but on the third trial all the stooges gave the same *wrong* answer (*critical trial*). There were 11 more critical trials (making 12 in all), and 4 more neutral trials between the critical trials (6 in all).

A minority of one faces a unanimous majority

Results (AO1)

The crucial measure was how often naive participants gave the same wrong answer as the stooges on the critical trials; this was a measure of conformity. Overall, there was a 32 per cent conformity rate – that is, participants agreed with the wrong answer in about a third of the critical trials.

However, there were important *individual differences.* For example, no one conformed on all the critical trials, and about 25 per cent didn't conform even once. About 75 per cent conformed at least once.

Conclusions (AO1)

Because the answers on the critical trials were obviously (objectively) incorrect, Asch's study shows the impact that a majority can have on an individual. However, the majority doesn't have the same impact on every individual. In fact, Asch was interested in the social and personal conditions that help individuals *resist* group pressure (see pages 169–172).

Evaluation (AO1/AO2)

- Asch's method for studying conformity has been adopted by many other researchers. It's the established way of 'doing' conformity research – the basic procedure (or **paradigm**).
- In the Asch paradigm, only one naive participant is tested at a time; this makes it uneconomical and time-consuming. Crutchfield (1954) tested participants in separate booths, each booth containing a panel of lights, which supposedly showed other participants' answers. This way, he was able to test several participants at once.
- In everyday life, we're unlikely to disagree with other people so fundamentally about the 'correct' answer. Real-life situations are rarely as clear-cut as this.
- In later experiments, Asch found that it wasn't the size of the majority that mattered: the crucial factor was whether or not the stooges all agreed with each other (that is, were they *unanimous*?). So, if one stooge gave a different answer from the rest (there was a *dissenter*), naive participants were more likely to give the correct answer – that is, they were more likely to resist group pressure. The dissenting stooge seemed to give the naive participant moral support ('If he disagrees with them, why shouldn't I?').
- In another experiment, Asch made the comparison lines more similar (making the task more ambiguous and, consequently, more difficult). Under these conditions, conformity rate *increased.*
- Other American (and British) researchers haven't always replicated Asch's findings. For example, some have found *lower* conformity rates than Asch, while others have found similar rates. This variation in results suggests that conformity in experiments may reflect current social and political conditions.

- Generally, people in western (*individualised*) cultures (such as the USA and UK) are less likely to conform than people in non-western (*collectivist*) cultures (such as Japan and Africa). Since most research using the Asch paradigm has been conducted in western countries, our impression of what determines conformity is *culturally biased.*
- According to Moscovici and Faucheux (1972), the numerical majority (the stooges) actually represent an unorthodox, unconventional (*minority*) viewpoint; the numerical minority (the naive participant) represents the conventional (*majority*) 'truth'. A way of interpreting Asch's results is to say that the unconventional, minority viewpoint (the stooges' answers on the critical trials) held sway over the conventional, majority view (the 'obvious', objectively correct answer) a third of the time (the overall conformity rate) (see Key Study 5.3).

How Science Works
Practical Learning Activity 5.2

- How might Asch have established that the Comparison-Of-Lines Experiment was unambiguous and that there was an objectively correct answer?
- Is there anything unethical about Asch's experiment? How might you get around this problem?
- Try replicating Asch's experiment – taking the ethical issues into account.

A famous study that's relevant to both conformity and obedience is Zimbardo *et al.*'s (1973) Prison Experiment (see Key Study 5.2).

Key Study 5.2: Zimbardo *et al.*'s (1973) Prison Experiment (PE)

Aim/hypothesis (AO1)

As well as its relevance to conformity and obedience, this study demonstrates the *power of social situations* on people's behaviour. Specifically, Zimbardo *et al.* were testing (and trying to find evidence *against*) the **dispositional hypothesis**, according to which the dehumanising effects of the prison system are due to prisoners' anti-social attitudes and behaviour, and guards' sadism and insensitivity. They favoured the alternative explanation – namely, the **situational hypothesis** (see the 'Conclusions' section below).

Method/design (AO1)

Participants were recruited through newspaper advertisements asking for male student volunteers for a two-week study of prison life. From 75 volunteers, 24 were selected; they were carefully screened for being emotionally stable, physically healthy and of 'normal to average' personality. They also had no history of psychiatric problems, and had never been in trouble with the police; they were all white, middle-class students from across the USA.

They were randomly assigned to the role of prisoner or guard. A mock (simulated) prison was deliberately created in the basement of the Stanford University psychology department (which is why the study is often referred to as the 'prison simulation experiment' or the 'Stanford prison study'). Zimbardo *et al.* wished to create a prison-like environment that was as *psychologically* real as possible.

Those allocated to the prisoner role were arrested by the local police: they were charged with a felony, read their rights, searched, handcuffed, and taken to the police station to be 'booked'. After being fingerprinted, each prisoner was taken, blindfold, to the basement prison. On arrival, they were stripped naked and issued with a loose-fitting smock. Their ID number was printed on the front and back, and they had a chain bolted around one ankle. They wore a nylon stocking to cover their hair, were referred to by their number only and were allocated to 6 x 9 ft 'cells' (three to a cell).

The guards wore military-style khaki uniforms and silver reflective sunglasses (making eye contact impossible). They carried clubs, whistles, handcuffs and keys to the cells. There were guards on duty 24 hours a day, each working eight-hour shifts. They had complete control over the prisoners, who were confined to their cells around the clock – except for meals, toilet privileges, head counts and work.

Results (AO1)

An initial 'rebellion' by the prisoners was crushed, after which they began to react passively as the guards stepped up their aggression. The prisoners began to feel helpless and no longer in control of their lives. Every guard at some time or another behaved in an abusive, authoritarian way; many seemed to really enjoy the newfound power and control that went with the uniform.

After less than 36 hours, one prisoner had to be released because of uncontrollable crying, fits of rage, disorganised thinking and severe depression. Three others developed the same symptoms and were released on successive days; another prisoner developed a rash over his entire body. They became demoralised and apathetic, and started to refer to themselves (and others) by their numbers.

Zimbardo *et al.* intended the experiment to run for two weeks. But it was abandoned after just six days, because of the prisoners' pathological reactions.

Conclusions (AO1)

Zimbardo *et al.* rejected the **dispositional hypothesis**. They argued that their findings supported the **situational hypothesis**, which claims that it's the conditions of prisons (physical, social and psychological) that are 'to blame' (*not* the characteristics of prisoners and guards). So, anyone given the role of guard or prisoner would probably behave as Zimbardo *et al.*'s participants did: a brutalising atmosphere, like the mock prison, produces brutality. If the roles had been reversed, the prisoners would have abused their power in just the same way: it's the prison environment that makes people act in 'typical guard' or 'typical prisoner' ways.

Evaluation (AO1/AO2)

- Both the environment and the behaviour (of guards and prisoners) were 'realistic' and the findings can be applied to real prisons. Although they may have been role playing at the beginning, they were soon taking their roles very seriously indeed – they became 'real'. So, the experiment has **high ecological validity**.
- Participants were merely acting out their prior expectations about how guards and prisoners *should* behave (based on TV programmes, films, etc.). In other words, they were *conforming*, but this wasn't so much yielding to group pressure as trying to be a 'typical' prisoner or guard (i.e. **role-playing**).
- Zimbardo *et al.* should have stopped the experiment long before day six, as Zimbardo himself later admitted. He became too involved in his role as prison supervisor and it took one of his students to remind him that he was also the psychologist in charge of the study! He **lost objectivity**.

How Science Works
Practical Learning Activity 5.3

- By randomly assigning the carefully screened participants to the prisoner or guard roles, what could Zimbardo *et al.* infer about the causes of any anti-social or sadistic behaviour they displayed?
- What do you think the *psychological reality* of a prison might involve? A way of thinking about this is to consider the *differences* between prisoners and guards.
- What kind of sample were the prisoners and guards?
- How do you think you'd have behaved if you'd been assigned to (a) the prisoner role and (b) the role of guard? Can you relate to the guards' enjoyment of their power over the prisoners?
- Interview people who know nothing about the experiment, asking them how they think they'd have behaved in one or other role. Then 'debrief' them by providing a brief summary of Zimbardo *et al.*'s results.
- Do we have to choose between the dispositional and situational hypotheses as explanations of how people in prisons behave?
- Do you agree with the 'mere role playing' criticism? Is it obvious how prisoners are meant to behave and, if so, were the prisoner participants conforming to this expectation?

Minority influence

We usually interpret the findings of Asch's experiments as showing how a powerful majority influences an isolated individual; in other words, conformity involves **majority influence** (see above). But is the numerical majority always more powerful? Even in Asch's original experiment, there was *no* conformity on two-thirds of the critical trials. What's more, the numerical minority can sometimes change the views of the majority (**minority influence**). This was demonstrated in a famous study by Moscovici *et al.* (1969), described in Key Study 5.3.

Key Study 5.3: Moscovici *et al.*'s (1969) Coloured Slide Experiment (CSE)

Aim/hypothesis (AO1)

Moscovici *et al.* were trying to demonstrate minority influence. The experimental task involved naming the colour of slides, which was objective (there was a right and wrong answer, as in Asch's experiment). Consequently, it might seem very unlikely that a minority could persuade the majority to give the wrong answer. However, Moscovici *et al.* predicted that a minority could exert influence over a majority if it *consistently* called a blue slide green.

Method/design (AO1)

Moscovici *et al.* used groups of six, four of whom were naive participants and the other two stooges. The stooges played the role of the minority. Before the experiment began, all the participants' colour vision was tested – and they all passed. This meant that the naive participants couldn't explain the stooges' wrong answers by claiming they were colour blind. All participants gave their answers aloud, with the stooges sitting either in the first and second position, or first and fourth.

On 36 separate trials, a slide that was clearly blue was presented on a screen.

- In the *consistent condition*, the stooges called it green *every time.*
- In the *inconsistent condition,* they answered 'green' 24 times and 'blue' 12 times.
- There was also a *control condition*, in which the groups comprised six naive participants.

Results (AO1)

- In the *control condition*, there were fewer than 1 per cent green responses. This showed how obvious the correct response was.
- In the *inconsistent condition*, 1.25 per cent of responses were green.
- In the *consistent condition,* green responses were made more than 8 per cent of the time. This was significantly more than in the other two conditions.
- 32 per cent of naive participants gave at least one green response.

Moscovici *et al.* found that there were really two types of group: in one, nobody was influenced by the minority; while, in the other, several participants were influenced. Where the stooges sat made no difference.

Conclusions (AO1)

The experiment clearly showed that a consistent minority can affect the judgements made by the majority. Although the minority doesn't have a numerical advantage, its consistent behavioural style makes it influential. In conformity experiments, the influence of the majority is evident from the start, while minority influence begins to show only after a while.

Evaluation (AO1/AO2)

- As with any study involving stooges, naive participants were deceived as to the true purpose of the experiment. This breaches a fundamental ethical principle – namely, **giving informed consent** (see page 164).
- As with Asch's experiments, the experimental task was very contrived (specially constructed for the purposes of the experiment) and far removed from real-life situations. In other words, the experiment lacked **external (ecological) validity.**

- Nemeth *et al.* (1974) showed that how the majority interprets the minority's answers also matters: they must relate to the stimulus (e.g. a colour slide) in some predictable way (stooges said 'green' in response to the *brighter* slides and 'blue-green' in response to the *dimmer* slides). So, there's more to minority influence than just consistency.

Explanations of conformity

How Science Works
Practical Learning Activity 5.4

- What motivates people to conform in everyday life? Taking different examples of conformity, try to identify different motives.
- What might be (some of) the reasons that people conform in the Asch experiment?
- Repeat the exercise for the Sherif experiment.

Deutsch and Gerard (1955) distinguished between **informational social influence** (ISI) and **normative social influence** (NSI). They felt that this distinction was crucial to understanding majority group influence.

Informational social influence (ISI)

We all have a basic need to feel confident that our ideas and beliefs are correct (a need for *certainty*). This makes us feel in charge of our lives and in control of the world. This is the motive underlying ISI. When we're unsure about something, we tend to seek other people's opinions: if we know what they think, we're in a better position to form our own opinions. This is more likely to happen in situations we're not familiar with (such as deciding who to vote for in your first election) or in ambiguous situations (such as reading a book or watching a film and not knowing what to make of it). Asking friends who *they're* voting for or what *they* made of the book or film helps you to make up your own mind.

The participants in Sherif's experiment were unsure how far the light moved (with good reason – it didn't actually move at all!). Similarly, when Asch made the comparison lines more similar, the situation became more ambiguous – the correct answer was now much less obvious.

If we conform because of ISI, it's very likely that we *really* believe the opinions we adopt. The whole point is that we're uncertain at first what to believe, which is why we compare our ideas with those of other people; so we come to share their views (we're 'converted'). When Sherif's participants were later tested individually (away from the group), they stuck to the answer they'd given while in the group; this shows that they genuinely (privately) believed that the group was correct. In other words, they said what they believed, and believed what they said. This describes a type of conformity called **internalisation** or **true conformity**.

In this way, other people help us define 'social reality'. But it also matters *who* these other people are (Brown, 1988): we're only likely to be influenced by others' opinions in an ambiguous situation if we see ourselves as sharing important characteristics with them (Abrams *et al.*, 1990). For example, you're more likely to internalise the views of other psychology students than those of, say, history students (assuming you're not doing history too).

Normative social influence (NSI)

The motive underlying NSI is the need to be accepted by other people. We want others to like and respect us, and being rejected is very painful. In these ways, people have the power to reward or punish us, and one way of ensuring their acceptance is to agree with them. But this doesn't necessarily mean that we truly believe in what we say.

For example, many of Asch's participants who'd conformed on the critical trials *knew* the stooges' answer was wrong. But if they'd given the correct answer, they risked being laughed at by the majority (a form of rejection). In the post-experimental debriefing, they said things such as 'I didn't want to look stupid' or 'I didn't want to be the odd one out'. So, what they *said* (publicly) and what they *believed* (privately) were *different*. This describes a type of conformity called **compliance**; it represents a compromise in situations where we face a *conflict* between our own and others' opinions. Sherif's participants didn't face any such conflict.

However, we only experience conflict if we disagree with others whom we see as similar to ourselves in some relevant way (as in ISI: see Abrams *et al.*, 1990). The example above, of being among other psychology students, applies here too.

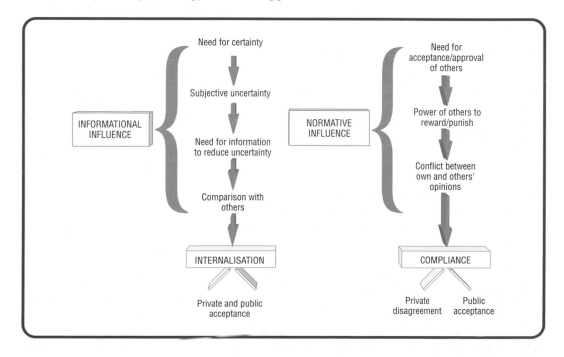

Figure 5.2: The relationship between different kinds of influence and different kinds of conformity

✔ Assessment Check 5.1

1. Define what's meant by the terms 'conformity', the 'Asch paradigm', and 'compliance'. (2 + 2 + 2 marks)
2. Outline TWO weaknesses of Asch's conformity research. (2 + 2 marks)
3. In relation to Zimbardo *et al.*'s prison study, define what's meant by the dispositional and situational hypotheses. (3 + 3 marks)
4. Outline TWO weaknesses of the prison study. (2 + 2 marks)
5. Distinguish ONE difference between informational and normative social influence. (3 marks)
6. Outline and evaluate psychological explanations of why people conform. (12 marks)

Obedience to authority

How Science Works
Practical Learning Activity 5.5

- What do you understand by the term 'obedience'?
- Try to observe some examples of obedience (see Practical Learning Activity 5.1).
- Draw up a list of differences between conformity and obedience.

Conformity	Obedience
No one tells us what to do. There's no explicit requirement to act in a particular way.	The authority figure orders us to do something. So there *is* an explicit requirement to act in a particular way.
The people who influence us are our *peers*, that is, our *equals*. They influence us by *example*, that is, we tend to behave as they do. In this way, everyone's behaviour becomes more similar.	The person who influences us has greater authority than we do in that particular situation. S/he influences us by *direction*, that is, by giving us orders or instructions. In this way, our behaviour is very different from the authority figure's.
We conform either because we want others to accept us, or because they provide us with important information. But we usually don't like to admit that we've been influenced by them.	We obey because we accept that society is organised in a *hierarchical* way, that is, some people have more influence than others. We don't mind admitting that we obey people 'in authority'.

Table 5.1: Comparison between conformity and obedience

Obedience can be defined as complying with the demands or instructions of an authority figure. The authority figure has greater power and influence in that particular situation.

The most famous – and one of the earliest – psychological studies of obedience is that of Milgram. Indeed, it's one of the best-known (and most controversial) studies in the whole of Psychology (see Key Study 5.4).

Key Study 5.4: Milgram's (1963) 'Shocking Obedience Study' (SOS)

Aim/hypothesis (AO1)

Milgram set out to test the 'Germans-are-different' hypothesis. This claims that (a) the Germans are a highly obedient nation and (b) Hitler couldn't have put into practice his plans to exterminate the Jews in the 1930s and 1940s without the cooperation of the German population. (It was really (a) that Milgram was trying to test.)

The American experiment described here was meant to be a *pilot study*, with the experiment proper to be carried out in Germany.

Method/design (AO1)

Participants volunteered for a study of memory and learning (see Figure 5.3), which was to take place in the Yale University Psychology Department. On arrival, they were met by the experimenter (who wore a grey lab coat), who introduced them to a Mr Wallace (a stooge pretending to be another participant).

The experimenter told the naive participant and Mr Wallace that the experiment was about the effects of *punishment* on learning, with one playing the role of 'teacher' and the other the 'learner'. The situation was rigged, such that Mr Wallace was always the learner and the participant the teacher.

The experimenter explained that the punishment would take the form of electric shocks. All three then went into an adjoining room, where the experimenter strapped Mr Wallace into a chair with his arms attached to electrodes. The teacher would deliver shocks via a shock generator, which was situated in an adjacent room. As the photograph on the next page shows, the generator had a series of switches, each clearly marked with a voltage level (starting at 15 volts)

Public Announcement

WE WILL PAY YOU $4.00 FOR ONE HOUR OF YOUR TIME

Persons Needed for a Study of Memory

*We will pay five hundred New Haven men to help us complete a scientific study of memory and learning. The study is being done at Yale University.

*Each person who participates will be paid $4.00 (plus 50c carfare) for approximately 1 hour's time. We need you for only one hour: there are no further obligations. You may choose the time you would like to come (evenings, weekdays, or weekends).

*No special training, education, or experience is needed. We want:

Factory workers	Businessmen	Construction workers
City employees	Clerks	Salespeople
Laborers	Professional people	White-collar workers
Barbers	Telephone workers	Others

All persons must be between the ages of 20 and 50. High school and college students cannot be used.

*If you meet these qualifications, fill out the coupon below and mail it now to Professor Stanley Milgram, Department of Psychology, Yale University, New Haven. You will be notified later of the specific time and place of the study. We reserve the right to decline any application.

*You will be paid $4.00 (plus 50c carfare) as soon as you arrive at the laboratory.

- -

TO:
PROF. STANLEY MILGRAM, DEPARTMENT OF PSYCHOLOGY, YALE UNIVERSITY, NEW HAVEN, CONN. I want to take part in this study of memory and learning. I am between the ages of 20 and 50. I will be paid $4.00 (plus 50c carfare) if I participate.

NAME (Please Print). . . . .

ADDRESS . . . .

TELEPHONE NO. . . . . Best time to call you . . . .

AGE . . . . OCCUPATION . . . . SEX . . . . . .
CAN YOU COME:

WEEKDAYS . . . . EVENINGS . . . . WEEKENDS . . . .

Figure 5.3: Announcement in a local newspaper to recruit participants

together with a verbal description (e.g. 'slight shock'). Each switch gave a shock 15 volts higher than the one before, going up to 450 volts (marked 'XXX').

The teacher was instructed to deliver a shock each time Mr Wallace made a mistake on a paired-associate word task; he indicated his answer by switching on one of four lights located above the shock generator. With each successive mistake, the teacher had to give the next highest shock (that is, 15 volts higher than the previous one).

At 300 volts, Mr Wallace kicked against the wall that adjoined the two rooms. After 315 volts, he stopped kicking and also stopped responding to the teacher's questions. The teacher was instructed to keep on shocking if Mr Wallace stopped answering.

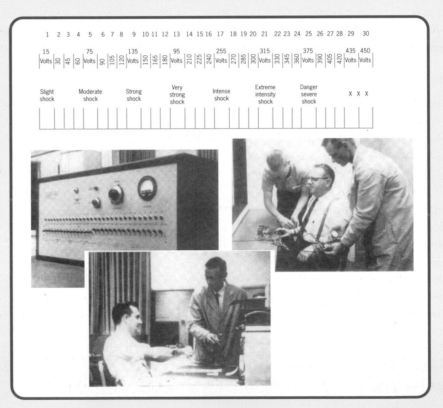

Shock generator and procedure used in the Milgram experiments (Milgram, 1974)

Results (AO1)

Obedience rate was defined as the percentage of participants who kept on giving shocks right up to the maximum 450 volts. Obedience rate was 65 per cent. Many participants showed extreme distress (such as twitching or giggling nervously, digging their nails into their flesh and verbally attacking the experimenter).

Whenever they threatened to pull out of the experiment, the experimenter would 'prod' them by saying things like:

- 'Please continue' (or 'Please go on')
- 'The experiment requires that you continue'
- 'It is absolutely essential that you continue'
- 'You have no choice, you *must* go on'.

Conclusions (AO1)

The 'Germans-are-different' hypothesis is clearly false. Milgram's participants were 40 'ordinary' Americans living in a fairly typical small town. Their high level of obedience showed that we all tend to obey people we regard as authority figures in particular situations: if we'd been living in Nazi Germany in the 1930s, we might well have acted just as obediently. As there was no reason to believe that these volunteers were unusually sadistic – or particularly subservient – the results strongly suggest that obeying those in authority is normal behaviour in a hierarchically organised society.

Evaluation (AO1/AO2)

- This represents the first major attempt to study obedience experimentally – that is, under controlled conditions. Milgram established a basic method (or *paradigm*) for studying obedience in the lab. This is equivalent to Asch's paradigm for studying conformity.
- Milgram's paradigm has been used in several other countries, including Italy, Australia, the UK, Jordan and Spain. However, methodological differences between these studies make it difficult to compare the results.
- Since it was intended as a pilot study, it might be fairer (and more useful) to consider the research that was stimulated by the 1963 study, rather than the study itself. Milgram had expected to find very *low* levels of obedience among his American participants, so he conducted several further studies to determine exactly *why* they were so obedient (see Key Study 5.5).

How Science Works
Practical Learning Activity 5.6

- Explain what is meant by a pilot study.
- Given that Milgram was planning to run the experiment in Germany, what can you infer about his belief regarding the Germans-are-different hypothesis?
- In one variation of the original experiment, the experimenter was called out of the room and asked an ordinary man to take over his role. Which characteristic of the experimenter (the 'obedience source') changed, and how do you think this affected the obedience rate?
- What ethical principles do you think Milgram's experiments have been criticised for breaching? You could hold a class debate, arguing against, or in defence of, Milgram's methods.

As noted above, Milgram conducted a series of experiments to try to pinpoint why his American sample had shown such a high obedience rate. Key Study 5.5 describes six of these variations on the original 1963 experiment.

Key Study 5.5: Some of Milgram's (1974) variations on his 'Shocking Obedience Study' (SOS)

Aim/hypothesis (AO1)

This was basically the same in all cases – namely, to change a *single* variable at a time in order to see its effect on obedience rate. The basic procedure remained the same as in the original 1963 experiment (called the *remote victim* condition).

How Science Works
Practical Learning Activity 5.7

- For each of the variations described below, try to predict the obedience rate Milgram actually found. Ask yourself why it should be higher or lower than the 65 per cent found in the original experiment.
- Repeat the exercise, this time with people unfamiliar with the original experiment. Give them a summary of the original, then a brief account of the variations (as below), asking them to write down the obedience rate for each one. (Don't worry about their reasons.)

Method/design (AO1)

- **(i) Voice feedback (VF):** the teacher heard a series of tape-recorded verbal responses, which, supposedly, were Mr Wallace's spontaneous reactions to the increasing shock levels. At first (75–105 volts) he made a little grunt. At 120 volts, he told the experimenter the shocks were getting painful. He then demanded to be let out, sometimes screaming in agony, sometimes refusing to give any more answers (150–315 volts). After 330 volts, there was silence!
- **(ii) Proximity (P):** the teacher was now in the same room as Mr Wallace. They sat about 1.5 ft (46 cm) apart, and the teacher could see as well as hear Mr Wallace's protests and screams.
- **(iii) Touch proximity (TP):** the teacher had to help keep Mr Wallace's arms down on the arms of the chair – the electric shock supposedly came through shock plates located on the arms.
- **(iv) Remote authority (RA):** the experimenter left the room after giving the teacher the essential instructions. He gave all subsequent instructions by phone.
- **(v) Two peers rebel (TPR):** the teacher was paired with two other (stooge) teachers. One stooge read out the list of word pairs, while the other told Mr Wallace whether his answer was correct or incorrect. The naive participant

delivered the shocks. At 150 volts, the first stooge refused to continue and moved to another part of the room. At 210 volts, the second stooge did the same. The naive participant had to take over the stooges' tasks.

- **(vi) A peer administers shock (PAS):** the teacher was paired with another (stooge) teacher. It was the stooge's job to 'throw the switch'.

Results (AO1)

- **VF:** 62.5 per cent. This became the new 'baseline'. In other words, in all the later experiments there was voice feedback, and some *other* variable was changed.
- **P:** 40 per cent.
- **TP:** 30 per cent.
- **RA:** 20.5 per cent.
- **TPR:** 10 per cent.
- **PAS:** 92.5 per cent.

Conclusions (AO1/AO2)

The 62.5 per cent obedience rate in VF is still frighteningly high. Based on P and TP, it seems easier to resist the demands of an authority figure (that is, to disobey) when you can see for yourself the effects that your behaviour has on the victim. RA suggests that it's easier to follow the dictates of our conscience when the authority figure isn't physically present. In TPR, participants see that it's *possible* to disobey and *how* to disobey. Some participants said they didn't realise they *could* – a demonstration of *conformity*.

Is Milgram's research valid?

According to Orne and Holland (1968), Milgram's experiments lacked **experimental (internal) realism/validity**. That is, participants didn't believe that the experimental situation they found themselves in was real; specifically, they didn't believe that Mr Wallace was really receiving electric shocks. They were actually responding to the **demand characteristics** of the experiment: they were simply picking up on the cues that showed them how they were *expected* to behave in that situation (see pages 68 and 151).

However, there's good reason to believe that participants *did* take the situation seriously. For example, many showed signs of distress and anxiety (see the 'Results' section in Key Study 5.4). According to Orne and Holland, this was a 'pretence', but in post-experimental interviews participants never indicated that they'd been pretending.

Sheridan and King (1972) found high levels of obedience when participants *must* have believed that the situation was real. This involved students training a puppy by punishing it with *actual* electric shocks whenever it made an error on a particular task. Although the shocks were small, the students could see and hear the puppy's squeals; 75 per cent of the students delivered the maximum shock.

To criticise Milgram's experiments for being unethical, you must first believe that participants *weren't* pretending. Only if you're convinced that they were really stressed could you condemn Milgram for exposing them to that stress (see page 165).

Orne and Holland also claimed that Milgram's experiments lacked **mundane (external) realism** (or **ecological validity**). That is, the findings cannot be generalised beyond the particular laboratory setting in which they were collected. So, we cannot learn from Milgram's research about how people behave in other situations. However, *naturalistic studies* of obedience suggest otherwise. For example, Hofling *et al.* (1966) studied 22 nurses working in various US hospitals. A stooge, 'Dr Smith', from the psychiatric department instructed them by phone to give his patient ('Mr Jones') 20 mg of a drug called Astrofen. Dr Smith was in a desperate hurry and would sign the drug authorisation form later when he came to see the patient.

Astrofen was in fact a dummy drug (a harmless sugar pill) invented just for the experiment. The label on the box clearly stated that the maximum daily dose was 10 mg. So, if the nurse obeyed Dr Smith's instructions, she'd be giving *twice* the maximum daily dose. Also, hospital rules required that doctors sign the authorisation form *before* any drug was given. Another rule demanded that nurses should be absolutely certain that 'Dr Smith' was a genuine doctor.

A total of 21 of the 22 nurses complied without hesitation. A control group of 22 nurses were asked what they *would have done* in that situation: 21 said they wouldn't have given the drug without written authorisation, especially as it exceeded the maximum daily dose.

Hofling *et al.* concluded that the power and authority of doctors proved to be a greater influence on the nurses' behaviour than basic hospital rules. Also, what people *say* they would do in a particular situation, and what they actually *do,* can be very different.

Why do people obey?

According to Milgram (1974), most of us would have behaved like his obedient participants. So, the explanation for such high levels of obedience must lie in aspects of the situation, rather than in individual characteristics.

Perception of legitimate authority

Obedient participants seemed to accept the power and status of the experimenter: in the context of the Yale University Psychology Department, he was 'in charge'.

Authority figures often possess highly visible symbols of their power and status; these make it much more difficult to disobey them. For example, the experimenter always wore a *grey* lab coat (a white one would have implied 'scientist' rather than 'authority figure'). Zimbardo *et al.*'s prison study (see Key Study 5.2) also showed the impact of uniforms and other trappings of power and authority.

The agentic state

When we obey, we see ourselves as the instrument, or agent, of the authority figure's wishes (the **agentic state**). We give up personal responsibility for our actions (the **autonomous state**) and transfer that responsibility onto the authority figure: 'I was only following orders' was the most common defence given by Nazi war criminals (including Eichmann, who ran the death camps).

Once we come to see ourselves in this way, the specific orders are largely irrelevant. Obedience always involves the same mental adjustment (the agentic state): 'obedience is obedience is obedience'.

Personal responsibility

The agentic and autonomous states are two sides of the same coin: anything that detracts from the authority figure's power increases feelings of personal responsibility. This was demonstrated in Milgram's Remote Authority (RA) variation. When the experimenter wasn't in the same room to give his instructions in person, participants were more likely to disobey.

This was also evident in the Proximity (P) and Touch Proximity (TP) experiments. It's much more difficult to deny responsibility if you're in the same room as Mr Wallace (instead of just hearing his screams, etc.). It's even more difficult if you physically have to force him to endure the shocks. In other words, it's easier to disobey when you can see for yourself the effects of your behaviour on the victim (see the 'Conclusions' section in Key Study 5.5).

However, when someone else actually 'throws the switch' (as in 'A peer administers shock' (PAS)), it's easier to *deny* personal responsibility ('*He* delivered the shock, not *me*').

The 'foot in the door'

Participants got 'sucked into' a situation that they found very difficult to escape from. They'd volunteered for what seemed like a 'harmless' study of learning and memory. There was no mention in the original announcement of punishment, let alone delivering electric shocks to another participant: it was first mentioned only after they'd already made the effort to get to the Psychology Department.

Once they were in the experimental situation, it became more difficult to leave. The deeper in you are, the greater the effort you must make to escape. If the original announcement had referred to punishment and/or electric shocks, perhaps fewer volunteers would have come forward. Or perhaps it would have attracted a more sadistic group of people!

Ethical issues arising from social influence research

Most people would agree that it's morally unacceptable (unethical) to harm another person (physically and/or mentally) in everyday life. It may also be illegal. Similarly, if we lie or deceive someone. But until Milgram's initial obedience experiment, psychologists didn't really discuss the ethics of their research in the way they do today.

The social influence research of Asch, Zimbardo *et al.*, Milgram and others has been criticised for being unethical. But this research has also helped to identify the crucial ethical issues that *all* psychologists must consider when planning and conducting their research: without these studies of social influence, there might not be an ethics debate – and ethical codes and guidelines – at all. Examples include the British Psychological Society's (BPS) Code of Ethics (BPS, 2007). (See pages 90–92.)

How Science Works
Practical Learning Activity 5.8

- Try to identify the ethical shortcomings of Milgram's, Zimbardo *et al.*'s and Asch's research. Are there any common themes?
- You could hold a debate around the topic of whether the breaching of basic ethical principles can ever be justified.

Deception and informed consent: Milgram's research

There's no question that Milgram deceived his participants. The original announcement states that the study was concerned with memory and learning. Only after volunteers were already in the experimental situation did the experimenter mention punishment and electric shock.

Even if the study had actually been about the effects of punishment on learning, Milgram would still have been deceiving his participants (Mr Wallace was an actor pretending to be another participant, he never actually received any electric shocks, etc.) – but, of course, it *wasn't*. The more serious deception was that it was really about obedience. This was never mentioned until after the experiment was over.

What all this means is that participants couldn't give their **informed consent** – they volunteered for a study without knowing its true purpose or what would happen. Had they known, they may not have volunteered in the first place. You could say that they were *tricked* into taking part.

Deception and informed consent: Zimbardo *et al.*'s research

Zimbardo *et al.*'s prison study was advertised as a study of prison life, which was its *true* purpose. In fact, the researchers produced an informed consent contract, which informed participants about everything that was going to happen to them (as far as this could be predicted). It was signed by every participant, thereby giving their permission for invasion of privacy, loss of civil rights, and harassment.

Participants were deceived about only one thing: they weren't told that those allocated to the role of prisoner would be arrested by the local police force. This was partly because the police didn't give their final approval until the last minute; but Zimbardo *et al.* (1973) also wanted the arrest to come as a surprise. Zimbardo *et al.* (1973) admitted that this was in breach of their own contract.

Deception and informed consent: Asch's research

Asch told his participants that the experiment was concerned with perception. Since it was actually about conformity, they were clearly deceived about its true purpose. This means, as with Milgram, that participants couldn't give their informed consent; also like Milgram, they didn't realise that the other group members were, in fact, stooges.

Is deception ever justified?

Most of Asch's participants were very enthusiastic. In post-experimental interviews, they said how they admired the elegance and significance of the experimental procedure.

Milgram defended his use of deception by reporting that he thoroughly *debriefed* his participants. He had a lengthy discussion with each participant individually as soon as the experiment was over (see below). He then sent each of them a detailed account of the procedure and results of all the experiments. He also sent them a follow-up questionnaire about their experience of taking part. Most of those who returned the questionnaire said they were glad, or very glad, to have taken part; many said they learned something important about themselves and that there should be more research like it.

Milgram took this to be the *crucial* justification for the use of deception: if participants didn't object, why should anybody else? Also, deception was necessary if participants were to behave in a 'realistic' way: as we noted earlier when discussing internal and external validity, participants had to believe they were delivering real shocks, otherwise we couldn't generalise the results to real-life obedience situations.

Protecting participants from psychological harm: Milgram's research

Baumrind (1964) accused Milgram of abusing his participants' rights and feelings. She argued that Milgram failed to protect them adequately from stress and emotional conflict. Milgram accepted that they did experience stress and conflict, but Baumrind's criticism assumes that the experimental outcome was *expected*. In fact, Milgram was as surprised as anyone by the high obedience rate. The most distressed participants tended to be those who were the most obedient. So, if Milgram expected very low obedience rates, he certainly didn't expect participants to experience high levels of conflict.

But shouldn't he have stopped his research as soon as he saw how distressed participants became? Also, the whole set-up was designed to make it difficult for participants to disobey: the experimenter's prods pressurised the participant into obeying. This made *withdrawal from the investigation* extremely difficult. In his defence, Milgram put forward the following arguments.

- At whatever point the participant stopped giving shocks, s/he was reunited with Mr Wallace, who was clearly unharmed. Milgram also revealed that the shocks weren't real, assuring obedient participants that their behaviour was completely normal and supporting the disobedient ones in their resistance to the experimenter's demands. This was all part of the *debriefing*, which Milgram had decided would take place as a matter of course (it would have happened anyway and wasn't a response to any criticisms).

- The experimenter *didn't* make the participant shock Mr Wallace (as Baumrind claimed). Indeed, this *couldn't* have happened: Milgram believed that people have free will, and so *choose* to obey or disobey.

Consent/informed consent	
For	**Against**
• Participants volunteered	• They volunteered for a study of learning and memory
Deception	
For	**Against**
• Debriefing – as a matter of course • Participants accept it • The end justifies the means	• Debriefing only needed because of deception • Prevents informed consent • Harmful to self-concept
Protection of participants	
For	**Against**
• Results weren't anticipated • Reunited with unharmed victim • Reassured after the experiment as part of debriefing • No evidence of long-term harm • Participants have free will	• Participants very distressed • Debriefing only needed because of participants' distress
Withdrawal from the investigation	
For	**Against**
• Participants free to leave at any time • 37.5% disobeyed (voice-feedback condition) • 62.5% obeyed (voice-feedback condition	• The whole situation made resistance (disobedience) difficult

Table 5.2: Summary of arguments in Milgram's defence ('for') and criticisms ('against') of his obedience experiments

Protecting participants from harm: Zimbardo *et al.*'s research

Zimbardo (1973) believes that the ethical concerns are even greater in the prison study than in Milgram's research. Volunteer prisoners suffered physical and psychological abuse over several days, and volunteer guards discovered that they enjoyed having power and abused it to make other human beings suffer. Although every participant signed an informed consent form (see above), this couldn't protect the prisoners from the guards' abuse. Nor could it protect the guards from what they learned about themselves. It took Zimbardo *et al.* six days to end the experiment, which was planned to run for two weeks. Why did it take them so long?

According to Savin (1973), the practical benefits of the prison study didn't justify the distress, mistreatment and degradation suffered by the prisoners: the end *didn't* justify the means.

Protecting participants from harm: Asch's research

Many of Asch's participants said that they conformed only because they didn't want to be laughed at or ridiculed (see page 155). When Asch ran the experiment using several naive participants and a single stooge, they openly ridiculed the stooge on the critical trials. Other studies have shown that participants' physiological stress levels increase on critical trials.

Assessment Check 5.2

1. Define what's meant by the terms 'obedience', 'experimental (internal) realism/validity', and 'demand characteristics'. (2 + 2 + 2 marks)
2. Outline TWO differences between conformity and obedience. (2 + 2 marks)
3. Outline and evaluate Milgram's research into obedience. (12 marks)
4. Give TWO reasons for believing that Milgram's experiments had mundane (external) realism (or ecological validity). (2 + 2 marks)
5. Define what's meant by the terms 'the agentic state', 'the autonomous state', and 'informed consent'. (2 + 2 + 2 marks)
6. Describe TWO explanations for why people obey. (6 marks)
7. Outline and evaluate the ethics of research into social influence. (8 marks)

Social influence in everyday life

Independent behaviour

What do we mean by independent behaviour?

Here, **independent behaviour** simply refers to resisting pressures to conform ('non-conformity') and to obey authority figures ('disobedience'). However, 'non-conformity' can mean different things.

Are all non-conformers alike?

According to Willis (1963), two dimensions are necessary in order to construct an adequate representation of conformity and non-conformity – namely (i) *dependence–independence* and (ii) *conformity–anti-conformity*. Taken together, these produce three major patterns of behaviour over a series of interactions:

(a) **conformity**, which involves a consistent movement *towards* social expectancy

(b) **independence**, which involves a *lack* of consistent movement either towards or away from social expectancy

(c) **anti-conformity**, which involves a consistent movement *away* from social conformity.

Both (b) and (c) represent *non-conformity*, but they differ, especially in relation to the dimension of independence. Whereas (a) implies dependence on (influence by) others, (b), as the word 'independent' implies, is (relatively) free of such dependence; (c) also involves dependence on (influence by) others, in the sense of dependence on some minority group's norms which are adopted in opposition to the majority's.

Willis saw conformity and non-conformity *not* as fixed personality characteristics, but as outcomes of interaction in a particular situation. Also, in western culture, (c) has a more negative valuation than (b). As Hollander (1981) puts it:

independence is probably seen as a more authentic, self-motivated, form of response than is the negativism of anticonformity.

Hollander and Willis (1964) found that participants responded differently to co-workers (jointly engaged on a task) according to whether they behaved in a conforming, independent or anti-conforming way. Even when co-workers were presented as being more competent than the participant with respect to the task, participants were influenced more by the independent, competent co-worker than by the anti-conforming co-worker. This supports Willis's claim that (b) and (c) are essentially different kinds of non-conformity.

While (b) and (c) can be seen as forms of *dissent* (disagreeing with the majority), (c) seems to represent a *refusal* to conform, a way of expressing one's *individuality* (i.e. not conforming on principle!). Dissent as a self-expressive act is particularly likely in social influence situations in which people have more options than simply agreeing or disagreeing with the majority opinion (e.g. there's a third option). According to Maslach *et al.* (1985), 'creative dissenters' have high self-esteem, low anxiety in social situations and a strong tendency to be *individuated* – that is, a willingness to act differently from others so as to stand out. Such people seem to have a strong need for self-expression and, when the opportunity presents itself, they take it (Zimbardo and Leippe, 1991).

Explanations of how people resist pressures to conform and obey authority

How Science Works
Practical Learning Activity 5.9

- Look back at the research of Asch and Milgram. What factors reduced conformity or obedience rates in their experiments?
- Ask your peers what would make them less likely to conform with current fashion (not just in clothes, but in music and other areas) and more likely to resist the demands of an authority figure (such as their teacher/lecturer and/or parents).

Resisting conformity

As we saw earlier (page 148), if naive participants hear a dissenter (one of the stooges) disagreeing with the majority wrong answer on critical trials, the conformity rate drops sharply. Dissenters provide the participant with moral support, even though they still give the wrong answer (but a different wrong answer from the majority); this 'frees' the participant to give the correct answer. The dissenter represents a form of *social support*. So, a major way of resisting conformity is to break the *unanimity* of the majority – if they don't *all* agree, their impact is greatly reduced.

Conformity is reduced even when the dissenter isn't competent in that particular situation. For example, Allen and Levine (1971) found that conformity was reduced on a task involving visual judgements, even by a 'partner' who wore glasses with thick lenses and admitted to having a sight problem. However, support that's received earlier is more effective than support received later: if you ever find yourself in a situation in which pressures towards conformity are increasing and you feel they should be resisted, try to speak out as quickly as possible. The sooner you do, the greater your chances of rallying others to your side and resisting the majority (Baron and Byrne, 1991).

We also saw that we don't necessarily conform with the majority simply because they are more numerous – they also have to be a group that we regard as being similar to ourselves in some relevant respect (e.g. in terms of the A-level subjects they're taking) (Abrams *et al.*, 1990).

Resisting obedience

Milgram's variations on his original experiment suggest that anything that (a) detracts from seeing the person giving orders as a legitimate authority and/or (b) increases our feeling of personal responsibility (i.e. decreases the *agentic state* and increases the *autonomous state*) will make obedience less likely to occur.

As we saw above (pages 160–161), when the experimenter gave subsequent instructions by phone (RA), and when the participant could see (as well as hear) the effects of the shocks (P and TP), obedience rates were substantially reduced. In all three cases, participants were forced to accept personal responsibility for their actions. When the experimenter said 'You have no other choice, you *must* go on', many participants *stopped* obeying: it brought home to them that they *did* have a choice and *were* responsible.

We also saw that *conformity* can play a crucial role in helping participants resist the experimenter. In TPR, participants witnessed disobedience on the part of others, which then made it easier for them to follow suit. The disobedient stooge teachers demonstrated both that it was *possible* to disobey, and *how* to do it. According to Milgram (1965):

The effects of peer rebellion are most impressive in undercutting the experimenter's authority.

The influence of individual differences on independent behaviour

Locus of control

One recurring theme in social psychological research is the extent to which people perceive themselves as being in control of their lives. Sometimes it's quite obvious that we either have or don't have control. But, where this is less obvious, some individuals tend to believe that their own actions make a difference, that they can affect the outcomes of situations (they have **high internal locus of control**), while others tend to believe that nothing they do will make any real difference, that things will turn out a certain way regardless of their own actions (they have **high external locus of control**).

In other words, *internal* locus of control (LOC) refers to the belief that things happen as a result of an individual's choices and decisions and acting upon these, while *external* LOC refers to the belief that things happen as a result of luck, fate and other uncontrollable outside forces. LOC was originally identified as a personality dimension by Rotter (1966); Strickland (1984) has described its effect on many aspects of social behaviour.

If you have high internal LOC, you accept responsibility for your actions (this is perhaps the flip-side of seeing yourself as being in charge of what happens to you). This may help explain why some people actively participate in attempts to bring about changes in society (often involving some degree of sacrifice and sometimes personal risk to themselves). They do this because they believe that their actions can bring about a worthwhile outcome. For example, African-American college students who participated in civil rights activities in the early 1960s were higher on internal LOC than those who weren't interested in taking part (Gore and Rotter, 1963; Strickland, 1984). Those with high internal LOC are also more likely to believe in a just world and so be critical of current injustices.

Learned helplessness

Related to LOC is **learned helplessness** (LH) (Seligman, 1975). This refers to the belief that nothing we do will make any difference to our situation.

Seligman strapped dogs into harnesses and gave them a series of electric shocks, from which they couldn't escape. Later, they had to jump a barrier within ten seconds of a warning signal (an avoidance response), otherwise they'd receive a painful shock. About two-thirds of the dogs failed to learn the avoidance response. They seemed passively resigned to suffering the shock. A control group of dogs (which hadn't been subjected to the unavoidable shock) learned the avoidance response easily.

Based on these observations, Seligman proposed that animals acquire a sense of helplessness when confronted with uncontrollable aversive stimulation. Later, this sense of helplessness impairs their performance in stressful situations that *are* controllable: they seem to lose the ability and motivation to respond effectively to painful stimulation. By extension, LH could help explain human depression. Seligman proposed that, like the dogs, many depressed people respond passively in the face of stress.

What relevance does this have for resisting social influence?

Abramson, Seligman & Teasdale (1978) combined the concept of LH with aspects of attribution theory (which accounts for how people assign causes to their own and others' behaviour). As with high external LOC, people displaying a *'depressed attributional style'* will see themselves as incapable of changing things for the better. If you attribute your successes to stable situational forces (things beyond your control) and your failures to the kind of person you are (also beyond your control), then you're likely to respond passively to other people's attempts to influence your behaviour. This can be thought of as a *fatalistic* view of the world: 'things happen in a certain way and there's nothing I can do about it'. There's an acceptance of the way things are (the *status quo*), which includes how our behaviour is shaped by our peers, as well as by those with greater power and authority than us.

Assessment Check 5.3

1. Define what's meant by the terms 'independent behaviour', 'locus of control', and 'learned helplessness'. (2 + 2 + 2 marks)
2. Describe ONE difference between independence and anti-conformity as two types of non-conformity. (3 marks)
3. Name THREE characteristics of 'creative dissenters'. (1 + 1 + 1 mark)
4. Outline TWO factors that are likely to increase resistance to conformity. (2 + 2 marks)
5. Outline and evaluate research into resisting obedience. (12 marks)
6. Explain the relevance of attributional style to understanding resistance to social influence. (6 marks)

Implications of research into conformity, obedience and independence for social change

For Moscovici (1976), minority influence is important for *innovation* – that is, the introduction and acceptance of new ideas and ways of doing things. It results from the *conflict* that minorities create, which, in turn, is created when they state their position with consistency, confidence and conviction. In this way, they disrupt the existing (majority) norm; this creates doubt and uncertainty in the minds of the majority (Fiske, 2004). They show that the existing norm (the *status quo*) isn't the only one.

When discussing resistance to obedience, we saw that in Milgram's TPR experiment, obedience rate fell to 10 per cent. This involved a kind of conformity in which participants were exposed to *disobedient models*, who displayed both that it was *possible* to disobey and *how* to do it. This represents one of three ways of reducing obedience, according to Milgram (1974); the others being:

1 *educating* people about the dangers of blind obedience; and

2 encouraging them to *question authority*.

According to Ross (1988), obedience would have been much less had there been a 'quit' button made visible and within easy reach of the participant: the button would have suggested both the appropriateness and the means of stopping their destructive obedience. Zimbardo and Leippe (1991) propose six steps that can be taken to counteract pressures to comply made by salespeople and, by extension, authority figures in general. These are described in Box 5.1.

Box 5.1: Six steps to counteract the demands of an authority figure (based on Zimbardo and Leippe, 1991)

1 Trust your intuition that 'something is wrong here'.

2 Don't accept the definition of the situation as presented to you by the other person, whose vested interests may conflict with yours.

3 Consider the 'worst case' scenario, and act on that possibility.

4 Figure out an escape plan and put it into effect as soon as possible.

5 Don't care what the other person may think of you – you can always apologise later when it's safe to do so if you were mistaken.

6 Think about the 'exit button' idea and mentally rehearse it as it applies to different situations in your life.

One way in which people might be educated about the dangers of blind obedience (Milgram's (1) above) is to inform them about the disturbing results of Milgram's own research: as they become widely known, they may produce desirable shifts within society (Baron and Byrne, 1991). Baron and Byrne cite the collapse of the Soviet Union and the overthrow of Communist regimes in (the former) East Germany, Poland, Czechoslovakia,

'People power': the 'collapse' of the Berlin Wall, 1989

Romania and elsewhere, as demonstrations of the ability to resist the power of totalitarian regimes. These changes, they say:

could not have occurred without the heroic acts of countless individuals who decided to shoulder the risks involved in resisting the authority of their own entrenched governments ...

In all these countries, courageous leaders emerged to serve as *disobedient models*, and large numbers of citizens decided that the established government didn't have their best interests at heart:

Together, these dramatic events suggest that no matter how great their authority or military might, tyrants cannot long remain in power when large numbers of citizens refuse to obey ... (Baron and Byrne, 1991).

SUMMARY

Social influence

- **Conformity** refers to the influence that a group has over an individual (**majority influence**). This is demonstrated in Asch's experiments, and the **Asch paradigm** has become the most widely used procedure for studying majority influence.

- Asch found that it's not the size of the majority that matters, but whether or not the majority is **unanimous**.

- Zimbardo *et al.*'s prison experiment rejected the **dispositional hypothesis** in favour of the **situational hypothesis**. The study also illustrates aspects of both conformity and influence.

- Moscovici and Faucheux reinterpreted Asch's findings, seeing the naive participant as representing the traditional, orthodox view of the world, and the stooge majority as embodying unorthodox, unconventional ideas. The latter is crucial to understanding **innovation** (how new ideas come to be accepted).

- **Minority influence** is also crucial for innovation, as demonstrated by Moscovici *et al.* To be influential, the minority needs to be **consistent**. However, consistency doesn't have to involve repeating the same response every time, provided there's a clear *pattern* in the minority's responses.

- Deutsch and Gerard's distinction between **informational social influence (ISI)** and **normative social influence (NSI)** is crucial for understanding why people conform. ISI and NSI correspond to **internalisation (true conformity)** and **compliance** respectively.

- **Obedience** refers to compliance with the demands/instructions of an **authority figure**. This is one of the important differences between obedience and conformity.

- The original idea for Milgram's obedience experiments was the **Germans-are-different hypothesis.** The original **remote-victim** experiment was followed by the **voice-feedback** experiment. Altogether, Milgram conducted 18 experiments, in each of which a different variable was manipulated in order to see its effect on obedience rate.

- Orne and Holland criticised Milgram's experiments for their lack of both **experimental (internal) realism/validity** and **mundane (external) realism** (or **ecological validity**). However, these criticisms seem unfounded. For example, naturalistic studies (such as Hofling *et al.*'s study of nurses) suggest that they *do* have mundane realism, and Milgram's findings have been replicated in several cross-cultural studies.

- We tend to obey people whom we perceive as a **legitimate authority**. When they give us orders, our usual **autonomous state** is replaced by the **agentic state**. These are all related, in turn, to our sense of **personal responsibility** for our own behaviour.

- Social influence research in general, and Milgram's obedience experiments in particular, have been criticised for being **unethical**. But they have also helped to identify the ethical issues central to the 'ethics debate' in psychology as a whole.

- Major ethical **principles** highlighted by this research include **consent/informed consent**, **deception** (and the related **debriefing**), **protecting participants from psychological harm**, and **withdrawal from the investigation**.

Social influence in everyday life

- **Independent behaviour** refers to resisting pressures to conform and to obey authority figures.

- '**Non-conformity**' can refer to both **independence** (a lack of consistent movement either towards or away from social expectancy) and **anti-conformity** (a consistent movement away from social conformity).

- Both independence and anti-conformity are forms of **dissent** (disagreeing with the majority). But anti-conformity represents a *refusal* to conform, a way of expressing one's **individuality**. 'Creative dissenters' have a strong tendency to be **individuated** (a willingness to act differently from others so as to stand out).

- In Asch's experiments, conformity rates were substantially reduced if one of the stooges was a *dissenter*, disagreeing with the majority wrong answer but also giving a different wrong answer. This represents a form of **social support** for the naive participant, breaking the **unanimity** of the majority.

- Conformity may also be reduced if we perceive the majority as being **dissimilar** from us in some relevant respect.

- Anything that makes us feel more personally responsible for our actions will reduce the impact of an authority figure (as when participants could see as well as hear the effects of their behaviour, or the experimenter gave later instructions by phone).

- Milgram also found that when stooge teachers displayed that it was possible to disobey – and how to do it – participants were much more likely themselves to disobey. This **peer rebellion** represents a form of **conformity**.

- One way of **educating** people about the dangers of blind obedience is to inform them of Milgram's experimental findings.

- People who actively try to bring about social change are likely to have a **high internal locus of control (LOC)** (Rotter). This involves a strong acceptance of responsibility for their actions and belief that their actions can bring about a worthwhile outcome. Those with high internal LOC are also likely to believe in a just world and so be critical of current injustices.

- Related to LOC is **learned helplessness (LH)**, the belief that nothing we do will make any difference to our situation. This sense of helplessness, which may arise in situations that are uncontrollable, then generalises to stressful situations that *are* controllable.

- Like high external LOC, people with a **depressed attributional style** see themselves as incapable of changing things for the better. This *fatalistic* view of the world involves an acceptance of the *status quo*, which includes how our behaviour is shaped by others – both our peers and authority figures.

AS Unit 2

Individual differences: psychopathology (abnormality)

6 Chapter

What's covered in this chapter?

You need to know about:

Defining and explaining psychological abnormality

- 'Deviation from social norms', definition and limitations
- 'Failure to function adequately', definition and limitations
- 'Deviation from ideal mental health', definition and limitations
- Key features of the biological approach to psychopathology
- Key features of the psychological approach to psychopathology, including:
  - psychodynamic approach
  - behavioural approach
  - cognitive approach

Treating abnormality

- Biological therapies, including drugs and ECT
- Psychological therapies including:
  - psychoanalysis
  - systematic desensitisation
  - cognitive behavioural therapy

Defining psychological abnormality

Abnormality is a difficult term to define, because abnormal behaviour can take many different forms and involve different features. There's no single feature that distinguishes between abnormal and normal behaviour. Despite this, attempts have been made to define abnormality.

The 'deviation from social norms' definition

Society sets norms, or unwritten rules, for acceptable behaviour. According to this definition, behaviour that deviates from these norms is considered abnormal. Abnormal behaviour is therefore whatever violates social norms. This approach takes into account the *desirability of behaviour*, as social norms identify those behaviours that are desirable for both the individual and society.

Limitations of the 'deviation from social norms' definition

- **Subjective:** the norms defined by society are subjective. They're often based on the opinions of elites within society rather than the majority opinion.

- **Change over time:** the norms defined by society are often related to moral standards that vary over time as social attitudes change. For example, the wearing of trousers by women and views on homosexuality.

- **Human rights abuse:** the use of the 'deviation from social norms' definition has allowed serious abuse of human rights to occur. According to Szasz (1962) the term 'mental illness' is a form of social control, a subjective concept that is used to label those who don't conform to the norms of society. Those seen as abnormal are labelled and discriminated against. For example, in the Soviet Union after the Second World War, political dissenters were frequently classified as mentally ill and sent to mental hospitals.

- **Value of breaking social norms:** it can also be beneficial to break social norms. Suffragette campaigners for women's votes broke many social norms and this led to positive electoral reform. Should such people really be classified as abnormal?

- **Situational and developmental norms:** deviating from social norms doesn't necessarily have any mental health consequences. On many occasions, the situation or context in which the norms are broken is important. For example, naturists do sometimes break social norms and yet they are not thought of as having mental problems. Indeed, there are some

Oscar Wilde (1854–1900), the Irish writer, was imprisoned for homosexuality in 1895

beaches where nudity is the prevalent social norm and remaining clothed may appear odd. Thus social norms change from area to area as well. Determining exactly what is the social norm in any given situation becomes more and more difficult. There are also developmental (or age) norms to consider. A temper tantrum by a 2-year-old is considered fairly normal behaviour but that would not be the case for a 42-year-old (Gross, 2005).

- **'Conforming neurotics'**: these are people who conform strictly to social norms, and this is precisely their problem. They've *such* a fear of rejection that they adhere strictly to all society's norms and worry excessively about them. Such cases aren't included within this definition.

- **Cultural differences**: social norms vary both within and across cultures. As such, it is often impossible to know when they are being broken. If a teacher turned up for work with their hair dyed green and a nose ring would that be taken as a sign of psychological abnormality? Would the same be said of an art student or rock musician?

- **Ethnocentric bias in diagnosis**: in the West, the social norms that are adopted often reflect the behaviour of the majority 'white' population. It is suggested that deviation from these norms by ethnic groups means that ethnic minorities are more likely to be over-represented in the mental illness statistics. This is supported by Cochrane (1977), who found that African-Caribbean immigrants are far more likely to be diagnosed as schizophrenic than whites or Asians. Of course, this might reflect the true incidence of schizophrenia in these groups. However, the high rate for African-Caribbean immigrants is found *only* in the UK, not in other countries. It's suggested that this reflects a cultural bias (or blindness) in diagnosis among British psychiatrists.

The 'failure to function adequately' definition

This means that a person is unable to live a normal life. Such people don't experience a 'normal' range of emotions or participate in a 'normal' range of behaviours. People's behaviour is considered abnormal if it causes great distress and torment in them, leading to dysfunction. That is, their behaviour disrupts their ability to work and/or conduct satisfying relationships with people. In effect, they cannot cope with day-to-day life.

Rosenhan and Seligman (1989) suggested that the concept of dysfunction includes:

- **personal distress** – this is a key feature of abnormality; this would include depression and anxiety disorders

- **maladaptive behaviour** – behaviour that stops individuals from attaining satisfactory goals, both socially and occupationally

- **unpredictability** – behaviour that wouldn't be expected given the particular circumstances (e.g. trying to commit suicide having failed a driving test)

- **irrationality** – behaviour that cannot be explained in a rational way

- **observer discomfort** – behaviour that causes distress or discomfort to others

- **violation of moral and ideal standards** – behaviour that doesn't fit in with society's standards.

The more of these indicators that are present, the more abnormal an individual is considered to be. This approach does recognise the *subjective experience* of the individual.

Limitations of the 'failure to function adequately' definition

● **Abnormality isn't always accompanied by dysfunction:** people with anti-social personality disorders (psychopaths) have been known to commit murders and still appear to lead a 'normal' life (e.g. Jeffrey Dahmer, Harold Shipman). Such people must surely be classified as abnormal despite not appearing to exhibit many of the features of dysfunction listed above.

Dr Harold Shipman: a serial killer while working as a GP

● **Subjective nature of Rosenhan and Seligman's components:** there are problems in defining some of Rosenhan and Seligman's components. For example, how is personal distress measured? People are likely to differ in their subjective experience. Similarly, there are people who experience inappropriate mania (unbounded joy for no good reason). Their behaviour doesn't appear to cause them distress, but would count as evidence for a psychological disorder. It would also appear to be abnormal *not* to suffer personal distress at various points during one's life – say when a close relative dies.

The 'deviation from ideal mental health' definition

This approach concentrates on defining the 'normal' characteristics people should possess. Abnormality is seen as a deviation from these ideals of mental health. Jahoda (1958) identified several criteria relating to ideal mental health. These factors are required for 'optimal living' (living life to the full).

● **Positive attitude towards oneself:** this is shown by having a fairly high self-regard (self-esteem).

● **Potential for growth and development:** this is shown by self-actualisation. Maslow

(1968) defines this as 'becoming everything that one is capable of becoming'. The more things you do, the healthier you are (psychologically).

- **Autonomy:** being able to make decisions on our own and not be dependent on other people.

- **Resistance to stress:** being able to cope with everyday anxiety-provoking situations.

- **Accurate perception of reality:** possessing an objective and realistic view of the world – for example, not being too pessimistic or optimistic. This can be summarised as 'seeing the world as it really is'.

- **Environmental mastery:** being able to meet the demands of any situation, and being flexible enough to adapt to changing life circumstances.

The further people are from these ideals, the more abnormal they are.

Limitations of the 'deviation from ideal mental health' definition

- **Over-demanding criteria:** most people don't meet all of these ideals. For example, self-actualisation is achieved by very few people. Therefore, according to this definition, most people could be classified as abnormal.

- **Subjective criteria:** many of the concepts aren't clearly defined. Measuring physical health is more of an objective science using well-established methods such as X-rays and blood tests. Diagnosing mental health is far more subjective, and relies to a large extent on patient self-reports. Some of these patients may actually be mentally ill, and so may not be particularly reliable!

- **Contextual effects:** as with some of the other definitions of abnormality, mental health criteria can be affected by context. Spitting in your Psychology lesson may be a sign of mental illness, whereas for the majority of Premiership football players it seems to be the norm while playing.

- **Changes over time:** mental health criteria also change over time. In thirteenth-century Europe, seeing visions was a sign of religious fervour, now it would most likely be seen as a sign of schizophrenia.

- **Mental health criteria vary across cultures:** many studies have found that 'abnormality' can vary across cultures (Berry *et al.*, 1992). For example, 'Koro' refers to an acute anxiety reaction whereby a man believes his penis is fatally retracting into his abdomen. This disorder is mainly reported in parts of Southeast Asia, Africa and China, and is an example of a culture-bound syndrome (CBS). It's assumed that the western concept of mental disorder is culture-free, but this may not be the case.

- **Collectivist societies:** collectivist societies that emphasise cooperation among their members would reject the importance of individual autonomy as a criterion for mental health. Nobles (1976) claimed that African people have a sense of 'we', instead of the 'me' view common in the West. Western cultures tend to be more concerned with individual attainment and goals.

Summary

It's extremely difficult to produce a culture-free definition of abnormality. What constitutes abnormal behaviour differs between cultures. This suggests that the concept of abnormality is a social construction. It's difficult enough to define abnormality *within* a culture without trying to produce one to use *between* cultures. As a result, all definitions of abnormality, diagnosis and classification of mental illness must be treated with caution.

How Science Works

Practical Learning Activity 6.1: The changing view of abnormal behaviour

Homosexuality was illegal in the UK among consenting adults up to the 1960s and was still included in the American Psychiatric Association *Diagnostic Statistical Manual* as a 'form of sexual abnormality' as recently as 1973. Indeed, the Japanese Society of Psychiatry and Neurology adopted this change only in 1993 (International Gay and Lesbian Human Rights Commission, 1995).

● Try to think of other examples where behaviour once regarded as abnormal is now considered normal. Has the behaviour changed or merely societies' attitudes to it?
● Try to find some examples of behaviours from other cultures that are considered normal but would be considered unusual in our society. Psychological 'normality' appears to be culturally defined, whereas physical 'normality' is universal.
● Which of the definitions of abnormality described above do you think is the best definition to use? Try to justify your choice.

✔ Assessment Check 6.1

1. Outline TWO attempts to define abnormality. (3 + 3 marks)
2. Give TWO limitations of the definition of abnormality in terms of 'deviation from ideal mental health'. (3 + 3 marks)
3. Describe the 'deviation from social norms' definition of abnormality. (2 marks)
4. Outline and evaluate TWO definitions of abnormality. (12 marks)
5. Alex does not wear shoes at any time during the year. He walks to and from school each day in his bare feet. Use any ONE definition of abnormality to try to explain Alex's behaviour. (3 marks)

Key features of the biological approach to psychopathology

This is the most widely used approach to the causes and treatment of mental illness in the West. It was developed by the medical profession, hence it's often referred to as the *medical model*.

The biological approach has a number of key features:

- **Similar to a disease, a physical cause:** abnormal behaviour may be compared to a disease. It's assumed that all mental illnesses have a physiological cause related to the physical structure and/or functioning of the brain. A distinction is made between 'organic' and 'functional' disorders. Organic disorders involve obvious physical brain damage and/or disease (say, a brain tumour), whereas functional disorders don't have an obvious physiological cause (e.g. depression).

- **Symptoms:** in medicine, physical illnesses have clear-cut symptoms. Doctors diagnose using well-established criteria. Psychiatrists also use diagnostic manuals for mental illness, and compare symptoms with set classifications of illnesses. There are slight differences between the *ICD 10* (*International Classification of Diseases*, 10th edn, 1992 – used in the UK) manual and *DSM IV* (*Diagnostic Statistical Manual*, 4th edn, 1994 – used in the USA). Brain scans can be used to help with diagnosis, particularly with organic disorders.

- **Genetic inheritance:** it's assumed that genes have a major effect on the likelihood of a person developing a mental illness. It's been found that people have a genetic predisposition to certain psychological disorders. Twin and family resemblance studies have shown that some mental illnesses 'run in the family'. Kendler *et al.* (1985) found that relatives of schizophrenics were 18 times more likely to develop the illness than a matched control group. More recently, Gurling *et al.* (2001) performed genetic linkage analysis in 13 large multiply affected families, to test the hypothesis that there is extensive genetic inheritance for certain types of schizophrenia. The 13 families contained multiple affected cases in three or more generations. DNA samples were taken from these families. They found strong evidence that certain chromosomes were indeed linked to schizophrenia and that these are passed on through the generations.

- **Biochemistry:** chemical imbalances in the brain may be involved in certain mental illnesses. Neurotransmitters (chemicals in the brain) play an important part in behaviour, and an excess of dopamine has been detected in the brains of schizophrenics. However, such findings involve correlations and don't prove cause and effect. For example, it might be that it's the schizophrenia itself that is causing the dopamine excess, rather than the other way round.

- **Infection:** this is a common cause of physical illness, but has also been found with some mental illnesses. Barr *et al.* (1990) found increased levels of schizophrenia among the children of mothers who had suffered from flu while they were pregnant, suggesting a possible link with the disorder.

Evaluation of the biological approach

✔ **Humane approach:** the biological approach attaches no blame to the mentally ill individual. People with a mental illness are just unlucky to develop it, in the same way that someone might catch an illness such as measles. This is a humane approach since mental illness, in practice, often invokes fear and stigma.

✔ **Effective treatments:** carefully controlled studies demonstrate the effectiveness of drugs. Possible side-effects don't outweigh the benefits. The case is less clear-cut for other biological therapies such as ECT (electro-convulsive therapy) and psychosurgery. However, patients are often pleased to have tried these 'last-ditch' treatments even if they haven't been successful (see pages 199–201).

✔ **Physiological evidence, well-established scientific principles:** the increased use of brain scans and post-mortems adds to the growing body of physiological evidence supporting the biological approach.

✔ **Reliability of diagnosis:** two reliability measures can be used. Different psychia-
✗ trists can be given the same patients to diagnose (*inter-rater reliability*) and the same patients can be assessed at different times by the same psychiatrist (*test–retest reliability*). Both types of reliability have increased since the introduction of the newest classification systems (post-1980). Pre-1980 diagnosis was not so accurate (see Key Study 6.1 below).

Key Study 6.1: 'On being sane in insane places' (Rosenhan, 1973)

Aim/hypothesis (AO1)

This study set out to test the hypothesis that psychiatrists cannot reliably distinguish between people who are mentally ill and those who aren't. In essence, Rosenhan was questioning whether the classification system used by psychiatrists to diagnose mental illness was valid. Rosenhan tested the hypothesis in two studies. One involved *pseudo-patients* trying to gain admittance to various mental hospitals while claiming to be hearing voices (auditory hallucinations). In the second experiment, Rosenhan told hospitals in a different area that he would replicate the first study and send them one or more pseudo-patients in the next three months to see if they could detect the sane from the insane (in fact, none were sent).

Method/design (AO1)

Both studies are regarded as field experiments since they took place in actual hospitals in the USA.

The first study (which is the best known and most widely reported) involved participant observation. In the first experiment the independent variable was the reported hearing of voices by the pseudo-patients and the dependent variable was the classification (mentally ill or not) by the psychiatrists of these pseudo-patients. Eight sane people sought admission to 12 separate hospitals by turning up at the admissions office complaining of hearing voices saying 'thud', 'empty' and 'hollow'. These were the only lies or inventions concerning the patients' history or circumstances used in the study. Immediately on entering the psychiatric ward, the pseudo-patients stopped simulating any symptoms of abnormality and behaved 'normally' as far as possible. Nursing reports described the pseudo-patients as 'friendly', 'cooperative' and 'exhibiting no abnormal indications'. The pseudo-patients made written notes of their experiences on the wards.

In the second study, the independent variable (IV) was the false information about the pseudo-patients reported to the psychiatrists at the hospitals, and the dependent variable (DV) was the number of patients staff suspected were pseudo-patients over the following three months.

Results (AO1)

Despite their public displays of sanity, none of the pseudo-patients was ever detected. With the exception of one, all were given a diagnosis of schizophrenia and 'schizophrenia in remission' (on discharge). The latter indicated that the label schizophrenia is very difficult to shake off even it is wrongly applied in the first place. The pseudo-patients remained in hospital for anything from 7 to 52 days (mean of 19 days), giving the psychiatrists plenty of time to assess their behaviour. Ironically, during the first three hospitalisations, 35 out of 118 genuine patients on the ward suspected the pseudo-patients were actually sane. It appeared that the mentally ill were better at diagnosing mental illness than the psychiatrists! Much of the pseudo-patients' behaviour was viewed as an indication of their mentally ill status. For example, their note-taking behaviour was seen as a behavioural manifestation of their disorder. Pacing the corridor was seen as an act of nervousness rather than the reality that the pseudo-patient was simply bored.

In the second experiment, staff at another teaching hospital were informed that one or more pseudo-patients would seek admittance over the next three months. They were asked to rate on a ten-point scale the likelihood that any patient seeking admission was a pseudo-patient. Of the 193 patients who sought admission, 41 were confidently judged to be pseudo-patients, with another 23 suspected by at least one psychiatrist. No patients were sent by Rosenhan; all the patients were genuine (on admission).

Conclusions (AO1)

Rosenhan concluded that psychiatrists cannot detect the sane from the insane, and that psychiatric diagnosis was unreliable.

Evaluation (AO1/AO2)

Reliability is usually measured by assessing diagnostic criteria between two or more psychiatrists examining the same patients. This was not the procedure used here. Spitzer (1976) has found that the diagnosis 'schizophrenia in

remission' is extremely rare in the research literature and concluded that the psychiatrists did successfully distinguish the sane from the insane, and this was reflected in their unusual diagnoses. Since Rosenhan's study, diagnostic procedures have been improved and, furthermore, psychiatrists don't expect to be deliberately misled or lied to by patients.

How Science Works

Practical Learning Activity 6.2: Detecting the sane from the insane

- Outline all the ethical considerations involved in Rosenhan's study.
- It seems doctors are more inclined to call a healthy person sick (a false positive – an example of a type two error) than to call a sick person healthy (a false negative – an example of a type one error). Explain why this might be.
- If you were one of the psychiatrists criticised in this study, what arguments would you put forward to defend yourself?
- Can we draw any firm conclusions from this study?

Evaluation of the biological approach (continued)

✔✘ **Validity of diagnosis:** this refers to whether the diagnosis is measuring what it's supposed to be measuring (i.e. is there an actual underlying illness called schizophrenia?). Research shows that diagnosis is valid for the general categories of mental disorder, but not for the sub-categories of disorders. However, the same could be said of physical illness diagnosis, which isn't always accurate.

✘ **Reductionist approach:** the biological approach reduces the diagnosis of mental illness to lists of physical symptoms. Greater emphasis should be placed on a patient's personal feelings and experiences.

✘ **Animal studies:** many biological experiments have been carried out using animals. Ethical and methodological issues arise here. Is it reasonable to exploit animals for the (possible) benefit of humans (so-called 'speciesism')? In addition, researchers cannot be certain that animals that display abnormal behaviours are experiencing a mental disorder in the same way that humans do.

✘ **Responsibility denied:** people aren't held responsible for their actions or their treatment. They become 'patients'. Responsibility for the therapy is 'passed over' to the 'great expert' (the psychiatrist). Therapy works best when people take more responsibility for their treatments and behaviour.

✘ **Relies on self-report, not objective tests:** unlike doctors, psychiatrists have few objective tests for mental illnesses. Instead, they rely on patient self-reports. This has led to cases where people have pretended to be mentally ill, which challenges the accuracy of mental illness diagnosis (see Key Study 6.1 above).

✔✘ **Treats symptoms, not causes:** physiological treatments alleviate the symptoms, but don't treat the root cause. Symptoms recur when physiological treatments stop. This leads many patients to be re-admitted to hospitals – the so-called 'revolving door' syndrome. However, if the main symptom of depression is the feeling of depression and drugs stop this, then perhaps the biological approach has succeeded. Indeed, the original cause of the depression may not be worth pursuing, since the main problem (feeling of depression) no longer exists. The root cause may also be impossible to detect.

✗ **Cause-and-effect problem:** it's not clear whether some physiological abnormalities are the cause of the illness or one of its effects. For example, does excess dopamine in the brain cause schizophrenia, or is it merely the effect?

✗ **Culture-bound syndromes:** not all mental illnesses are universal. Those that occur only in particular cultures are called 'culture-bound syndromes' (as explained above). Such syndromes aren't easily explained by the biological model.

✗ **The myth of mental illness:** Szasz (1962) was a leading member of the so-called anti-psychiatry movement. He believed that since the mind doesn't exist as a physical organ, it can't be diseased. Abnormal behaviours are thus viewed as 'problems in living'. Szasz believed that diagnosis of mental illness is used as a form of 'social control'. Laing (1959) also controversially viewed mental illness as a sane response to an insane world.

✗ **Labelling and stigma:** the biological approach tends to lead to the labelling of patients. Labels are definitions that, when applied to people, identify what they are. Mental illness terms often identify the whole person ('schizophrenic' rather than 'a person with schizophrenia'). This doesn't occur to the same extent with physical illnesses. Labelling may lead to a *self-fulfilling prophecy*, whereby a person identified as mentally ill *actually* becomes mentally ill. Once labelling has occurred, stigma can result. Stigma means a 'mark' that sets people apart on the basis of an undesirable characteristic. The mentally ill often suffer from such stigma.

Psychological approaches to psychopathology
Key features of the psychodynamic approach to psychopathology

The psychodynamic approach explains the forces or dynamics that determine behaviour. The best-known example of this was proposed by Sigmund Freud. Although subsequently developed by others, there are some commonly agreed key assumptions, as listed below.

● **Mental illness is psychological in origin:** the psychodynamic approach suggests that abnormality occurs as a result of psychological, not physical, problems (in contrast to the biological approach).

● **The importance of the unconscious:** although, by definition, the unconscious isn't accessible to the conscious mind, it plays a major role in determining behaviour. The term 'dynamic unconscious' is used to explain why people don't know the reasons for their behaviour. There's an assumption that abnormal behaviours occur due to unconscious problems or forces.

● **Three components to the personality – id, ego superego:** Freud stated that there are three components to the personality or psyche. The *id* is present at birth. This represents a person's instinctual, basic drives related to sex and aggression. Later, people are socialised into the moral standards of their culture and develop a *superego*. This represents their conscience. These two parts of the personality are in conflict and therefore need to be managed by the third part of the personality: the ego. When this balance isn't achieved, abnormal behaviour may result. For example, anxiety disorders may result

from an over-developed superego (conscience). Since these processes occur at an unconscious level, people aren't aware of them.

- **Importance of childhood experiences:** Freud argued that childhood experiences play a crucial part in adult development. Particularly distressing events in childhood may also become part of the unconscious. Although unconscious, they may be expressed in later abnormal behaviours.

- **Psychosexual developmental stages:** Freud argued that children pass through a number of psychosexual stages. Conflicts that occur during these stages can affect later behaviour. The stages are as follows.

  (a) **Oral stage (0–1 year):** the primary source of pleasure is the mouth and sucking.

  (b) **Anal stage (1–3 years):** the primary source of pleasure involves the membranes of the anal region.

  (c) **Phallic stage (3–6 years):** the primary source of pleasure comes from the genitals.

  (d) **Latency stage: (6–12 years):** the development of other activities means less concentration on sexual areas.

  (e) **Genital stage (puberty onwards):** the primary source of pleasure is through heterosexual relationships.

Freud believed that people can become stuck or 'fixated' at any of these stages. This will also affect later behaviour. For example, someone who smokes is described as having an 'oral' personality, since they gain pleasure through the mouth. Someone who is excessively tidy and obsessive might be described as having an 'anal' personality.

- **Defence mechanisms:** childhood conflicts cause anxiety, and the ego uses a number of defence mechanisms to keep these thoughts in the unconscious. *Repression* is the major defence mechanism, whereby traumatic events are forced into the unconscious. Defence mechanisms help to reduce anxiety, but don't resolve deep psychological problems.

Evaluation of the psychodynamic approach

✔ **Psychological factors:** Freud was the first to stress the importance of psychological factors causing abnormal behaviour. He argued that psychological problems can result in physical symptoms – an accepted viewpoint today. However, physiological factors are largely ignored.

✔ **Importance of childhood:** most psychologists would accept that childhood is an important, influential factor in future adult development. Indeed, many people suffering from psychological problems can recount childhood difficulties.

✗ However, the original model over-emphasised childhood influences and ignored the everyday problems faced by the adult patients. Current, psychodynamic therapy recognises this.

✔ **Importance of the unconscious:** many people would agree that unconscious processes do have an effect on human behaviour.

✔ **Influential theory:** Freud remains the best-known psychologist of all time and psychoanalysis the most influential theory. His ideas appear strange to some, while others pay for therapy based on them. Freud's ideas have found expression in many other domains, including art, film, literature, and so on. Surely an unimportant theory would have been dismissed years ago. In addition, Freudian terminology has been adopted into everyday language and conversation.

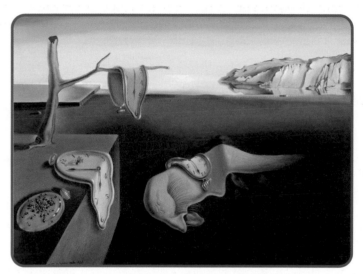

'The Persistence of Memory', 1931, by Salvador Dali. Dali was deeply influenced by Freud's ideas on the unconscious and dreams

✗ **Problems validating the theory:** it's impossible to scientifically test some of the psychodynamic model. The subtlety and complexity of the theory means it's not suited to empirical research. The strength of the evidence remains variable (Andrews and Brewin, 2000). Sometimes, interpretation plays a major part in the theory. For example, if a patient 'uncovers' painful childhood memories this can be taken as a cause of any later abnormal behaviour. If they don't uncover or recall anything, it can be claimed that the childhood trauma still happened but that it remains hidden in their unconscious. Both interpretations can be used to support the model!

✗ **Poor methodology:** the dominant use of case studies in psychodynamic therapy is unscientific (see pages 78–79). Evidence produced by therapists is subjective and biased. Indeed, Freud was accused by his own patients of exaggerating the effectiveness of his therapy. Freud's patients were mainly middle-class Viennese women. Whether findings from such a sample can be generalised into a universal theory is open to question.

✗ **Over-emphasis on sexual factors:** Freud believed that sexual factors were a major cause of abnormal behaviour. Nowadays, other factors, such as social relationships, are recognised as important. Indeed, it's argued that inadequate interpersonal relationships can also cause sexual problems. Freud's ideas on sexual repression may be less relevant in today's sexually permissive society.

✗ **Blames parents:** since people cannot really influence their own personality, it's assumed that they aren't to blame for their illness. However, given the importance of childhood conflicts, parents might feel to blame for any subsequent abnormal behaviour in their children. The individual is seen as the result of his/her parenting. Child abuse cases are cited as evidence to support this, although so-called 'recovered memory syndrome' has been questioned.

189

Key features of the behavioural approach to psychopathology

The behavioural model concentrates on observable behaviour, not on physical or psychological processes. It's associated with maladaptive behaviour, not mental illness.

- **All behaviour is learnt:** all behaviour (both normal and abnormal) is learnt through the processes of classical and operant conditioning.

  (a) *Classical conditioning* is 'learning through association'. It was first proposed by Ivan Pavlov, who noticed that his laboratory dogs had learnt to salivate to the sound of the footsteps of the man who fed them. They'd learnt to associate the footsteps with food. Later, Pavlov classically conditioned the dogs to salivate to the sound of a bell that he rang before giving them their food.

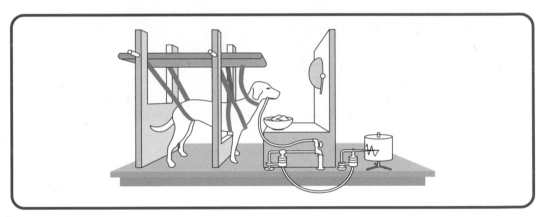

Figure 6.1: The apparatus used by Pavlov in his experiments on conditioned reflexes

  (b) *Classical conditioning* can help explain abnormal behaviour. For example, a phobia may develop when children see the fear of their parents when confronted by a spider. They learn to associate the fear with the spider.

Arachnophobia can be treated successfully using systematic desensitisation (see page 205)

Key Study 6.2: The case of Little Albert (Watson and Rayner, 1920)

Aim/hypothesis (AO1)

J.B. Watson was the founder of behaviourism and believed that even the complex range of human emotions (CERs or conditioned emotional responses) are learnt as a result of environmental experiences. The aim was to provide a convincing empirical demonstration of how CERs are acquired.

Method/design (AO1)

Watson and Rayner used a laboratory study with a single participant. The participant was an 11-month-old boy known as Albert B., who was 'unemotional' and living in the hospital in which Watson worked. Albert B. was presented with various stimuli, such as a white rat, rabbit, cotton wool, and so on. His responses were recorded. At this stage, he showed no fear reaction to any of the stimuli. Next came the learning part. Watson developed a technique to try to develop a fear reaction in Albert. On presentation of the white rat, Watson would strike a hammer on a four-foot steel bar suspended just behind Albert and out of his view. Albert immediately showed distress at this unexpected sound and started to cry. Variations of these conditioning techniques continued over the next three months. Watson and Rayner kept detailed recordings using a diary method of investigation.

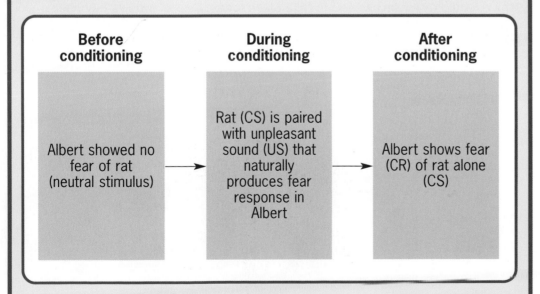

Figure 6.2: The classical conditioning of Little Albert

Results (AO1)

After repeated pairings, Albert showed a fear response to the sight of the stimulus alone. He had developed a conditioned emotional response towards the white rat. Albert also displayed a CER to other similar animals and these CERs persisted at a slightly lower intensity for over one month.

Conclusions (AO1)

Watson and Rayner concluded that conditioned emotional responses (including love, fear and phobias) are acquired as a direct result of environmental experiences and these can transfer and persist for at least one month, but possibly indefinitely unless removed by counter-conditioning.

Evaluation (AO1/AO2)

There is some dispute as to the extent of the fear response that Albert actually exhibited. It is mentioned in the original paper that Albert's fear reactions were 'slight'. Indeed, the entire study has been subject to so many discrepancies that it has acquired mythical status. Even Watson himself subsequently (mis)reported details of the original study (Watson and Watson, 1921). Given this lack of academic rigour it is difficult to draw firm conclusions from the study. The 'Little Albert' study could not be replicated and thus the findings could not be checked. It is also impossible to conclude that the fear reaction would have persisted indefinitely in Albert.

Serious ethical issues lie at the heart of this study. There is no doubt that this study would never be allowed to take place today. One of today's key ethical rules – namely, the protection of the participant from psychological and physical harm – was broken. Albert appeared to suffer a great deal of stress in the study

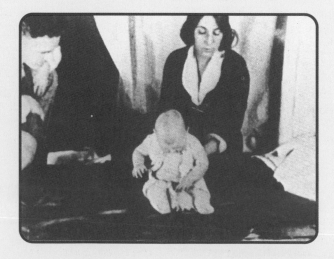

A very rare photograph of John Watson and Rosalie Rayner during the conditioning of Little Albert

and he left the hospital before Watson and Rayner had a chance to remove or recondition his fear responses.

- Using your knowledge of conditioning, suggest ways that Watson and Rayner might have reconditioned Little Albert.
- Explain why this study is criticised for having low external validity (see page 90).
- Consider other ethical issues associated with this study.

(c) *Operant conditioning* is 'learning through the consequences of behaviour'. If a behaviour is rewarded (reinforced) then it will be maintained or will increase. If it is punished, then it will cease. Skinner investigated operant conditioning using rats and pigeons in a laboratory. Again, operant conditioning can help explain abnormal behaviour. For example, adolescents who are criticised or ridiculed (punished) for being fat, may stop eating to reduce their weight and develop an eating disorder.

- **Abnormal behaviour can be unlearnt using the same learning (conditioning) principles:** the case of Little Albert demonstrates how a phobia can be acquired through classical conditioning. Watson and Rayner proposed to rid Little Albert of his fears through counter-conditioning. They planned to do this by pairing a pleasurable stimulus or reward (e.g. a sweet) with the sight of the rat. Unfortunately, they didn't get the chance to do this as Albert was withdrawn from the study.

Evaluation of the behavioural approach

✔ **Experimentally tested:** the principles of learning have been, and continue to be, tested empirically in a laboratory. The focus on observable behaviour means that it can be objectively measured.

✔ **Present, not past:** the behavioural approach concentrates on the 'here and now' rather than delving into the past. This is advantageous since many people don't know the past causes of their abnormal behaviour and it is more important to sort out present symptoms. But it's important to try to uncover the causes, otherwise the abnormal behaviour may reappear.

✔ **Effective treatments:** behavioural treatments are effective for certain disorders, such as obsessive-compulsive disorders and phobias. They are less effective for more serious disorders, such as schizophrenia.

✔ **Accounts for cultural differences:** the behavioural model recognises the importance of the environment in shaping behaviour. Thus, it does take into account cultural differences.

✗ **Simple, mechanistic model:** the behavioural approach suggests that humans are simple mechanisms at the mercy of environmental stimuli. The approach ignores people's complex thought processes. This is a reductionist, dehumanising approach.

✗ **Animal studies:** the principles of learning have been tested mainly on animals and such findings may not be totally applicable to more complex human behaviour.

193

✗ **Ethical treatment?** Some behavioural treatments are used without the consent of patients. In addition, certain treatments use punishments to change behaviour, and these can cause pain or discomfort to patients. Behaviourists would agree that this is undesirable, but necessary. Behavioural techniques can be used as a form of 'social control' to manipulate people's behaviour (see pages 204–208).

How Science Works

Practical Learning Activity 6.3: Explain that behaviour

1 Sunil is afraid of flying.
2 Samantha can't stand cabbage.
3 Phillip dislikes public speaking.
4 Helen is a chocaholic and eats ten bars of chocolate a day.

- Using your knowledge of the behavioural approach to abnormality, suggest how each of these people might have acquired their fears/behaviours.
- Read the section on behavioural therapy below (pages 204–208) and suggest ways in which their fears/behaviours might be overcome.

Key features of the cognitive approach to psychopathology

Inevitably, the cognitive (often called the cognitive behavioural) approach concentrates on the individual's thought processes and their behaviour. The disturbed individual's behaviour is affected by disturbed thoughts. This approach sees the individual as an active processor of information. It's the way individuals perceive, anticipate and evaluate events, rather than the events themselves, that have the greatest impact on behaviour. The psychologists most associated with this approach are Aaron Beck and Albert Ellis.

- **Cognitions affect behaviour:** behaviour is primarily affected by an individual's thoughts and cognitions. Healthy cognitions lead to normal behaviour, whereas faulty cognitions lead to abnormal behaviour. Beck (1967a) called these irrational thoughts 'cognitive errors'.

- **'Cognitive errors':** individuals try to make sense of their world through cognitive processes. *Automatic thoughts* are the assumptions people make about the world (i.e. their schemas). People with psychological problems tend to have more negative automatic thoughts. *Attributions* refer to people's attempts to make sense of and explain their own and others' behaviour. People with psychological problems may make more inaccurate attributions – for example, they may attribute a failed relationship to their own lack of social skill. In addition, people suffering from psychological problems may have inaccurate *expectations*. For example, they may *expect* their relationships to end in failure. Such expectations will make this more likely to happen in reality – a *self-fulfilling prophecy*. In effect, people with psychological problems may lack confidence in their own ability to achieve the goals they want to in life. These illogical thoughts may not reflect reality. Nevertheless, these negative thoughts will adversely affect their behaviour.

- **Cognitive processes can be faulty in many ways.** These include the following.

  (a) *Over-generalisation*: a conclusion is reached on the basis of one event or incident. For example, failing a class test means you are completely useless in life.

  (b) *Magnification and minimisation*: this involves magnifying failures and minimising successes – the glass is half-empty rather than half-full.

- **Cognitions can be monitored and altered:** it's assumed that all biased cognitions can be replaced by more appropriate ones (see the section on 'cognitive behavioural therapy', below).

- **Cognitive change will lead to behaviour change:** it is assumed that changing faulty thinking will lead to a change in behaviour.

Evaluation of the cognitive approach

✔ **Concentrates on current cognitions:** the cognitive model doesn't delve into the past to try to sort out problems. It concentrates on the individual's current thought processes.

✔ **Research evidence:** many people suffering from anxiety disorders and/or depression do appear to report irrational thought processes.

✔ **Influential and popular model:** currently, the cognitive approach seems to be favoured in many fields of psychology. This is also true of the cognitive approach to abnormality, and many cognitive therapists practise within the NHS.

✔ **Empowers the individual:** the individual is given responsibility to change her/his cognitions. As such, it presents a positive view of mankind.

✘ **Underplays physiological and environmental influences:** evidence suggests that physiological factors and past events can affect an individual's behaviour. These social aspects are largely ignored with this approach. This (over)emphasis on cognitive processes has led to criticisms that the cognitive model is reductionist and mechanistic.

✘ **Unscientific:** since thoughts cannot be observed or measured, it's been claimed that the cognitive approach is unscientific.

✘ **Cause and effect problem?** It's uncertain whether irrational beliefs cause the anxiety disorder/depression, or whether they are merely a by-product (effect) of the disorder.

✘ **Individual blame:** since disorders result from an individual's faulty thinking, it's clear that any blame for a disorder rests with the individual. This can have the unfortunate side-effect of making the disorder worse. It might also be unfair, since factors beyond the individual's control might be seen as contributing to their mental disorder.

✘ **Is thinking irrational?** There are two associated problems with questioning someone's thought processes. First, given the state of some people's lives, is their thinking so irrational? Depression may be a rational response to one's (miserable) life. It's been claimed that many depressives have a more realistic view of life than 'normal' people. Viewing the world through rose-coloured spectacles might be equally irrational yet psychologically healthy! Second, should a therapist argue that someone is thinking irrationally when their life circumstances appear to support that pessimistic view?

Assessment Check 6.2

1. Outline TWO key features of the biological approach to psychopathology. (3 + 3 marks)
2. Outline key features of the psychodynamic approach to psychopathology. (6 marks)
3. Explain ONE way in which the behavioural approach differs from the cognitive approach. (3 marks).
4. Evaluate the cognitive approach to psychopathology. (6 marks)

Treating abnormality

Biological therapies, including drugs and ECT

Biological (or somatic) therapies ('soma' means 'body' in Greek) derive from the biological model of abnormality. This assumes that altering bodily functioning will be effective in treating certain abnormal behaviours. The two main biological treatments are drug therapy (chemotherapy) and ECT (electroconvulsive shock treatment).

Drug therapy

Approximately 25 per cent of all drugs prescribed by the NHS are for mental health problems. In 1992/1993, spending on psychiatric drugs was £159 million, or 5.2 per cent of the NHS drugs budget. Psychiatric drugs modify the working of the brain, and affect mood and behaviour (Mind, 2007). People suffering from mental disorders are frequently prescribed more than one drug.

Drugs work by entering the bloodstream in order to reach the brain. The amount of drug absorbed by the brain depends on the extent to which the drug gets absorbed, excreted or converted into inactive substances. When consumed orally, drugs are absorbed by the gut and pass into the liver, which breaks down much of the drug. Drugs that are injected into the bloodstream bypass the liver, hence smaller amounts are needed than with oral doses. Slow-acting injections are the exception to this, where release of an appropriate drug can occur over a month or so. Because different people's bodies work in slightly different ways, different doses may be required depending on the individual.

Drugs affect transmission of chemicals in the nervous system. Some neural transmission occurs when chemicals cross the gaps between nerves. This is called 'synaptic transmission'. These chemicals are called *neurotransmitters* and have a variety of effects on behaviour. The main neurotransmitters are dopamine, serotonin, acetylcholine, noradrenaline and GABA. Basically, drugs work by either increasing or decreasing the availability of these neurotransmitters and hence modify their effects on behaviour. A drug that blocks the effects of a given neurotransmitter is called an *antagonist* (meaning enemy). A drug that mimics or increases the effects of a neurotransmitter is called an *agonist*.

Drugs can exert their effects in numerous ways, by:

• facilitating or inhibiting production of a neurotransmitter

• increasing or decreasing the release of a neurotransmitter, or

• altering what happens to it after it attaches to the receptor.

Specification Hint

There are a number of different drug types and they have slightly different strengths and weaknesses. However, since specific drug types are not mentioned in the Specification the examiners cannot ask you about them specifically. You need to know about drug use and be able to evaluate drugs in general for the treatment of mental disorder.

Obviously, there are different drugs available for different mental disorders. *Anti-psychotic* or *neuroleptic* drugs (*major tranquillisers*) are used to treat schizophrenia, the manic phase of manic depression, and other psychotic symptoms. They work by lowering dopamine activity in the brain. *Anxiolytics* or *anti-anxiety drugs* (*minor tranquillisers*) are among the most widely prescribed. They're given for anxiety or stress-related symptoms, and occasionally for short-term management of phobias. Unsurprisingly, *antidepressant* drugs are used to relieve persistent low moods and other symptoms of depression. *Anti-manic*, or mood-stabilising, drugs are used to control moods. They're used to treat bipolar affective disorder (manic depression) and severe depression. *Stimulants* are used to improve mood, alertness and confidence.

Evaluation of drug therapy

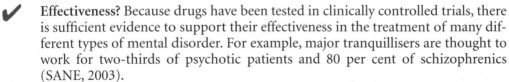

Effectiveness? Because drugs have been tested in clinically controlled trials, there is sufficient evidence to support their effectiveness in the treatment of many different types of mental disorder. For example, major tranquillisers are thought to work for two-thirds of psychotic patients and 80 per cent of schizophrenics (SANE, 2003).

Not cures: it is often claimed that, although drugs help to reduce the symptoms in carefully controlled trials, they don't cure the illness. Nevertheless, symptom reduction can significantly improve many people's lives. Indeed, in the case of depression, a temporary alleviation of depression through the use of drugs can lead to a cure. Provided that the choice of drug is appropriate, about 75 per cent of patients 'remain free from depression for long periods of their lifetime' (SANE, 2003).

Side-effects: the continued use of drugs can lead to side-effects. For example, the older tranquillisers (e.g. phenothiazines) often cause movement disorders (extra-pyramidal symptoms) such as tremors, slowing of body and facial features, and abnormal body movements. Newer anti-psychotic drugs (e.g. dibenzazepines) seem to be even more effective and have fewer side-effects. The

197

reason for these side-effects is that drugs are blunt instruments and interfere with brain mechanisms other than those causing the mental disorder. Some minor tranquillisers can be very addictive and it is essential to monitor patients' tolerance and dependence on the drug. Some of the drugs are poisonous and an overdose can lead to death. Side-effects of other drugs can involve nausea, diarrhoea, headaches and sleeping difficulties.

✔ **Tolerance to side-effects:** most patients develop a tolerance to side-effects during their treatment, and the risks can be minimised by a short period when the patient takes a very low dose of the drug.

✗ **Delayed effects:** with antidepressants, side-effects can occur immediately after taking the drug, but the relief of symptoms often only becomes apparent after two to four weeks. Some patients thus stop taking a drug before it has started to work. It's unclear why this effect is delayed, since the effect on the neurotransmitters is immediate.

✗ **Agents of social control?** It has been claimed that some drugs (e.g. major tranquillisers) have been over-used to control patients, particularly in institutionalised settings such as care homes. Their use in such circumstances has been compared to the use of straitjackets in the past. Indeed, they have been called 'pharmacological straitjackets' or 'chemical lobotomies'.

The placebo effect

A *placebo* is an inactive treatment (e.g. sugar pill) that nevertheless appears to produce some improvement in patients. The *placebo effect* refers to treatment responses in a placebo group compared to the responses of those patients taking an active treatment (e.g. an active drug). The effects on the active treatment group are then compared to those on the control group taking the placebo.

It's not unusual for a placebo effect to be found in 50 per cent of patients in any medical study (Schatzberg and Nemeroff, 1999). Obviously, the active treatment has to improve patients by a statistically significant level compared to the placebo control group.

It's unclear how placebos work but it's thought that factors such as patient expectations and attitudes, and patients' production of their own painkillers (*endorphins*) may play a part in the placebo effect.

GPs aren't allowed to use placebos other than in clinical trials where patients have given their informed consent. Of course, patients in such trials don't know which condition or group they're in (active treatment or control group).

A controversial analysis of 19 double blind (see page 95) clinical drug trials involving 2318 depressed patients concluded that there was a 0.9 correlation between placebo effect and drug effect (see Figure 6.3). Kirsch and Sapirstein (1998) found that the inactive placebos produced improvement that was 75 per cent of the effect of the active drug. Furthermore, the authors concluded that approximately one-quarter of the drug response is due to the administration of an active medication, one half is a placebo effect, and the remaining quarter is due to other non-specific factors.

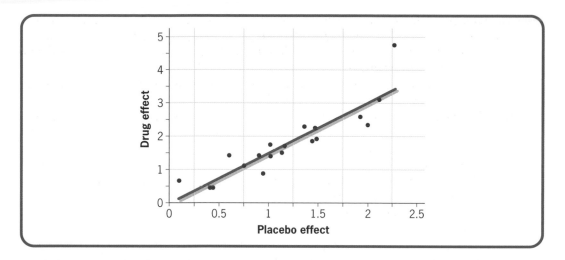

Figure 6.3: The placebo response as a predictor of the drug response

Electroconvulsive therapy (ECT)

ECT is a medical treatment used with drug-resistant depressive disorders. It tends to be used when drugs and psychotherapy have failed or cannot be tolerated. Approximately 22,000 people receive ECT in the UK every year.

A course of treatment with ECT usually consists of about 6–12 treatments given several times per week. Nowadays, the patient is given a general anaesthetic and a muscle relaxant that ensures s/he doesn't convulse or feel pain (despite Hollywood's continual portrayal of this). The patient's brain is then stimulated using electrodes placed on their head, with a brief controlled series of electrical pulses. This 110 mv stimulus causes a seizure within the brain that lasts about a minute. After 5–10 minutes, the patient will regain consciousness (APA, 2003).

ECT has changed considerably since its portrayal in the Oscar-winning film One Flew Over the Cuckoo's Nest

There are two types of ECT. *Unilateral ECT* occurs when only one side of the head is stimulated (the non-dominant hemisphere – the right hemisphere for right-handed people). *Bilateral ECT* involves stimulation on both sides. There are continuing arguments about the mechanism underlying the effectiveness of ECT. It's suggested that ECT induces changes in various neurotransmitters including an increased sensitivity to serotonin in the hypothalamus, and an increase in the release of GABA, noradrenaline and dopamine (Sasa, 1999).

Evaluation of ECT

 Effectiveness? ECT can have an immediate beneficial effect. Some patients swear by its effectiveness and others swear at its continued use! Weiner and Coffey (1988) report that ECT produces a substantial improvement in at least 80 per cent of depressed patients, and Sackheim *et al.* (1990) have found this for patients with medically resistant depression. In terms of electrical dosage and placement of the electrodes, it appears that suprathreshold doses (2.5 times the electricity needed to produce a seizure) and bilateral ECT are more effective than low-dose, unilateral ECT (see Figure 6.4) (Sackheim *et al.*, 1993).

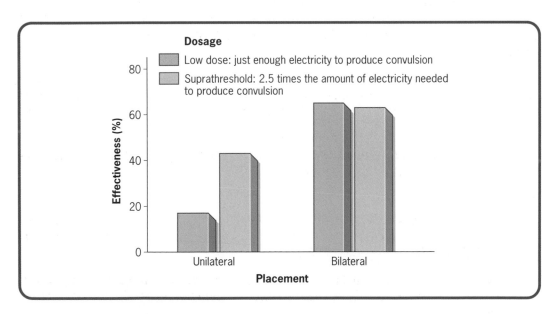

Figure 6.4: Effectiveness rates based on electrode placement and electricity amount (Sackheim et al., 1993)

 Effectiveness? However, a study has shown that despite the fact that ECT should be used only after other treatments have failed, as many as 18 per cent of people had been offered no other treatment. Also 78.5 per cent of the people that took part in the study said that they would never have ECT again (UKAN, 1995).

 Effectiveness? Geddes and the UK ECT Review Group (2003) reviewed 73 studies using depressed patients and compared ECT to placebo ECT and drug therapy. They showed there was a significant benefit of ECT over the placebo and

✗   drug treatments. However, there was a slightly increased risk of cognitive impairment in ECT patients, usually involving temporary amnesia.

✔   **Side-effects?** Some researchers have found no evidence that ECT damages the brain (Weiner, 1984). It's argued that people can have many epileptic seizures and these don't consistently harm the brain. Indeed, ECT-induced seizures take place under far more controlled conditions than epilepsy. Coffey *et al.* (1991), using MRI brain scans, could find no evidence for ECT brain damage.

✗   **Method of social control?** It's generally agreed that ECT has a troubled history and may have been used in the past to control awkward or troublesome patients. The far stricter guidelines in place today suggest that this is now unlikely to occur.

Psychological therapies

Psychoanalysis

Psychoanalysis is derived specifically from Freud's ideas, although most psychoanalytic therapists don't practise the therapy in exactly the same way that he did. We've already covered some of the key principles of psychoanalytic theory (see pages 187–189). You'll recall that psychoanalysis places an importance on childhood and repressed impulses and conflicts.

The goal of psychoanalytic therapy is to try to bring these repressed feelings into conscious awareness ('to make the unconscious conscious') where the patient (called an *analysand*) can deal with them. Through gaining 'insight' (see page 203) in this way, the analysand can work through any buried feelings they have.

There are a number of techniques used by psychoanalytic therapists to help the analysand recover repressed conflicts. Some of these are described below.

Free association

Free association involves an analysand lying on the couch and talking about whatever comes to mind, regardless of whether it makes any sense, relates to an earlier point or is related to their problems. (See Box 6.1 below.)

The analysand can say absolutely anything, regardless of whether it appears unimportant, embarrassing, shameful or dirty. The therapist usually doesn't react at all, and certainly not in a negative way.

The analysand is relieved of any responsibility for what s/he says. It's assumed that, using this technique, the internal 'censor' of the unconscious will relax so unconscious material can emerge, at least symbolically.

> ## Box 6.1: Example of an instruction given to an analysand during free association (Ford and Urban, 1963)
>
> *As you talk, various thoughts will occur to you which you like to ignore because of certain criticisms and objections. You'll be tempted to think, 'That is irrelevant or unimportant or nonsensical', and to avoid saying it. Do not give in to such criticism. Report such thoughts in spite of your wish not to do so. Later, the reason for this will become clear. Report whatever goes through your mind. Pretend that you are a traveller, describing to someone beside you the changing views which you see inside the train window.*

The analysand's collection of thoughts provides the analyst with clues to help understand their unconscious conflicts. Another related technique, **word association**, involves single words being presented to the analysand, who has to respond as quickly as possible with the first word that comes to mind. Words thought to be emotionally significant to the analysand are included among common words. The significance of the response is judged subjectively. In addition, some significance is attached to how long it takes the analysand to respond. A long delay in responding suggests that *resistance* or a censoring of thoughts is occurring (see below).

Dream analysis

Freud believed dreams were 'the royal road into the unconscious' that influences so much of our lives. Freud believed that, during sleep, the ego defences are lowered, allowing repressed material to surface in a disguised, symbolic form. It's disguised in order to stop unacceptable thoughts from waking us up (e.g. dreaming of a lollipop rather than a penis).

Anxieties and concerns are 'hidden' (the **latent content**) in dreams, whereas the **manifest content** is what is immediately apparent in the dream (what we can recall). The analyst guides the analysand in recalling and analysing their dreams, the goal being to reveal the latent content. For example, a dream of a collapsing bridge (manifest content) might symbolise the analysand's anxiety about their marriage (latent content).

There are a number of therapeutic stages that occur during free association and/or dream analysis, as follows:

- **Resistance** involves anything that prevents the progress of the therapy. Resistance can be either conscious (e.g. deliberately changing the subject or arriving late) or unconscious. Any resistance noted by the analyst can provide further clues as to the unconscious conflict experienced by the analysand.

- **Transference** involves the analysand transferring attitudes from the past towards the therapist. Analysands respond to the analyst as though they were one of the important people in their past. Freud believed that transference is a vital technique for explaining to analysands the childhood origin of some of their anxieties and fears. The analysand must work through the transference process if success is to be achieved. Analysts encourage transference by remaining in the background as much as possible and revealing little about their own lives and views.

- **Interpretation** is another technique used in psychoanalysis. This is where the analyst points out and interprets the hidden meanings in what the analysand says and does. The analyst should offer interpretations that the analysand is on the verge of making – they can't be forced on analysands. The analyst may point out what certain reported memories, events or dreams really mean. Interpretation should help the analysand to re-examine how their present-day behaviour may have evolved from conflicts originating in their childhood. An analysand may show resistance or denial of an interpretation. The analyst may point out why the analysand resists or denies the interpretation and sometimes the denial is taken as further evidence that the interpretation is correct. An analysand's 'no' may actually be a 'yes'.

- **Insight** occurs when the analysand gains self-knowledge and understanding of the nature and origin of their neuroses. The analysand understands how the unconscious conflicts they've faced relate to their present-day problems. This can take a considerable time and develop very gradually.

Evaluation of psychoanalysis

✗ **Difficulties of measuring effectiveness?** There's no agreed way of measuring the effectiveness of psychoanalysis. Some studies use analysand self-report, others rely on the analyst to judge the treatment outcome. This is likely to lead to either demand characteristics or a *self-serving bias* (the analysand exaggerates the success of their treatment). Allied to this problem of measuring outcomes, there are problems of lack of standardised diagnoses and a lack of control over sampling procedures. In addition, it's been claimed that the success of psychoanalysis sometimes becomes apparent only some years after the treatment has ended!

✔ **Appropriateness?** It is suggested that neurotic analysands (e.g. those with anxiety disorders) are helped more by psychoanalysis than psychotic analysands (e.g. those with severe disorders such as schizophrenia). Even Freud maintained that psychoanalysis wouldn't work with schizophrenics, because such analysands ignore their therapist's insights and are resistant to treatment (Dolnick, 1998). If one accepts some biological cause to certain mental disorders such as schizophrenia, then it might be considered ridiculous to think that a 'talking cure' can have any effect. Would you treat a broken leg or diabetes with 'talk' therapy or by interpreting the analysand's dreams? It's also believed that psychoanalysis favours the YAVIS (Young, Attractive, Verbal, Intelligent, Successful) person. Luborsky *et al.* (1993) conclude that psychoanalytic treatment tools are limited by the analysand's capacity to use them.

✗ **Scientific status?** Psychoanalysis is based on Freudian theory and this has been criticised for its lack of scientific evidence (see page 189). The methods of free association and dream analysis are incapable of being scientifically tested and are based on subjective speculation on the part of the analyst.

✗ **Practicalities?** Psychoanalysis tends to be costly, time-consuming (several sessions per week) and lengthy (often taking a number of years).

✗ **Studies of effectiveness?** One of the most frequently cited studies of the effectiveness of psychoanalysis was that published by Eysenck (1952). Eysenck included patients who'd dropped out of therapy prior to completion and judged the 'success' level at 39 per cent. However, Bergin (1971) didn't include such patients and arrived at a 91 per cent success rate. This highlights how data can be viewed in different ways to obtain various measures of 'success rates' (see Figure 6.5).

Eysenck even went on to claim that 'spontaneous remission rates' (people who improve over time without undergoing any treatment) are better than those who undergo psychoanalysis. He stated: 'the more the psychotherapy, the smaller the recovery rate'.

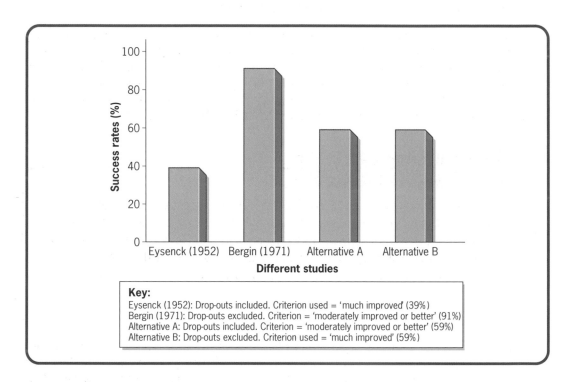

Figure 6.5: Different ways of interpreting the success rates of psychotherapy

A more recent review showed that, at the end of psychotherapy, the 'average' patient is better off than 80 per cent of untreated patients (Lambert and Bergin, 1994) and that this beneficial effect is such an effective treatment that it would be unethical to withhold it from patients (Ursano and Silberman, (1994). There are many associated benefits of psychoanalytic therapy. Dossman *et al*. (1997) found, in a study of 666 patients, that therapy decreased medical visits by 30 per cent, lost work days by 40 per cent and days in hospital by 66 per cent.

Behavioural therapies

The aim of behavioural therapy is to change maladaptive behaviour by replacing it with appropriate learnt behaviour. Behavioural therapy was defined by Wolpe (1958) as:

the use of experimentally established laws of learning for the purposes of changing unadaptive behaviour.

According to behaviourist theory, abnormal behaviours can be measured objectively and therapies can be planned to modify them using conditioning principles. They fit into two types:

1 behaviour therapy based on classical conditioning principles

2 behaviour modification based on operant conditioning principles.

Behaviourists seek to treat the symptoms, not the causes, of abnormal behaviour. They believe that the symptoms are the problem and that searching for the causes is likely to be fruitless. After all, if you can alleviate the symptoms of depression, what does it matter what the underlying causes are? Critics claim that symptoms are merely the 'tip of the iceberg', underlying causes remain, and 'symptom substitution' will occur – that is, other abnormal symptoms will replace the symptoms that have been removed.

 Specification Hint

There are a number of different behavioural therapies, such as flooding and those involving the use of token economies. However, only systematic desensitisation is named in the Specification and, for this reason, this therapy alone can be asked about in the exam.

Systematic desensitisation therapy

According to classical conditioning theory, a phobia is a reflex acquired to a non-dangerous stimulus. The normal fear of a dangerous stimulus, such as a poisonous snake, becomes generalised to non-poisonous ones as well. If a person were to be exposed to the non-dangerous stimulus over and over again (e.g. non-dangerous snakes), then the phobia would gradually extinguish. Since this is unlikely to occur naturally, behaviour therapy can help by exposing phobics to their fears in a safe and controlled setting.

Systematic desensitisation is a form of *counter-conditioning* where a person is trained to substitute a relaxation response for the fear response in the presence of the phobic stimulus.

The principle of *reciprocal inhibition* suggests that it's impossible to hold two opposite emotions (e.g. fear and anxiety) at the same time. Since relaxation is incompatible with the feeling of fear or anxiety, it helps to counter the fear response when confronted by a phobic object (they 'cancel each other out'). Counter-conditioning is used very gradually to introduce the feared stimulus in a step-by-step way, and is thus called systematic desensitisation (SD) (Wolpe, 1958). SD involves three steps:

1 training the patient to relax (using deep muscle relaxation or tranquillisers)

2 establishing an *anxiety hierarchy* of the stimuli involved

3 counter-conditioning relaxation as a response to each feared stimulus, beginning first with the least anxiety-provoking stimulus (e.g. toy spider) and then systematically moving on to the next least anxiety-provoking stimulus (e.g. spider in glass box); this continues until all the items listed in the anxiety hierarchy have been dealt with successfully.

Key Study 6.3: The case of Little Peter (Jones, 1924)

Aim/hypothesis (AO1)

This case was regarded as a sequel to Watson and Rayner's (1920) Little Albert study. The aim was to determine the most effective method of removing a fear response in a child.

Method/design (AO1)

Peter was two years and 10 months old when the study began. He was afraid of a white rat and this fear generalised to a rabbit, fur coat and other similar stimuli. As Jones put it, Peter 'seemed almost to be Albert grown a bit older'. A diary was kept of the procedure. The procedure involved Peter and three other children being brought into the laboratory for a play period. The other children showed no fear reaction whatsoever to the rabbit. At other times, Peter was brought in alone so that his reactions could be observed. New situations requiring closer contact with the rabbit were gradually introduced and the degree to which these situations were tolerated gave the measure of improvement. There were 16 such graduated steps, starting from the rabbit being '12 feet away in a cage', moving through to 'sitting beside the rabbit' and finally to 'fondling the rabbit affectionately'. Later on in the study, a pleasant stimulus (food) was produced whenever the rabbit was present. This and the presence with other children contributed to the 'unconditioning' procedure.

Results (AO1)

In the last session, Peter showed no fear at all even despite another child being present who showed a marked disturbance at the sight of the rabbit. Peter was happy to stay on his own in the room with the rabbit and even allowed the rabbit onto the tray of his high chair. The removal of the fear of the rabbit was also generalised to other stimuli such as cotton, fur coat and feathers.

Conclusions (AO1)

Many emotional reactions, such as fear, can be extinguished through a process of counter-conditioning. Systematic desensitisation using a gradual anxiety hierarchy appears to be a successful method in this respect. Pairing a pleasant stimulus such as food with the presentation of the feared object is an important part of the procedure. Furthermore, the elimination of a specific fear (the rabbit in this case) appears to generalise to other similar objects.

Evaluation (AO1/AO2)

- Marks (1987) suggests that it is the exposure to the feared stimulus that is the most important feature of SD, not the pairing of the pleasant stimulus (see below). Perhaps the presentation of the food had little effect on Peter, but the design of the study makes it impossible to determine which of these factors had the greatest effect.

● There are ethical issues raised by the study. Peter did exhibit fear during the study and the experimenters deliberately set up situations to measure this. However, the study ended with Peter's fears removed so the benefits to him outweighed the costs. Nevertheless, it was not certain at the start of the study that Peter's fears would be removed successfully.

In summary, SD is a type of counter-conditioning in which a state of relaxation is classically conditioned to a hierarchy of gradually increasing anxiety-provoking stimuli.

How Science Works

Practical Learning Activity 6.4

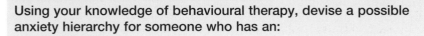

Using your knowledge of behavioural therapy, devise a possible anxiety hierarchy for someone who has an:

● ichthyophobia
● aquaphobia
● pogonophobia
● vestiphobia
● ceraunophobia
● aichmophobia or belonephobia.

(You'll probably have to look up what the above terms mean!)

Evaluation of behavioural therapies

 Effective treatments: simple or specific phobias have been quite effectively treated with behaviour therapy (Marks, 1987). Wolpe and Wolpe (1988) claim that behaviour therapy is an extremely effective treatment. They claim: 'alone among the systems of psychotherapy, behaviour therapy yields a percentage of recoveries significantly above the baseline: 80 to 90 percent of patients are either apparently cured or much improved after an average of twenty-five to thirty sessions'. Barlow and Lehman (1996) reviewed 12 studies on the efficacy of behavioural methods. They found an average panic-free rate of 77 per cent following behavioural treatment. Also, these were the preferred choice of treatments for their patients.

In a study by Klosko *et al.* (1990), SD treatment was as good as or better on all measures of outcome at the end of treatment than the most popular drug. Results were:

● SD treatment group – 87 per cent of patients free of panic

● drug – 50 per cent of patients free of panic

- placebo condition – 36 per cent of patients free of panic
- left on waiting list condition – 33 per cent of patients free of panic.

✔ **Cognitive sense:** the therapies developed by Wolpe and others may appear rather obvious and have been applied for years by non-professionals. Once formally stated, however, they can be rigorously applied, tested and improved.

✔ **Patient responsibility for SD therapy:** since the patient is responsible, with their therapist, for creating their own anxiety hierarchy, they can be seen as being in control of their therapy. Furthermore, if the patient finds that too much anxiety is being caused then s/he can decide to go back down their anxiety hierarchy.

✗ **Ethical issues?** Some form of behavioural therapies such as *flooding* cause a great deal of anxiety and stress in patients. So-called 'sink or swim' methods such as flooding can also make the symptoms worse. Flooding is a process whereby a person confronts their fears for a prolonged time until the fear fades away. Due to the graded anxiety hierarchy used with SD, it is considered a more ethical form of behaviour therapy compared to flooding.

✗ **Impractical method?** It's not always practical for an individual to be desensitised by confronting real situations. Real-life hierarchies in SD can be difficult to arrange and control. In addition, some patients' imaginations may not be vivid enough to produce the desired effect. However, the use of therapies involving imagination means that abstract fears, such as fear of failure, can also be dealt with.

✗ **Restricted application:** these two therapies (SD and flooding) work well only for minor anxiety disorders such as phobias.

✗ **Is relaxation or an anxiety hierarchy necessary?** It has been claimed that the relaxation techniques used aren't essential for the therapy but merely help the patient to confront their fears. It is exposure to the feared situation that is of paramount importance, *not* the reciprocal inhibition aspect of the therapy. In addition, the graded anxiety hierarchy merely helps a patient build up to facing their fear, but isn't an essential part of the therapy.

Cognitive behavioural therapy

Cognitive behaviour therapy (CBT) is based on the assumption that much abnormal behaviour occurs as the result of disordered cognitions or thinking. CBT is an umbrella term for a number of different therapies, but arguably the two best known are Rational Emotive Behaviour Therapy (REBT), proposed by Albert Ellis (1975, 1990), and Aaron Beck's ideas for the 'treatment of negative automatic thoughts' (1967b, 1993).

Rational Emotive Behavior Therapy (REBT) (Ellis, 1975)

Ellis argues that irrational thoughts cause emotional distress and behaviour disorders. Irrational thoughts cause negative self-statements and therapy involves making a client's irrational and negative thoughts more rational and positive. Ellis (1990) identified 11 basic irrational 'musturbatory' beliefs that are emotionally damaging and can lead to psychological problems. These include: 'I must be loved by everybody'; I must be excellent in all respects ... otherwise I'm worthless', and so on. The therapist's aim is to challenge the client's thinking and to show how irrational their thoughts are. Clients are explicitly told to practise positive and optimistic thinking. One technique used by Ellis (1975) involves the 'ABC technique' of irrational beliefs. It involves three steps to analyse the way a person has developed their irrational beliefs.

A = Activating event: the client records the event that led to the disordered thinking (e.g. exam failure).

B = Beliefs: the client records the negative thoughts associated with the event (e.g. I'm useless and stupid).

C = Consequence: the client records the negative thoughts or behaviour that follows (e.g. feeling upset and thinking about leaving college or school).

Therapy involves *reframing* – that is, challenging – these negative thoughts by reinterpreting the ABC in a different light. For example, the exam was difficult, there was little time for revision, and so on. In its simplest form, REBT involves looking on the bright side of life and trying to see life in a more optimistic way.

Treatment of automatic thoughts (Beck, 1967b, 1993)

Beck's cognitive therapy is often used for depression. Beck proposed that depressed people become depressed as a result of their negative thoughts or schemas. They see the world negatively. Depressed people expect to fail in life, blame themselves and have a negative view of themselves. These negative schemas contribute to the '*negative cognitive triad*', where a client has negative thoughts about themselves, about the world and about the future (these form the triad). Beck identified a number of cognitive biases and distortions that occur in depressed individuals. Five of these are:

1 *arbitrary inference* – the drawing of an unjustified conclusion based on little or no evidence

2 *selective abstraction* – the focusing of attention on one detail without regard to the rest of the picture

3 *over-generalisation* – the drawing of a general conclusion based upon a limited event

4 *magnification* – making mountains of molehills; a small problem becomes magnified

5 *minimisation* – an undervaluation of positive attributes; any positive aspects in life are minimised.

How Science Works
Practical Learning Activity 6.5: Cognitive bias in real life

Review the five cognitive biases identified by Ellis (1975) listed above.

- Think of some real-life examples to illustrate each of these biases.

Therapy is collaborative process between the client and therapist. The first step involves identifying the problem and the desired goal. The next step involves challenging negative thoughts associated with the depression. The client may be asked to undertake 'homework' between sessions to test these thoughts – for example, recording the number of times someone is rude to them. They may be pleasantly surprised that people aren't 'always

nasty' to them as they thought. The last step involves the client monitoring their own perceptions accurately. Clients are taught to monitor negative automatic thoughts and examine the evidence that supports them. In this way, they may learn to see why they hold distorted thoughts.

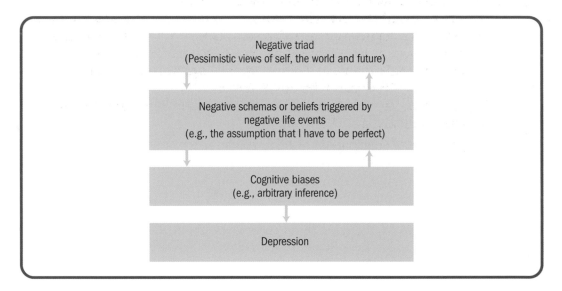

Figure 6.6: The interrelationships between different kinds of cognitions in Beck's theory of depression

Evaluation of cognitive behavioural therapy (CBT)

✔ **Effectiveness?** CBT has been shown to be effective in over 400 studies in both children and adults. It is seen as effective for a wide range of disorders, including post-traumatic stress disorder, obsessive compulsive disorder, depression and eating disorders. This therapy is recognised as being reputable enough to be made available through the NHS.

✗ **Is it more rational?** It is not necessarily more rational to see life through rose-coloured spectacles, but it may be more psychological healthy to do so.

✗ **Doesn't work for all:** cognitive therapy depends on an individual being able to talk about their thought processes lucidly. Hence, the method doesn't work for particularly severe mental disorders such as schizophrenia. CBT can take a long time. Teaching clients to recognise their faulty thinking and alter it can take months of effort.

✗ **Theoretical problems:** a fundamental problem with CBT is whether the theory behind it is correct. Can we be sure that a depressed person's disordered thinking causes depression rather than the other way round? Many cognitive behavioural therapists agree that, in reality, the relationship probably works both ways (Gross, 2005).

Assessment Check 6.3

1. Discuss the use of ECT. (12 marks)
2. Outline and evaluate psychoanalysis. (12 marks)
3. Katy is afraid of spiders. Her doctor recommends that she attend a course on systematic desensitisation. Describe how this therapy might be carried out to overcome Katy's fear of spiders. (6 marks)
4. Outline the main features of the cognitive approach for the treatment of abnormal behaviour. (6 marks).
5. Explain ONE way in which cognitive behavioural therapy differs from psychoanalysis. (3 marks)

SUMMARY
Defining and explaining psychological abnormality

- Psychologists do not agree on the best definition for the term '**abnormality**'.

- The **'deviation from the social norms' definition** refers to any behaviour that does not follow the unwritten rules for normality of a particular society as abnormal.

- The **'failure to function adequately' definition** suggests that a person is considered abnormal if they cannot cope with daily life. Unusual or strange behaviour that does not cause distress would not be considered 'abnormal'.

- The **'deviation from ideal mental health' definition** lists different criteria that indicate 'normal' behaviour. Any deviation from these criteria can be considered abnormal.

- All these definitions suffer from a number of limitations. One of these relates to whether they can be applied to all cultures. In practice, it's difficult to produce an adequate definition *within* a culture, much less one that is of use *between* cultures.

- The **biological (medical) approach to psychopathology** assumes an underlying physical cause. Studies involving **genetics**, **brain damage** and **biochemistry** support this. Classification of abnormal behaviour concentrates on patient symptoms.

- The **psychodynamic approach to psychopathology** assumes that mental disorders are **psychological in origin. Childhood experiences** and the **conflict in the personality (id, ego** and **superego)** play an important part in the development of mental disorders. Traumatic events are placed in the **unconscious** through **repression**. The model remains **controversial** and is difficult to evaluate **scientifically**.

- The **behavioural approach to psychopathology** isn't associated with mental disorders but **maladaptive behaviour**. It assumes that **all behaviour is learnt** through the process of **classical and operant conditioning**, and thus can be unlearnt using the same principles. This approach is **scientifically tested** and proven to be **effective** for the less serious disorders.

- The **cognitive approach to psychopathology** assumes that abnormal behaviour is caused by an **individual's disturbed thoughts**. It assumes that **thoughts affect behaviour**. Individuals make '**cognitive errors**' such as magnifying failure and minimising success. This approach is both **modern and popular**.

Treating abnormality

- The two main biological therapies involve the use of **drugs and ECT (electro-convulsive therapy)**.

- Approximately 25 per cent of all drugs prescribed by the NHS are for mental health problems. **Drugs** work by entering the bloodstream to reach the brain. Drugs **affect transmission** of chemicals in the nervous system. They affect transmission of neurotransmitters in the nervous system, either increasing or decreasing their availability, and hence modifying their effect on behaviour. **A placebo** is an inactive treatment (e.g. sugar pill) that nevertheless appears to produce some improvement in patients.

- **Drugs** have to be shown to be effective in clinical trails. The five major drug types are **antipsychotic (major tranquillisers); anti-anxiety drugs (minor tranquillisers); antidepressants; anti-manics and stimulants**.

- **Electro-convulsive therapy (ECT)** is a medical treatment used to treat drug-resistant depressive disorders. It's used as a last resort when drugs and psychotherapy have failed or cannot be tolerated. There are two types: **unilateral ECT** (in which just one hemisphere/side of the brain is stimulated) and **bilateral ECT** (both hemispheres).

- ECT has an immediate beneficial effect with up to 80 per cent of depressed patients. ECT does not seem to have *major* side-effects.

- Psychoanalysis is derived from **Freudian theory**, though most psychoanalytic therapists don't practice today in the same way that Freud did.

- Psychoanalysis places an **importance on childhood** and repressed impulses and conflicts. The goal of psychoanalytic therapy is to try to bring these repressed feelings into conscious awareness, to make the '**unconscious conscious**'.

- By gaining **insight** in this way, the patient, or **analysand**, can work through any buried feelings they have.

- There are a number of **techniques** that psychoanalysts use, including **free association** and **dream analysis**. Freud believed dreams were the '**royal road to the unconscious**'.

- It is difficult to measure the **effectiveness of psychoanalysis** since there's no agreed way of measuring its success. Psychoanalysis appears to be more

effective with **neurotic patients**, rather than those with severe personality disorders such as schizophrenia.

- Psychoanalysis is based on **Freudian theory**. Many of the **criticisms** of psychoanalysis can also therefore be applied to the therapy. These include practical issues of **time** and **cost**.

- **Behavioural therapy** is the use of the experimentally established laws of learning for the purposes of changing maladaptive behaviour.

- Behavioural therapies based on **classical conditioning** ('learning by association') include **systematic desensitisation**.

- Systematic desensitisation involves training a person to substitute a relaxation response with the fear response usually produced by the phobic stimulus. It is based on the principle of **reciprocal inhibition**, which suggests it is impossible to hold two opposite emotions at the same time. The relaxation helps to counter the fear response.

- These behavioural therapies are **effective** and **work relatively quickly**. They can be rigorously applied, tested and improved.

- However, there are **ethical issues** involved in the use of behavioural therapies, particularly with flooding, that causes a great deal of anxiety and stress to the patient.

- Cognitive behavioural therapy (CBT) is based on the assumption that much abnormal behaviour occurs as the result of disordered cognitions and thinking. CBT involves **cognitive restructuring.**

- The two best-known therapies are **Rational Emotive Behaviour Therapy (REBT),** proposed by **Ellis** (1975), and **Beck's Treatment of Negative Automatic Thoughts** (1993).

- CBT appears to be a particularly **effective therapy** for post-traumatic stress disorder, obsessive-compulsive disorder and depression.

- A major problem with CBT is its theoretical basis: it remains uncertain that a person's disordered thinking causes depression rather than the other way round.

References

Abrams, D., Wetherell, M., Cochrane, S., Hogg, M.A. and Turner, J.C. (1990) Knowing what to think by knowing who you are: self-categorisation and the nature of norm formation. *British Journal of Social Psychology*, *29*, 97–119.

Abramson, L.Y. and Martin, D.J. (1981) Depression and the causal inference process. In J.M. Harvey, W. Ickes and R.F. Kidd (eds) *New Directions in Attributional Research*, Vol. 3. Hillsdale, NJ: Erlbaum.

Abramson, L.Y., Seligman, M.E.P. and Teasdale, J.D. (1978) Learned helplessness in humans: critique and reformulation. *Journal of Abnormal Psychology*, *87*, 49–74.

Ainsworth, M.D.S. (1967) *Infancy in Uganda: Infant Care and the Growth of Love*. Baltimore, MD: Johns Hopkins University Press.

Ainsworth, M.D.S., Bell, M.S.V. and Stayton, D.J. (1971) Individual differences in strange-situation behaviour of one-year-olds. In H.R. Schaffer (ed.) *The Origins of Human Social Relations*. New York: Academic Press.

Ainsworth, M.D.S., Blehar, M.C., Waters, E. and Wall, S. (1978) *Patterns of Attachment: A Psychological Study of the Strange Situation*. Hillsdale, NJ: Lawrence Erlbaum Associates Inc.

Allen, V. and Levine, J.M. (1971) Social support and conformity: the role of independent assessment of reality. *Journal of Experimental Social Psychology*, *7*, 48–58.

Anderson, C. (2004) An update on the effects of playing violent video games. *Journal of Adolescence*, *27*, 113–122.

Andrews, B. and Brewin, C.B. (2000) What did Freud get right? *The Psychologist*, *13*, 605–607.

Anokhin, P.K. (1973) The forming of natural and artificial intelligence. *Impact of Science on Society*, *23(3)*.

APA (2003) www.apa.org (accessed 21 June 2003).

Asch, S.E. (1951) Effect of group pressure upon the modification and distortion of judgements. In H. Guetzkow (ed.) *Groups, Leadership, and Men*. Pittsburgh, PA: Carnegie Press.

Atkinson, R.C. and Shiffrin, R.M. (1968) Human memory: a proposed system and its control processes. In K.W. Spence and J.T. Spence (eds) *The Psychology of Learning and Motivation*, Vol. 2. London: Academic Press.

Atkinson, R.C. and Shiffrin, R.M. (1971) The control of short-term memory. *Scientific American*, *224*, 82–90.

Baddeley, A.D. (1966) The influence of acoustic and semantic similarity on long-term memory for word sequences. *Quarterly Journal of Experimental Psychology*, *18*, 302–309.

Baddeley, A. (2005) *Human Memory*. Psychology Press.

Baddeley, A.D. and Hitch, G. (1974) Working memory. In G.H. Bower (ed.) *Recent Advances in Learning and Motivation*, Vol. 8. New York: Academic Press.

Baddeley, A.D., Grant, S., Wight, E. and Thomson, N. (1973) Imagery and visual working. In P.M.A. Rabbitt and S. Darnit (eds) *Attention and Performance V*. London: Academic Press.

Bahrick, H.P., Bahrick, P.O. and Wittinger, R.P. (1975) Fifty years of memory for names and faces: a cross-sectional approach. *Journal of Experimental Psychology: General*, *104*, 54–75.

Bandura, A. (1965) Influence of model's reinforcement contingencies on the acquisition of imitative responses. *Journal of Personality and Social Psychology*, *1*, 589–595.

Barlow, D.H. and Lehman, C.L. (1996) Advances in the psychosocial treatment of anxiety disorders: implications for national health care. *Archives of General Psychiatry*, *53*, 727–735.

Baron, R.A. and Byrne, D. (1991) *Social Psychology* (6th edn). Boston: Allyn & Bacon.

Barr, C.E., Mednick, S.A. and Munk-Jorgenson, P. (1990) Exposure to influenza epidemics during gestation and adult schizophrenia: a forty-year study. *Archives of General Psychiatry*, *47*, 869–874.

Bartlett, D. (1998) *Stress: Perspectives and Processes*. Buckingham: Open University Press.

Bartlett, F.C. (1932) *Remembering*. Cambridge: Cambridge University Press.

Bauman, K. (1973) Volunteer bias in a study of sexual knowledge, attitudes, and behavior. *Journal of Marriage and the Family*, *35(1)*, 27–31.

Baumrind, D. (1964) Some thoughts on the ethics of research: after reading Milgram's behavioural study of obedience. *American Psychologist*, *19*, 421–423.

Beck, A.T. (1967a) *Cognitive Therapy and the Emotional Disorders*. New York: International Universities Press.

Beck, A.T. (1967b) *Depression: Causes and Treatment*. Philadelphia: University of Philadelphia Press.

Beck, A.T. (1993) Cognitive therapy: past, present and future. *Journal of Consulting and Clinical Psychology, 61(2)*, 194–198.

Bekerian, D.A. and Baddeley, A.D. (1980) Saturation advertising and the repetition effect. *Learning and Verbal Behaviour, 19*, 17–25.

Bekerian, D.A. and Dennett, J.L. (1993) The cognitive interview technique: reviving the issues. *Applied Cognitive Psychology, 7*, 275–297.

Bekker, M.H.J. (2000) The gendered body: body and gender and the inter-relationships with health. In L. Sherr and J.S. St Lawrence (eds) *Women, Health and the Mind*. Chichester: John Wiley & Sons Ltd.

Belsky, J. and Rovine, M.J. (1988) Non-maternal care in the first year of life and the infant–parent attachment. *Child Development, 59*, 157–167.

Bergin, A.E. (1971) The evaluation of therapeutic outcomes. In A.E. Bergin and S.L. Garfield (eds) *Handbook of Psychotherapy and Behavior Change* (4th edn). New York: John Wiley & Sons.

Berry, J.W., Poortinga, Y.H., Segall, M.H. and Dasen, P.R. (1992) *Cross-cultural Psychology*. Cambridge: Cambridge University Press.

Blurton Jones, N. (1967) An ethological study of some aspects of social behaviour of children in nursery school. In D. Morris (ed.) *Primate Ethology*. London: Weidenfeld & Nicolson.

Bornstein, B., Christy J., Witt, C., Cherry, K. and Greene, E. (2000) The suggestibility of older witnesses. In M.B. Rothman, B.D. Dunlop and P. Entzel (eds) *Elders, Crime, and the Criminal Justice System: Myth, Perceptions, and Reality in the 21st Century*. Springer Series on Life Styles and Issues in Aging. New York, NY: Springer.

Bowlby, J. (1951) *Maternal Care and Mental Health*. Geneva: World Health Organization.

Bowlby, J. (1953) *Child Care and the Growth of Love*. Harmondsworth: Penguin.

Bowlby, J. (1969) *Attachment and Loss, Vol. 1: Attachment*. Harmondsworth: Penguin.

Bowlby, J. (1973) *Attachment and Loss, Vol. 2: Separation*. Harmondsworth: Penguin.

Bowlby, J., Ainsworth, M., Boston, M. and Rosenbluth, D. (1956) The effects of mother–child separation: a follow-up study. *British Journal of Medical Psychology, 24(3/4)*, 211–247.

BPS (British Psychological Society) (2007) Ethical principles for conducting research with human participants, http://www.bps.org.uk/the-society/ethics-rules-charter-code-of-conduct/code-of-conduct/ethical-principles-for-conducting-research-with-human-participants.cfm (accessed 15 May 2007).

Bradley, L.A. (1995) Chronic benign pain. In D. Wedding (ed.) *Behaviour and Medicine* (2nd edn). St Louis, MO: Mosby-Year Book.

Brady, J.V. (1958) Ulcers in executive monkeys. *Scientific American, 199*, 95–100.

Bromley, D. (1986) *The Case Study Method in Psychology and Related Disciplines*. Chichester: Wiley.

Brown, R. (1986) *Social Psychology: The Second Edition*. New York, NY: Free Press.

Brown, R.J. (1988) Intergroup relations. In M. Hewstone, W. Stroebe and G.M. Stephenson (eds) *Introduction to Social Psychology* (2nd edn). Oxford: Blackwell.

Burt, C. (1955) The evidence for the concept of intelligence. *British Journal of Educational Psychology, 25*, 158–177.

Cannon, W.B. (1927) The James-Lange theory of emotions: a critical examination and an alternative theory. *American Journal of Psychology, 39*, 106–124.

Chisolm, K., Carter, M.C., Amers, E.W. and Morison, S.J. (1995) Attachment security and indiscriminately friendly behaviour in children adopted from Romanian orphanages. *Development and Psychopathology, 7*, 283–294.

Clarke, A. and Clarke, A. (2000) *Early Experience and the Life Path*. London: Jessica Kingsley.

Clarke-Stewart, K.A. (1989) Infant day care: maligned or malignant? *American Psychologist, 44*, 266–273.

Cochrane, R. (1977) Mental illness in immigrants in the UK. *Social Psychiatry, 12*, 23–35.

Coffey, C.E., Weiner, R.D., Djang, W.T., Figiel, G.S., Soady, S.A.R., Patterson, L.J., Holt, P.D., Spritzer, C.E. and Wilkinson, W.E. (1991) Brain anatomic effects of ECT: a prospective magnetic resonance imaging study. *Archives of General Psychiatry, 115*, 1013–1021.

Cohen, G. (1990) Memory. In I. Roth (ed.) *Introduction to Psychology*, Vol. 2. Buckingham: Open University Press.

Cohen, G. and Faulkner, D. (1989) Age differences in

source forgetting: effects on reality monitoring and on eyewitness testimony. *Psychology and Aging*, *4*, 10–17.

Cohen, F. and Lazarus, R. (1979) Coping with the stresses of illness. In G.C. Stone, F. Cohen and N.E. Ader (eds) *Health Psychology: A Handbook*. San Francisco, CA: Jossey-Bass.

Cohen, S., Tyrrell, D.A.J. and Smith, A.P. (1991) Psychological stress and susceptibility to the common cold. *New England Journal of Medicine*, *325*, 606–612.

Coolican, H. (2004) *Research Methods and Statistics in Psychology* (4th edn). London: Hodder Arnold.

Coxon, P. and Valentine, T. (1997) The effects of the age of eyewitnesses on the accuracy and suggestibility of their testimony. *Applied Cognitive Psychology*, *11*, 415–430.

Crowder, R.G. (2003) Sensory memory. In J.H. Byrne (ed.) *Learning and Memory* (2nd edn). New York, NY: Macmillan, 607–609.

Crutchfield, R.S. (1954) A new technique for measuring individual differences in conformity to group judgement. *Proceedings of the Invitational Conference on Testing Problems*, 69–74.

Curtiss, S. (1977) *Genie: A Psycholinguistic Study of a Modern Day 'Wild Child'*. New York, NY: Academic Press.

Darley, J. and Batson, C. (1973) From Jerusalem to Jericho: a study of situational and dispositional variables in helping behaviour. *Journal of Personality and Social Psychology*, *27*, 100–108.

Darley, C.F., Tinklenberg, J.R., Hollister, L.E. and Atkinson, R.C. (1973) Marijuana and retrieval from short-term memory. *Psychopharmacologia*, *29*, 231–238.

Davison, G.C. and Neale, J.M. (2001) *Abnormal Psychology* (8th edn). New York, NY: John Wiley & Sons Inc.

De Ridder, D.T.D. (2000) Gender, stress and coping: do women handle stressful situations differently from men? In L. Sherr and J.S. St Lawrence (eds) *Women, Health and the Mind*. Chichester: John Wiley & Sons Ltd.

Deese, J. (1959) On the prediction of occurrence of particular verbal intrusions in immediate recall. *Journal of Experimental Psychology*, *58*, 17–22.

Deffenbacher, K.A. (1983) The influence of arousal on reliability of testimony. In S.M.A. Lloyd-Bostock and R.B. Clifford (eds) *Evaluating Witness Evidence: Recent Psychological Research and New Perspectives*. Chichester: John Wiley & Sons.

Deffenbacher, K.A., Bornstein, B., Penrod, S. and McGorty, K. (2004) A meta-analytic review of the effects of high stress on eyewitness memory. *Law and Human Behavior*, *28(6)*, December, 687–706.

DeLongis, A., Coyne, J.C., Dakof, G., Folkman, S. and Lazarus, R.S. (1982) The impact of daily hassles, uplifts and major life events to health status. *Health Psychology*, *1*, 119–136.

Dent, H.R. (1988) Children's eyewitness evidence: a brief review. In M. Gruneberg, P.E. Morris and R. Sykes (eds) *Practical Aspects of Memory: Current Research and Issues. Volume I Clinical and Educational Implications*. Chichester: Wiley.

Deutsch, M. and Gerard, H.B. (1955) A study of normative and informational social influence upon individual judgements. *Journal of Abnormal and Social Psychology*, *51*, 629–636.

Dolnick, E. (1998) *Madness on the Couch – Blaming the Victim in the Heyday of Psychoanalysis*. New York, NY: Simon & Schuster.

Dossman, R., Kutter, P., Heinzel, R. and Wurmser, L. (1997) The long-term benefits of intensive psychotherapy. A view from Germany. In S. Lazar (ed.) *Psychoanalytic Inquiry Supplement, Intensive Dynamic Psychotherapy: Making the Case in an Era of Managed Care*. Florence, KY: Analytic Press.

Durkin, K. (1995) *Developmental Social Psychology: From Infancy to Old Age*. Oxford: Blackwell.

Elias, M.F., Elias, J.W. and Elias, P.K. (1990) Biological and health influences on behavior. In J.E. Birren and K. Warner Schaie (eds) *Handbook of the Psychology of Aging*. New York, NY: Academic Press, 70–102.

Ellis, A. (1975) *A New Guide to Rational Living*. Englewood Cliffs, NJ: Prentice Hall.

Ellis, A. (1990) Rational and irrational beliefs in counselling psychology. *Journal of Rational-Emotive and Cognitive-Behavior Therapy*, *8(4)*, 221–233.

Eysenck, H. (1952) The effects of psychotherapy: an evaluation. *Journal of Consulting Psychology*, *16*, 319–324.

Eysenck, M.W. (1986) Working memory. In G. Cohen, M.W. Eysenck and M.A. Le Voi (eds) *Memory: A Cognitive Approach*. Milton Keynes: Open University Press.

Fernandez, A. and Glenberg, A.M. (1985) Changing environmental context does not reliably affect memory. *Memory and Cognition*, *13*, 333–345.

Fisher, R.P. and Geiselman, R.E. (1992) Memory-enhancing techniques for investigative interviewing. *Journal of Verbal Learning and Verbal Behaviour*, 6, 618–628.

Fisher, R.P., Geiselman, R.E. and Amador, M. (1989) Field test of the cognitive interview: enhancing the recollection of actual victims and witnesses of crime. *Journal of Applied Psychology*, 74, 722–727.

Fiske, S.T. (2004) *Social Beings: A Core Motives Approach to Social Psychology*. New York, NY: John Wiley & Sons Inc.

Folkman, S. (1984) Personal control and stress and coping processes: a theoretical analysis. *Journal of Personality and Social Psychology*, 46, 839–852.

Folkman, S. and Lazarus, R.S. (1980) An analysis of coping in a middle-aged community sample. *Journal of Health and Social Behaviour*, 21, 219–239.

Ford, D.H. and Urban, H.R. (1963) *Systems of Psychotherapy: A Comparative Study*. New York, NY: Wiley.

Forshaw, M. (2002) *Essential Health Psychology*. London: Arnold.

Foster, R.A., Libkuman, T.M., Schooler, J.W. and Loftus, E.F. (1994) Consequentiality and eyewitness person identification. *Applied Cognitive Psychology*, 8, 107–121.

Frankenhauser, M. (1983) The sympathetic-adrenal and pituitary-adrenal response to challenge: comparison between the sexes. In T.M. Dembroski, T.H. Schmidt and G. Blumchen (eds) *Behavioural Bases of Coronary Heart Disease*. Basle: S. Karger.

Friedman, M. and Rosenman, R.H. (1974) *Type A Behaviour and Your Heart*. New York, NY: Harper & Row.

Fruzzetti, A.E., Tolland, K., Teller, S.A. and Loftus, E.F. (1992) Memory and eyewitness testimony. In M. Gruneberg and P. Morris (eds) *Aspects of Memory. Vol. 1: The Practical Aspects* (2nd edn). London and New York, NY: Routledge.

Funk, S.C. (1992) Hardiness: a review of theory and research. *Health Psychology*, 11(5), 335–345.

Gathercole, S.E. and Baddeley, A. (1993) *Working Memory and Language*. Hillsdale, NJ: Lawrence Frlbaum Associates.

Geddes, J. and UK ECT Review Group (2003) Efficacy and safety of electroconvulsive therapy in depressive disorders: a systematic review and meta-analysis. *The Lancet*, 361(9360), 799–808.

Geiselman, R.E., Fisher, R.P., MacKinnon, D.P. and Holland, H.L. (1985) Eyewitness memory enhancement in the police interview: cognitive retrieval mnemonics versus hypnosis. *Journal of Applied Psychology*, 70, 401–412.

Ginet, M. and Py, J. (2001) A technique for enhancing memory in eye witness testimonies for use by police officers and judicial officials: the cognitive interview. *Le Travail humain*, 64, 173–191.

Godden, D. and Baddeley, A.D. (1975) Context-dependent memory in two natural environments: on land and under water. *British Journal of Psychology*, 66, 325–331.

Goldfarb, W. (1943) The effects of early institutional care on adult personality. *Journal of Experimental Education*, 12, 106–129.

Goodwin, D.W., Powell, B., Bremer, D., Hoine, H. and Stern, J. (1969) Alcohol and recall: state dependent effects in man. *Science*, 163, 1358.

Gore, P.M. and Rotter, J.B. (1963) A personality correlate of social action. *Journal of Personality*, 31, 58–64.

Gottfried, A.E., Gottfried, A.W. and Bathurst, K. (2002) Maternal and dual-earner employment status and parenting. In M.H. Bornstein (ed.) *Handbook of Parenting*, Vol. 2 (2nd edn). Mahwah, NJ: Erlbaum.

Greer, S. and Morris, T. (1975) Psychological attributes of women who develop breast cancer: a controlled study. *Journal of Psychosomatic Research*, 19, 147–153.

Gregory, R.L. and Wallace, J.G. (1963) Recovery from early blindness: a case study. *Experimental Society Monograph*, No. 2. Cambridge: Heffers.

Griffiths, M. and Parke, J. (2005) The psychology of music in gambling environments: an observational research note. *Journal of Gambling Issues*, 13, March, 1–12.

Groome, D., Dewart, H., Esgate, A., Gurney, K., Kemp, R. and Towell, N. (1999) *An Introduction to Cognitive Psychology: Processes and Disorders*. Hove, UK: Psychology Press.

Gross, R. (2003) *Key Studies in Psychology* (4th edition). London: Hodder & Stoughton.

Gross, R. (2005) *Psychology: The Science of Mind and Behaviour* (5th edn). London: Hodder Arnold.

Gruneberg, M. and Morris, P.E. (eds) (1992) *Aspects of Memory. Volume 1: Practical Aspects*. London: Routledge.

Gurling, H., Kalsi, G., Brynjolfsson, J. *et al.* (2001) Genomewide genetic linkage analysis confirms the presence of susceptibility loci for schizophrenia, on chromosomes 1q32.2, 5q33.2, and 8p21–22 and provides support for linkage to schizophrenia, on chromosomes 11q23.3–24 and 20q12.1–11.23. *American Journal of Human Genetics*, *68(3)*, March, 661–673.

Harlow, H.F. (1959) Love in infant monkeys. *Scientific American*, *200*, 68–74.

Hayward, S. (1998) Stress, health and psychoneuro-immunology. *Psychology Review*, *5(1)*, 16–19.

Herrmann, D. and Palmisano, M. (1992) The facilitation of memory performance. In M.M. Gruneberg and P.E. Morris (eds) *Aspects of Memory. Vol. 1: The Practical Aspects*. Chichester, UK: Wiley.

Hetherington, E.M. and Stanley-Hagan, M. (1999) The adjustment of children with divorced parents: a risk and resiliency perspective. *Journal of Child Psychology and Psychiatry*, *40(1)*, 129–140.

Hilts, P. (1995) *Memory's Ghost: The Nature of Memory and the Strange Tale of Mr M*. New York, NY: Simon & Schuster.

Hinsliff, G. (2004) Baby, what shall I do? *Observer*, 9 May, 19.

Hodges, J. and Tizard, B. (1989) Social and family relationships of ex-institutional adolescents. *Journal of Child Psychology and Psychiatry*, *30*, 77–97.

Hofling, K.C., Brotzman, E., Dalrymple, S., Graves, N. and Pierce, C.M. (1966) An experimental study in the nurse–physician relationship. *Journal of Nervous and Mental Disorders*, *143*, 171–180.

Hollander, E.P. (1981) *Principles and Methods of Social Psychology*. New York, NY: Oxford University Press.

Hollander, E.P. and Willis, R.H. (1964) Conformity, independence and anticonformity as determiners of perceived influence and attraction. In E.P. Hollander (ed.) *Leaders, Groups and Influence*. New York, NY: Oxford University Press.

Holmes, T.H. and Rahe, R.H. (1967) The social readjustment rating scale. *Journal of Psychosomatic Research*, *32*, 561–572.

International Gay and Lesbian Human Rights Commission (1995) Japanese psychiatrists remove homosexuality from list of disorders, http://www.iglhrc.org/site/iglhrc/section.php?id=5anddetail=313 (accessed 29 May 2007).

Jacobs, J. (1887) Experiments on 'prehension'. *Mind*, *12*, 75–79.

Jahoda, M. (1958) *Current Concepts of Positive Mental Health*. New York, NY: Basic Books.

Jones, M.C. (1924) A laboratory study of fear: the case of Peter. *Pedagogical Seminary*, *31*, 308–315.

Judd, J. (1997) Working mothers need not feel guilty. *Independent on Sunday*, 27 November, 5.

Kanner, A.D., Coyne, J.C., Schaefer, C. and Lazarus, R.S. (1981) Comparison of two modes of stress measurement: daily hassles and uplifts versus major life events. *Journal of Behavioural Measurement*, *4*, 1–39.

Kendler, K.S., Masterson, C.C. and Davis, K.L. (1985) Psychiatric illness in first degree relatives of patients with paranoid psychosis, schizophrenia, and medical controls. *British Journal of Psychiatry*, *147*, 524–531.

Kiecolt-Glaser, J.K., Garner, W., Speicher, C.E., Penn, G.M., Holliday, J. and Glaser, R. (1984) Psychosocial modifiers of immunocompetence in medical students. *Psychosomatic Medicine*, *46*, 7–14.

Kiecolt-Glaser, J.K., Marucha, P.T., Malarkey, W.B., Mercado, A.M. and Glaser, R. (1995) Slowing of wound healing by psychological stress. *The Lancet*, *346*, 1194–1196.

King, M.A. and Yuille, J.C. (1987) Suggestibility and the child witness. In S.J. Ceci, M.P. Toglia and D.F. Ross (eds) *Children's Eyewitness Memory*. New York, NY: Springer-Verlag, 24–35.

Kirsch, I. and Sapirstein, G. (1998) Listening to Prozac but hearing placebo: a meta-analysis of antidepressant medication. *Prevention and Treatment*, *1*, Article 2a.

Klosko, J.S., Barlow, D.H., Tassinari, R. and Cerny, J.A. (1990) A comparison of alprazolam and behavior therapy in treatment of panic disorder. *Journal of Consulting and Clinical Psychology*, *58*, 77–84.

Kobasa, S. (1979) Stressful life events, personality and health: an inquiry into hardiness. *Journal of Personality and Social Psychology*, *37*, 1–11.

Kobasa, S. (1986) How much stress can you survive? In M.G. Walraven and H.E. Fitzgerald (eds) *Annual Editions: Human Development*, *86/87*. New York, NY: Dushkin.

Koluchova, J. (1972) Severe deprivation in twins: a case study. *Journal of Child Psychology and Psychiatry*, *13*, 107–114.

Koluchova, J. (1991) Severely deprived twins after 22 years' observation. *Studia Psychologica*, *33*, 23–28.

Kremer, J. (1998) Work. In K. Trew and J. Kremer (eds) *Gender and Psychology*. London: Arnold.

Laing, R.D. (1959) *The Divided Self – An Existential Study in Sanity and Madness*. New York, NY: Pelican Books.

Lambert, M.J. and Bergin, A.E. (1994) The effectiveness of psychotherapy. In A. Bergin and S. Garfield (eds) *Handbook of Psychotherapy and Behavior Change* (4th edn). New York, NY: John Wiley & Sons.

Latané, B. (1981) The psychology of social impact. *American Psychologist*, *36*, 343–356.

Latané, B. and Nida, S. (1980) Social impact theory and social influence: a social engineering perspective. In P. Paulus (ed.) *The Psychology of Group Influence*. Hillsdale, NJ: Lawrence Erlbaum.

Latané, B. and Wolf, S. (1981) The social impact of majorities and minorities. *Psychological Review*, *88*, 438–453.

Lazarus, R.S. (1999) *Stress and Emotion: A New Synthesis*. London: Free Association Books.

Lazarus, R.S. and Folkman, S. (1984) *Stress, Appraisal and Coping*. New York, NY: Springer.

Lee, S.G. (1969) Spirit possession among the Zulu. In J. Beattie and J. Middleton (eds) *Spirit Mediumship and Society in Africa*. New York, NY: Africana.

Loftus, E.F. (1975) Leading questions and the eyewitness report. *Cognitive Psychology*, *1*, 560–572.

Loftus, E.F. and Palmer, J.C. (1974) Reconstruction of automobile destruction: an example of the interaction between language and memory. *Journal of Verbal Learning and Verbal Behavior*, *13*, 585–589.

Loftus, E.F., Levidow, B. and Duensing, S. (1991) Who remembers best? Individual differences in memory for events that occurred in a science museum. *Applied Cognitive Psychology*, *6(2)*, 93–107.

Loftus, E.F., Miller, D.G. and Burns, H.J. (1978) Semantic integration of verbal information into visual memory. *Journal of Experimental Psychology: Human Learning and Memory*, *4(1)*, 19–31.

Lopata, H.Z. (1993) The support systems of American urban widows. In M.S. Stroebe, W. Stroebe and R.O. Hansson (eds) *Handbook of Bereavement*. New York, NY: Cambridge University Press.

Lorenz, K.Z. (1935) The companion in the bird's world. *Auk*, *54*, 245–273.

Luborsky, L., Diguer, L., Luborsky, E., McLellan, A.T.,

Woody, G. and Alexander, L. (1993) Psychological health as predictor of the outcomes of psychotherapy. *Journal of Consulting and Clinical Psychology*, *61*, 542–548.

Luria, A.R. (1968) *The Mind of a Mnemonist*. London: Jonathan Cape Ltd.

Maccoby, E.E. (1980) *Social Development – Psychological Growth and the Parent–Child Relationship*. New York, NY: Harcourt Brace Jovanovich.

Marks, I. (1987) *Fears, Phobias and Rituals*. Oxford: Oxford University Press.

Marmot, M.G. and Theorell, T. (1988) Social clan and cardiovascular disease: the contribution of work. *International Journal of Health Services*, *18*, 659–674.

Marmot, M., Bosma, H., Hemingway, H., Brunner, E. and Stansfield, S. (1997) Contribution of job control and other risk factors to social variation in health disease incidence. *The Lancet*, *350*, 235–239.

Martz, D.M., Handley, K.B. and Eisler, R.M. (1995) The relationship between feminine gender role stress, body image, and eating disorders. *Psychology of Women Quarterly*, *19*, 493–508.

Maslach, C., Stapp, J. and Santee, R.T. (1985) Individuation: conceptual analysis and assessment. *Journal of Personality and Social Psychology*, *49*, 729–738.

Maslow, A. (1968) *Towards a Psychology of Being* (2nd edn). New York, NY: Van Nostrand Reinhold.

McCloskey, M. and Zaragoza, M.S. (1985) Misleading post-event information and memory for events: arguments and evidence against memory impairment hypotheses. *Journal of Experimental Psychology: General*, *114*, 1–16.

McKibbin, C.L., Koonce-Volwiler, D., Cronkite, R.C. and Gallagher-Thompson, D. (2000) Psychological, social, and economic implications of bereavement among older women. In L. Sherr and J.S. St Lawrence (eds) *Women, Health and the Mind*. Chichester: John Wiley & Sons Ltd.

Meichenbaum, D. (1977) *Cognitive-Behaviour Modification: An Integrative Approach*. New York, NY: Plenum.

Meichenbaum, D. (1997) The evolution of a cognitive-behaviour therapist. In J.K. Zeig (ed.) *The Evolution of Psychotherapy: The Third Conference*. New York, NY: Brunner/Mazel.

Memon, A., Cronin, Ó., Eaves, R. and Bull, R. (1993) The cognitive interview and child witnesses. In G.M.

Stephenson and N.K. Clark (eds) *Children, Evidence and Procedure. Issues in Criminological and Legal Psychology, 20*, 3–9 (Leicester: British Psychological Society).

Memon, A., Holley, A., Milne, R., Köhnken, G. and Bull, R. (1994) Towards understanding the effects of interviewer training in evaluating the cognitive interview. *Applied Cognitive Psychology, 8*, 641–659.

Memon, A., Cronin, O., Eaves, R. and Bull, R. (1996) An empirical test of the mnemonic components of the cognitive interview. In G.M. Davies, S. Lloyd-Bostock, M. McMurran and C. Wilson (eds) *Psychology, Law and Criminal Justice*. Berlin: De Gruyter, 135–145.

Milgram, S. (1963) Behavioural study of obedience. *Journal of Abnormal and Social Psychology, 67*, 391–398.

Milgram, S. (1965) Liberating effects of group pressure. *Journal of Personality and Social Psychology, 1*, 127–134.

Milgram, S. (1974) *Obedience to Authority*. New York, NY: Harper & Row.

Miller, G.A. (1956) The magical number seven, plus or minus two: some limits on our capacity for processing information. *Psychological Review, 63*, 81–97.

Mind (2007) http://www.mind.org.uk/Information/Factsheets/Treatments+and+drugs/Psychosurgery.htm (accessed 12 July 2007).

Morris, P.E., Tweedy, M. and Gruneberg, M.M. (1985) Interest, knowledge and the memorising of soccer scores. *British Journal of Psychology, 76*, 415–425.

Moscovici, S. (1976) *Social Influence and Social Change*. London: Academic Press.

Moscovici, S. and Faucheux, C. (1972) Social influence, conforming bias and the study of active minorities. In L. Berkowitz (ed.) *Advances in Experimental Social Psychology*, Vol. 6. New York, NY: Academic Press.

Moscovici, S. and Lage, E. (1976) Studies in social influence: III. Majority and minority influence in a group. *European Journal of Social Psychology, 6*, 149–174.

Moscovici, S., Lage, E. and Naffrechoux, M. (1969) Influence of a consistent minority on the responses of a majority in a colour perception task. *Sociometry, 32*, 365–380.

Murdock, B.B. (1962) The serial position effect in free recall. *Journal of Experimental Psychology, 64*, 482–488.

Nemeth, C., Swedlund, M. and Kanki, G. (1974) Patterning of the minority's responses and their influence on the majority. *European Journal of Social Psychology, 4*, 53–64.

Nobles, W.W. (1976) Extended self: rethinking the so-called Negro self-concept. *Journal of Black Psychology, 2*, 99–105.

Ochsner, J.E., Zaragoza, M.S. and Mitchell, K.J. (1999) The accuracy and suggestibility of children's memory for neutral and criminal eyewitness events. *Legal and Criminological Psychology, 4*, 79–92.

Orne, M.T. (1962) On the social psychology of the psychological experiment: with particular reference to demand characteristics and their implications. *American Psychologist, 17*, 776–783.

Orne, M.T. (1965) Psychological factors maximising resistance to stress with special reference to hypnosis. In S. Klausner (ed.) *The Quest for Self-control*. New York, NY: Free Press.

Orne, M.T. and Holland, C.C. (1968) On the ecological validity of laboratory deceptions. *International Journal of Psychiatry, 6*, 282–293.

Patry, P. (2001) Informed consent and deception in psychological research. *Kriterion, 14*, 34–38.

Paulescu, E., Frith, C.D. and Frackoviak, R.S.J. (1993) The neural correlates of the verbal component of working memory. *Nature, 362*, 342–345.

Penny, G. (1996) Health psychology. In H. Coolican (ed.) *Applied Psychology*. London: Hodder & Stoughton.

Peters, D.P. (1988) Eyewitness memory in a natural setting. In M.M. Gruneberg, P.E. Morris and R.N. Sykes (eds) *Practical Aspects of Memory: Current Research and Issues: Vol. 1. Memory in Everyday Life*. Chichester: Wiley, 89–94.

Peterson, L.R. and Peterson, M.J. (1959) Short-term retention of individual verbal items. *Journal of Experimental Psychology, 58*, 193–198.

Piliavin, I.M., Rodin, J. and Piliavin, J.A. (1969) Good Samaritanism: an underground phenomenon? *Journal of Personality and Social Psychology, 13*, 289–299.

Rack, P. (1982) *Race, Culture and Mental Disorder*. London: Tavistock.

Raho, R.H., Mahan, J. and Arthur, R. (1970) Prediction of near-future health-change from subjects' preceding life changes. *Journal of Psychosomatic Research, 14*, 401–406.

Richards, M.P.M. (1995) The International Year of the

Family – family research. *The Psychologist*, 8, 17–20.

Riley, V. (1981) Psychoneuroendocrine influence on immuno-competence and neoplasia. *Science*, 212, 1100–1109.

Roberts, K. and Lamb, M. (1999) Children's responses when interviewers distort details during investigative interviews. *Legal and Criminological Psychology*, 4, 23–31.

Robertson, J. and Robertson, J. (1967–1973) Film Series: *Young Children in Brief Separation*: No. 3 (1969) John, 17 months, 9 days in a residential nursery. London: Tavistock. Also, Robertson, J. and Robertson, J. (1969) *John, aged Seventeen Months, for Nine Days in a Residential Nursery*. www.robertsonfilms.info and www.concordvideo.co.uk.

Robertson, J. and Robertson, J. (1989) *Separation and the Very Young*. London: Free Association Books.

Roger, D. and Nash, P. (1995) Coping. *Nursing Times*, 91(29), 42–43.

Rogoff, B. (2003) *The Cultural Nature of Human Development*. New York, NY: Oxford University Press.

Rolls, G. (2005) *Classic Case Studies in Psychology*. London: Hodder Arnold.

Rolls, G. (2007) *A Picture is Worth 1000 Words. Taking the Proverbial: The Psychology of Proverbs and Sayings*. UK: Chambers Harrap.

Rosenhan, D.L. (1973) On being sane in insane places. *Science*, 179, 365–369.

Rosenhan, D.L. and Seligman, M.E. (1989) *Abnormal Psychology*. New York, NY: Norton.

Ross, L.D. (1988) Situationist perspectives on the obedience experiments. Review of A.G. Miller's *The Obedience Experiments*. *Contemporary Psychology*, 33, 101–104.

Rotter, J.B. (1966) Generalised expectancies for internal versus external control of reinforcement. *Psychological Monographs*, 30(1), 1–26.

Rutter, M. (1981) *Maternal Deprivation Reassessed* (2nd edn). Harmondsworth: Penguin.

Rutter, M. (2006) The psychological effects of institutional rearing. In P. Marshall and N. Fox (eds) *The Development of Social Engagement: Neurobiological Perspectives*. New York, NY: Oxford University Press.

Rutter, M. and the English and Romanian Adoptee (ERA) Study Team (2004) Are there biological programming effects for psychological development?

Findings from a study of Romanian adoptees. *Developmental Psychology*, 40, 81–94.

Rutter, M. and the ERA Study Team (2007) Early adolescent outcomes for institutionally-deprived and non-deprived adoptees: disinhibited attachment. *Journal of Child Psychology and Psychiatry*, 48(1), 17–30.

Sackheim, H.A., Prudic, J. and Devanand, D.P. (1990) Treatment of medication resistant depression with electroconvulsive therapy. In A. Tasman, S.M. Goldfinger and C.A. Kaufman (eds) *Review of Psychiatry*, Vol. 9. Washington, DC: American Psychiatric Press, Inc.

Sackheim, H.A., Prudic, J., Devanand, D.P., Kiersy, J.E., Fitzsimons, L., Moody, B.J., McElhiney, M.C., Coleman, E.A. and Settembrino, J.M. (1993) Effects of stimulus intensity and electrode placement on the efficacy and cognitive effects of electroconvulsive therapy. *New England Journal of Medicine*, 328(12), 882–883.

SANE (2003) www.sane.org.uk (accessed 12 July 2007).

Sasa, I.K. (1999) Mechanism underlying the therapeutic effects of ECT on depression. *Japanese Journal of Pharmacology*, 80(3), 185–189.

Savin, H.B. (1973) Professors and psychological researchers: conflicting values in conflicting roles. *Cognition*, 2(1), 147–149.

Scarr, S. (1998) American child care today. *American Psychologist*, 53(2), 95–108.

Schaffer, H.R. (1971) *The Growth of Sociability*. Harmondsworth: Penguin.

Schaffer, H.R. (1996) *Social Development*. Oxford: Blackwell.

Schaffer, H.R. (1998) Deprivation and its effects on children. *Psychology Review*, 5(2), 2–5.

Schaffer, H.R. (2004) *Introducing Child Psychology*. Oxford: Blackwell Publishing.

Schaffer, H.R. and Emerson, P.E. (1964) The development of social attachments in infancy. *Monographs of the Society for Research in Child Development*, 29 (whole No. 3).

Schatzberg, A.F. and Nemeroff, C.B. (1999) *Textbook of Psychopharmacology*. Washington, DC: American Psychiatric Press Inc.

Schliefer, S.J., Keller, S.E., Camerino, M., Thornton, J.C. and Stein, M. (1983) Suppression of lymphocyte stimulation following bereavement. *Journal of the*

American Medical Association, 250, 374–377.

Sears, D.O. (1986) College sophomores in the laboratory: influences of a narrow data base on social psychology's view of human nature. *Journal of Personality and Social Psychology, 51*, 515–530.

Seligman, M.E.P. (1975) *Helplessness: On Depression, Development and Death*. San Francisco, CA: W.H. Freeman.

Selye, H. (1956) *The Stress of Life*. New York, NY: McGraw-I lill.

Shallice, T. and Warrington, E.K. (1970) Independent functioning of verbal memory stores: a neurophysiological study. *Quarterly Journal of Experimental Psychology, 22*, 261–269.

Sheridan, C.L. and King, R.G. (1972) Obedience to authority with an authentic victim. *Proceedings of the 80th Annual Convention, American Psychological Association, 7(1)*, 165–166.

Sherif, M. (1935) A study of social factors in perception. *Archives of Psychology, 27* (whole No. 187).

Sims, K. (1999) How reliable are child eyewitnesses? *The Psychologist, 12(4)*, 191.

Smith, M. (1983) Hypnotic memory enhancement of witnesses: does it work? *Psychological Review, 94*, 387–407.

Smith, P.K., Cowie, H. and Blades, M. (1998) *Understanding Children's Development* (3rd edn). Oxford: Blackwell.

Spitz, R.A. (1945) Hospitalism: an enquiry into the genesis of psychiatric conditions in early childhood. *Psychoanalytic Study of the Child, 1*, 53–74.

Spitz, R.A. (1946) Hospitalism: a follow-up report on investigation described in Vol. 1, 1945. *Psychoanalytic Investigation of the Child, 2*, 113–117.

Spitz, R.A. and Wolf, K.M. (1946) Anaclitic depression. *Psychoanalytic Study of the Child, 2*, 313–342.

Spitzer, R.L. (1976) More on pseudoscience in science and the case for psychiatric diagnosis. *Archives of General Psychiatry, 33*, 459–470.

Stanton, A.L., Danoff-Burg, S., Cameron, C.L. and Ellis, A.P. (1994) Coping through emotional approach: problems of conceptualisation and confounding. *Journal of Personality and Social Psychology, 66*, 350–362.

Stone, A.A. and Neale, J.M. (1984) New measure of daily coping: developments and preliminary results. *Journal of Personality and Social Psychology, 46*, 892–906.

Strickland, B.R. (1984) This week's Citation Classic. *Current Contents, Social and Behavioural Sciences, 16(5)*, 20.

Stroebe, M.S. (1998) New directions on bereavement research: explorations of gender differences. *Palliative Medicine, 12*, 5–12.

Szasz, T.S. (1962) The myth of mental illness. *American Psychologist, 15*, 113–118.

Taylor, S.E., Peplau, L.A. and Sears, D.O. (1994) *Social Psychology* (8th edn). Englewood Cliffs, NJ: Erlbaum.

Temoshok, L. (1987) Personality, coping style, emotions and cancer: towards an integrative model. *Cancer Surveys, 6*, 545–567 (supplement).

Tizard, B. (1977) *Adoption: A Second Chance*. London: Open Books.

Tizard, B. and Hodges, J. (1978) The effects of early institutional rearing on the development of eight-year-old children. *Journal of Child Psychology and Psychiatry, 19*, 99–118.

Tulving, E. (1974) Cue dependent forgetting. *American Scientist, 62(1)*, 74–82.

Tulving, E. and Pearlstone, Z. (1966) Availability versus accessibility of information in memory for words. *Journal of Verbal Learning and Verbal Behavior, 5(4)*, 381–391.

Tulving, E. and Thomson, D.M. (1973) Encoding specificity and retrieval processes in episodic memory. *Psychological Review, 80*, 352–373.

Turner, J.C. (1991) *Social Influence*. Milton Keynes: Open University Press.

Ucros, C.G. (1989) Mood state-dependent memory: a meta-analysis. *Cognition and Emotion, 3*, 139–167.

UKAN (1995) *United Kingdom Advocacy Network ECT Survey*. Sheffield: UKAN.

Ursano, R. and Silberman, E.K. (1994) Psychoanalysis, psychoanalytic psychotherapy, and supportive psychotherapy. In E. Hales, S.C. Yudofsky and J. Talbott (eds) *The American Psychiatric Press Textbook of Psychiatry* (2nd edn). Washington, DC: American Psychiatric Press.

Ussher, J.M. (2000) Women and mental illness. In L. Sherr and J.S. St Lawrence (eds) *Women, Health and the Mind*. Chichester: John Wiley & Sons Ltd.

Van Ijzendoorn, M.H. and Kroonenberg, P.M. (1988) Cross-cultural patterns of attachment: a meta-analysis of the strange situation. *Child Development*, *59*, 147–156.

Van Ijzendoorn, M.H. and Schuengel, C. (1999) The development of attachment relationships: infancy and beyond. In D. Messer and S. Millar (eds) *Exploring Developmental Psychology: From Infancy to Adolescence*. London: Arnold.

Watson, J.B. and Rayner, R. (1920) Conditioned emotional reactions. *Journal of Experimental Psychology*, *3*, 1–14.

Watson, J.B. and Watson, R. (1921) Studies in infant psychology. *Scientific Monthly*, *13*, 493–515.

Waynforth, D. and Dunbar, R.I.M. (1995) Conditional mate choice strategies in humans: evidence from 'lonely hearts' advertisements. *Behaviour*, *132*, 755–779.

Weiner, R.D. (1984) Does electroconvulsive therapy cause brain damage? *The Behavioral and Brain Sciences*, *7*, 1–22.

Weiner, R.D. and Coffey, C.E. (1988) Indications for use of electroconvulsive therapy. In A.J. Frances and R.E. Hales (eds) *Review of Psychiatry*, Vol. 7. Washington, DC: American Psychiatric Press Inc.

Weinman, J. (1995) Health psychology. In A.M. Colman (ed.) *Controversies in Psychology*. London: Longman.

Williams, J.M.G. and Hargreaves, I.R. (1995) Neuroses: depressive and anxiety disorders. In A.A. Lazarus and

A.M. Colman (eds) *Abnormal Psychology*. London: Longman.

Willis, R.H. (1963) Two dimensions of conformity–nonconformity. *Sociometry*, *26*, 499–513.

Wilson, S., Brown, N., Mejia, C. and Lavori, P. (2002) Effects of interviewer characteristics on reported sexual behavior of California Latino couples. *Hispanic Journal of Behavioral Sciences*, *24(1)*, 38–62.

Wolpe, J. (1958) *Psychotherapy by Reciprocal Inhibition*. Stanford, CT: Stanford University Press.

Wolpe, J. with Wolpe, D. (1988) *Life Without Fear*. Oakland, CA: New Harbinger Publications.

Word, C., Zanna, M. and Cooper, J. (1974) The non-verbal mediation of self-fulfilling prophecies in interracial interaction. *Journal of Experimental Social Psychology*, *10*, 109–120.

Yuille, J.C. and Cutshall, J.L. (1986) A case study of eyewitness testimony of a crime. *Journal of Applied Psychology*, *71*, 291–301.

Zimbardo, P.G. (1973) On the ethics of intervention in human psychological research with special reference to the 'Stanford Prison Experiment'. *Cognition*, *2(2)*, 243–255.

Zimbardo, P.G. and Leippe, M. (1991) *The Psychology of Attitude Change and Social Influence*. New York, NY: McGraw-Hill.

Zimbardo, P.G., Banks, W.C., Craig, H. and Jaffe, D. (1973) A Pirandellian prison: the mind is a formidable jailor. *New York Times Magazine*, 8 April, 38–60.

Index